Translated Texts for Byzantinists

The intention of the series is to broaden access to Byzantine texts from 800 AD, enabling students, non-specialists and scholars working in related disciplines to access material otherwise unavailable to them. The series will cover a wide range of texts, including historical, theological and literary works, all of which include an English translation of the Byzantine text with introduction and commentary.

Liverpool University Press gratefully acknowledges the generous support of Dr Costas Kaplanis, alumnus of King's College London, who suggested the idea of the series to Professor Herrin and has underwritten the initial expenses.

General Editors
Judith Ryder, Oxford
Elizabeth Jeffreys, Oxford
Judith Herrin, King's College London

I0593108

Editorial Committee
Michael Angold, Edinburgh
Mary Cunningham, Nottingham
Charalambos Dendrinos, Royal Holloway
Niels Gaul, Edinburgh
Tim Greenwood, St Andrews
Anthony Hirst, London
Liz James, Sussex
Michael Jeffreys, Oxford
Costas Kaplanis, King's College London
Marc Lauxtermann, Oxford
Fr Andrew Louth, Durham
Ruth Macrides, Birmingham
Rosemary Morris, York
Leonora Neville, University of Wisconsin-Madison
Charlotte Roueché, King's College London
Teresa Shawcross, Princeton
Paul Stephenson, Lincoln
Mary Whitby, Oxford

Translated Texts for Byzantinists
Volume 7

The Chronicle
of the Logothete

Translated with introduction, commentary
and indices by STAFFAN WAHLGREN

Liverpool
University
Press

First published 2019
Liverpool University Press
4 Cambridge Street
Liverpool, L69 7ZU

This paperback edition first published 2020

British Library Cataloguing-in-Publication Data
A British Library CIP Record is available.

ISBN 978-1-78694-207-4 hardback
ISBN 978-1-78962-807-4 paperback

Typeset by Carnegie Book Production, Lancaster

CONTENTS

ACKNOWLEDGEMENTS

I would like to thank the General Editors of Translated Texts for Byzantinists, Judith Ryder, Judith Herrin and Elizabeth M. Jeffreys, for allowing me to publish my translation in their series, for untiring encouragement and for countless suggestions and corrections. In addition, my sincere thanks are due to the anonymous readers provided by the Press for their various suggestions; to Sebastián Ernesto Salvadó, who corrected my English and made many suggestions for improvements; and to Claudia Sode, who read parts of my translation and let me profit from her critical sense and knowledge. Last but not least, I acknowledge my undiminished debt to all those who made it possible for me to carry through the project of editing the Greek text of the Chronicle of the Logothete—friends, colleagues, family.

Staffan Wahlgren, June 2018

INTRODUCTION

World Chronicles

The world chronicle is a literary genre in which the recent history of a people of (Late) Antiquity or medieval times is connected to the beginnings of mankind as told in the Old Testament. It is an essentially Christian genre, ideologically underpinned by passages in the Bible (especially the Book of Daniel), and it shows history as an instrument to reveal God's plan for this world.

Thus, in its fully developed Byzantine form, the patriarchs of old (from Adam onwards) are seen as the direct predecessors of their Byzantine counterparts, the emperors, and the Byzantines stand forth as God's Chosen People. The history of other peoples is primarily included in the narrative in order to cover the gaps between these beginnings and the Christian Roman empire of the Byzantines themselves. In the Chronicle of the Logothete, the text translated in this volume, this is illustrated by the attention paid to the Assyrian–Median–Persian kings, the Ptolemaic rulers of Egypt, and the emperors of pagan Rome: they are all links in a chain.

Notwithstanding the main perspective, even the most focused of chronicles gives occasional titbits of information not belonging to the main thread of the narrative. Homer, the epic poet, may be mentioned, or Romulus, the founder of Rome: according to our text, Homer lived in the time of King Solomon, and Romulus was a contemporary of the prophet Isaiah. However, because of its lack of function in the overall scheme, information about these pagans is endangered—as, indeed, is most knowledge about pagan antiquity. The loss of this is indicative of an age in which the collective memory of the Greeks is being transformed in its foundations.

In sum, two principles are at work: synchronisation and unification. That Homer is mentioned together with King Solomon, or Romulus with

Isaiah, is an example of how pagan history has been synchronised with that of the Jews and Christians. To avoid such reference is typical of the unifying principle: world history is conceived as one narrative only.

(Sextus) Iulius Africanus (ca. AD 160–240), a native of Jerusalem, is considered the inventor of a world chronicle of this kind, and may be styled the 'Father of Christian Chronography.' His work, the *Chronographiae*, has been lost, but, since it was often cited by various later writers, it can be reconstructed in its general design.[1] Accordingly, we know that it was divided into five books, starting with the Creation of the World and reaching until ca. AD 221.

The second name of importance is that of Eusebius of Caesarea (ca. AD 260–340). Apart from theological works, and a *Church History*, he is the author of the so-called *Pantodape Historia* (*Miscellaneous/Universal History*), which consisted of two parts, the *Chronographia* and a set of *Canones* (*Tables*). Although most of this has been lost in Greek, and has to be studied in the existing Latin and Armenian versions, there is no doubt that it exerted a tremendous influence on later Byzantine chronography.

From these beginnings we come to texts that have been preserved to us. We will mention the main ones (written in Greek) of the following centuries.[2] The first of these is the *Chronographia* of John Malalas (ca. AD 490–570 or later).[3] In eighteen books (some text has been lost), the work begins with Adam and biblical history, but also incorporates a fair share of the history of the Egyptians, the pagan Greeks, and so on. Special attention is paid to Antioch, John's home town. The text ends in AD 563.

The anonymous *Chronicon Paschale* (so-called because of its system of chronology, based on the Paschal cycle) was probably written shortly after the last events recorded.[4] It treats the history of the world from Adam until AD 628.

---

1 The fragments are edited and translated in Wallraff 2007.

2 There is no satisfactory history of Byzantine literature. For an overview—of the history of literature as well as the general history of Byzantium—the reader may turn to L. James, *A Companion to Byzantium*, Blackwell Companions to the Ancient World, Chichester: Wiley-Blackwell, 2010, and E. Jeffreys/J. Haldon/R. Cormack, *The Oxford Handbook of Byzantine Studies*, Oxford: Oxford University Press, 2008. Valuable but idiosyncratic are W. Treadgold, *The Early Byzantine Historians*, Basingstoke: Palgrave Macmillan, 2007, and W. Treadgold, *The Middle Byzantine Historians*, Basingstoke: Palgrave Macmillan, 2013. A recent addition is Neville 2018.

3 Translated by Jeffreys/Jeffreys/Scott et al. 1986.

4 An annotated partial translation is available in Whitby/Whitby 1989.

The Constantinopolitan patriarch Nikephoros (ca. AD 758–828) wrote a very incomplete account of the period 602–769 (the *Historia syntomos*, or *Short History*), but also a (very short) world chronicle from Adam, called *Chronographikon syntomon* (*Short Chronography*).[5]

From the same time as Patriarch Nikephoros there is the combined world chronicle of George Synkellos[6] (reaching from the Creation of the World until AD 285) and Theophanes the Confessor[7] (continuing George's narrative into the early ninth century). George contains a lot of material pertaining to various ancient civilisations, and he takes great interest in chronology, including the calculation of years from the Creation. Theophanes is concerned with Late Antiquity and Byzantine times but, since his work is conceived as a continuation of George, it deserves a place in an overview of world chronicles. Theophanes is extremely influential in Byzantium, as seen by reflections of his work in the Chronicle of the Logothete and others. In addition, he is somewhat of a favourite among modern historians: in part, modern histories of Byzantium read like a running commentary to Theophanes. A characteristic feature of this text is the annalistic arrangement, in which the material is arranged as per year, a concept anticipated in George Synkellos.

The Chronicle of George the Monk covers the time from the Creation of the World until the re-establishment of orthodoxy after the iconoclast controversy (this was in AD 843; the work was probably finished around 870).[8] The text is remarkable for the number of manuscripts preserved (more than a hundred). It is structurally similar to many later texts, including the Chronicle of the Logothete, and there is reason to believe that it was very influential.

Finally, in the tenth century, there is a whole complex of texts associated with the name of Symeon the Logothete. The most widely transmitted form of this is the object of this translation. I will refer to it as the Chronicle of the Logothete (or, sometimes, as 'Symeon's Chronicle'). In the following section, it is discussed in greater detail. First, however,

---

5 For a translation with commentary of the *Short History* see Mango 1990, who also gives an overview of the contents of the *Short Chronography* (pp. 3–4), although, as pointed out by Mango (who calls the text an 'almanac'), it hardly makes sense to call this short, impersonal piece a chronicle at all.

6 Translated with commentary by Adler/Tuffin 2002.

7 Translated with commentary by Mango/Scott 1997.

8 There is no translation of George the Monk's chronicle into English, and a satisfactory critical edition is sorely needed.

we will take a look at some other texts within the wider family of Symeon the Logothete.[9]

The so-called Chronicle of Pseudo-Julius Pollux is a text covering the period from the Creation of the World until the emperor Valens, in the late fourth century AD (the text ends abruptly, since the main manuscript has been damaged).[10] The first part of it, until the time of Julius Caesar, is more or less identical with the Chronicle of the Logothete. In my opinion, the two texts reflect a common source lost to us.

Theophanes continuatus is the conventional name given to texts collected in the MS Vaticanus gr. 167 (and also preserved in some insignificant copies of this). The collection is divided into six books. Of these, the first four constitute a work in their own right.[11] The fifth book, a biography of emperor Basil I known as the *Vita Basilii*, is yet another, quite independent work, with its own style and character.[12] The sixth book is a version of the Chronicle of the Logothete.

Pseudo-Symeon is the name given to the text preserved in the MS Parisinus gr. 1712 (and in one insignificant copy of this). The text is partly a version of the Chronicle of the Logothete, partly dependent on other sources. Unfortunately, it has never been edited in full, and there is no translation into a modern language.[13]

The Chronicle of the Logothete: The Text and Its Author

The Chronicle of the Logothete encompasses the period from the Creation of the World to the burial of emperor Romanos I Lekapenos in the summer of AD 948. If we deduce a medieval text's importance and success from the number of extant manuscripts, this work must score highly. While some medieval chronicles have come down to us in only one manuscript, about thirty manuscripts transmit the Chronicle of the Logothete in its main form. If we include versions and texts dependent upon it in some way or

---

9 Unfortunately there is no good overview as yet of the tangled web of relevant texts and versions. For the time being, the reader is referred to the Introduction (in German) to my edition (Wahlgren 2006).

10 This text has not been published since the eighteenth century, and there is no translation. A critical edition is in preparation by me.

11 Edited and translated by Featherstone/Signes-Codoñer 2015.

12 Edited and translated by Ševčenko 2011.

13 An edition by A. Markopoulos is expected.

other, we arrive at a much higher number of manuscripts. In addition, the chronicle was translated into Old Slavonic at least twice.[14]

In spite of the work's popularity, the chronicler himself remains obscure. Judging from the text itself, he should be styled Symeon *magistros* and *logothetes*. It has been suggested that this could be Symeon Metaphrastes, an illustrious Byzantine literate who collected and (re-)wrote saints' Lives (and who later became a saint himself).[15] However, bearers of the titles of *magistros* and *logothetes* abound in this period, and Symeon is a common name. Perhaps also the work of the chronicler are some poems: one written by a Symeon on the death of Stephanos Lekapenos († 963), once co-emperor, another written by a Symeon *magistros* and *logothetes* of the *stratiotikon* on the occasion of the death of emperor Constantine VII in AD 959.[16]

In sum, little or nothing is known about the chronographer except for what the text itself can tell. We can assume that he was active in the second half of the tenth century, since, as mentioned above, the text runs until the summer of 948. In fact, it would seem that Symeon wrote after the death of Constantine VII in 959: the emperor's passing is mentioned in Chapter 135, § 1, and, if this is not an interpolation, it gives us a *terminus post quem* for the chronicle, or at least for the placement of the finishing touches to it. In any case, it is certain that the chronicle already existed in some form in the year 1013, for in this year the earliest extant and securely dated manuscript (the Parisinus gr. 1711) was written.

In addition to these observations, when attempting to establish a date of composition it may be beneficial to look for ideological or political bias in the chronicle. The work ends with a description of the death and burial of emperor Romanos I Lekapenos. The prominent position thus given to him

---

14 For a fuller treatment of the issues discussed here, the reader is, once more, referred to the Introduction to my edition of the Greek text (Wahlgren 2006).

15 The Metaphrast was active in the second half of the tenth century and died ca. AD 1000.

16 The identity of the chronicler and the Metaphrast has been maintained by A. Markopoulos (A. Markopoulos, Η χρονογραφία του Ψευδοσυμεών και οι πηγές της, Ioannina 1978) in particular. I. Ševčenko has collected the existing information about people named Symeon engaged in letters in the tenth century (I. Ševčenko, 'Poems on the deaths of Leo VI and Constantine VII in the Madrid Manuscript of Scylitzes,' *Dumbarton Oaks Papers* 23/24 (1969/1970), pp. 187–228). It may perhaps be mentioned that a web search for 'Symeon the Logothete' is likely to lead to the Metaphrast: there is an article in (English) Wikipedia named 'Symeon the Metaphrast' (or 'Symeon the Logothete') in which the Chronicle is, although with doubt, attributed to the Metaphrast.

in the text might itself be significant. There are also many statements about this emperor that seem intended to influence the reader favourably. An example is Chapter 136, §§ 83–84, where the circumstances of Romanos' dethronement are described, and he is the object of sympathy. Here, one might almost feel as if we were reading a saint's life. On the other hand, the author has abstained from every opportunity to picture Romanos as the fairly coarse and unsophisticated person that he probably was.

Conversely, we may also think that the opponents of the Lekapenoi, the Macedonian emperors, are depicted in a negative or, at the very best, indifferent way. This especially holds true with regard to their founding father, Basil I. He is depicted as the coarse, brutal, and unsophisticated person that *he* almost certainly was. To give some examples of how this is achieved, he is directly and without excuses staged as the murderer of a prominent member of the imperial family and member of government, Caesar Bardas (see Chapter 131, § 33 and onwards), and of his predecessor as emperor, Michael III (see Chapter 131, § 46 and onwards), and he is not, as in other works, given an elevated ancestry.[17]

Now, if we accept it as true that there is a pro-Lekapenian, anti-Macedonian bias here, the question poses itself whether this can tell us anything about the most likely date of the chronicle's completion and publication (supposing, first, that tenth-century Byzantium was a dangerous place with censorship and repression, and, second, that the author did not keep the text for himself but had it published). The reign of Nikephoros II Phokas—that is, AD 963–969—has been suggested as the most likely period of time meeting these conditions.

Beyond these issues, some words on the composition of the chronicle and its structure are due. Below, a short overview of the chronicle's contents is provided. It is clear that Symeon, whoever he was, did not write all this himself. This is proven by the existence of older texts that contain identical passages, such as the chronicles of Theophanes and George the Monk, and by the identical passages in Pseudo-Julius Pollux. However, although the existence of borrowed material is uncontroversial, it is neither certain in what form it reached Symeon's desk, nor what his own contribution was.

The question is whether Symeon was a compiler, putting several larger pieces of text together, or a continuator who worked on the basis

---

17 This is in particularly stark contrast to the story told in the *Vita Basilii* (see Ševčenko 2011).

of one, previously existing text (in both instances we may assume that he added a contribution of his own towards the end of the chronicle). As to working methods, we may ask whether he read the texts of his predecessors thoroughly and reflected on them, or not. As to the question of Symeon's working methods, it is my opinion that these were, at the very least, careless, and that he used the material of his predecessors without much reflection or correction. As far as the first question is concerned (that of the size and characteristics of the chunks of text taken over by Symeon), the following is a summary of current opinion. It has been supposed that there existed a chronicle from the Creation of the World until Justinian II (who reigned around the year AD 700); that this chronicle was added upon, until AD 842, by an anonymous continuator; and that Symeon's chronicle proper is the part covering the period from the year 842. This last part of the chronicle, covering the years 842–948, may in its turn be divided into segments. According to the view advocated by A. Kazhdan, three such segments can be discerned: one covering the years 842–886 (emperors Michael III and Basil I), a second covering the years 886–913 (emperors Leo VI and Alexander), and a third covering the years 913–948 (Constantine VII and Romanos I). Of these, according to Kazhdan, the third and last probably depended on the personal recollections of the author.[18]

To prove all this, observations about the text's homogeneity (or its lack thereof) have been adduced, as well as parallels in other chronicles. Personally, I feel that there is still a lot of this that we do not understand properly. It may be stressed that there are structuring devices in the text that transcend the boundaries sketched above (that is, the boundaries at ca. AD 700, 842 and so on). In these cases, we may think that Symeon has either put his stamp on the whole of the text or that he shares structuring devices with predecessors—in other words, that the narrative devices under consideration have been inherited from others.

The structuring of the text into chapters is one such cohesive feature. For the Byzantine part of the text, one chapter is devoted to each emperor's reign, and the parts dealing with periods earlier than Byzantium are structured in a similar way: a leader of people is always present in the text as the main agent, all the way back to Adam, who assumes a role similar to that of a Byzantine emperor (cf. the beginning of this Introduction). That this feature is not Symeon's invention is clear, since it exists in earlier texts,

---

18 See *Oxford Dictionary of Byzantium* (ed. A. Kazhdan, New York: Oxford University Press, 1991), s.v. *Symeon the Logothete*, or my edition (Wahlgren 2006), p. 5*.

such as the Chronicle of George the Monk. However, the question remains whether it existed in the sources that Symeon actually used (as I tend to believe) or was a feature imposed by him on these sources.

There are also structuring devices within chapters. First of all, there is a tendency to let the emperor stand in the centre of attention, and to give priority to his story. Further, there is a tendency to provide a kind of narrative arc: to let stories centre upon one crucial moment, and often, prior to this, to tell the prehistory of the crucial event and then its aftermath. Thus, centres of narrative gravity on a micro-level are provided. In my opinion there is little doubt that very similar methods are present also in other texts, and are not unique to Symeon.[19]

Translation

Already in the Middle Ages, the Chronicle of the Logothete text was translated into (Old) Slavonic at least twice, and some early prints are accompanied by a Latin translation. A forthcoming English translation of excerpts of the text is announced by P. Stephenson on his website, and Walter K. Hanak (†) was preparing an English translation of one of the Old Slavonic translations.[20] However, the only full-scale translation into a modern language actually published is that into Russian by A. Vinogradov.[21] This is an odd piece of work, in which the Greek text (taken from my edition) has been used, with additions taken from one of the Old Slavonic versions, in the belief that the Slavonic text is the more authentic Symeon. It is extremely unfortunate that the translator does not at all take into account the analysis of the manuscript tradition provided by me (and others). His is an uncritical way of dealing with evidence, and it is very difficult not to suspect that there is some wishful thinking with regard to Old Slavonic as the key to understanding Byzantium.

About my own translation, the following can be said. The translation is based on my edition of the Greek text, the only critical edition in existence. As is usual in the chronographic genre, the text is transmitted in a fairly

---

19 For this aspect of Symeon's literary technique there are the studies of Jenkins 1965 and Treadgold 1979. A text that would deserve the attention of a similar study is the Chronicle of George the Monk.

20 See <http://www.paulstephenson.info/trans/logothete.html>, accessed 14 November 2018.

21 A. Vinogradov, *Hronika Simeona Magistra i Logofeta* (Tom 1), Moscow 2014.

open way. This means that scribes have felt much freer to introduce changes than they would have if they were copying a more prestigious work, such as that of an ancient author. Much has been added in the centuries after Symeon, and later manuscripts often contain more than the earlier ones. In other cases, scribes have left out a lot of text, or rewritten it using their own words. My translation does not take this secondary variation into account, and readers who want to get a picture of the form the text assumed in later centuries I can only advise to go to my edition and study the Greek.

The translation aims at readability. This means that it favours a certain redundancy wherever I consider this helpful. For instance, I often supply a name where the text only gives a pronoun. Needless to say, such redundancy often amounts to an interpretation on my part.

Readability sometimes stands in conflict with an ambition to preserve the flavour of the original text. This ambition accounts for the use made of such features as historical present and connectives; here I often deviate from normal English usage. However, it should be stressed that, in these cases, we are also often far away from normal Greek. For it is not the flavour of normal Greek, but that of this particular Greek, that shall be preserved, and it seems wrong to make the text look smoother and more normal than it is.

As has been explained above, the chronicle is to a great extent a compilation. Sentences or whole paragraphs and chapters can be found in a more or less identical form in other existing texts, and later chroniclers have used Symeon's text, too. Some such texts are already accessible in excellent modern translations, e.g. the chronicles of Theophanes (a forerunner) and Skylitzes (a follower).[22] My translation often differs from these, even when the original wording is identical. This does not need to mean that anyone is wrong, for the same text can be correctly translated in many ways. It only means that, although I am aware of the work of others, I have chosen to do my own translation independently, and to consult others only in special cases.

Commentary

The main purpose of the commentary is to provide a basic framework for the reader. The overall chronology is kept track of, and explicit dates are

---

22 See Mango/Scott 1997 (Theophanes) and Wortley 2010 (Skylitzes) respectively.

translated into modern style and discussed when problematic. Persons and places are identified, and important parallels to other texts, including explicit references, are commented upon. Apart from this, there are two further features of my commentary worth mentioning in particular.

The first is that I have tried to keep an eye on the text as a piece of literature and as testimony to Byzantine mentality, conceptions of history and collective memory. Anachronisms provide a good example of this: the behaviour and attitudes of a later age are often ascribed to people of ancient times. This is, in my opinion, a phenomenon that deserves attention.

The second characteristic feature of my commentary derives from the fact that I am also the editor of the text. I have therefore seen it as my special duty not only to inform the reader about any passages that I have difficulty in understanding (although they may be correctly transmitted) but in particular to indicate any case where I see reason to doubt that the text has been correctly transmitted.

Some translations of related texts, such as Theophanes (Mango/Scott 1997) and Skylitzes (Wortley 2010), are accompanied by commentaries, too, and the reader may turn to these with profit. The Theophanes commentary is of great value, also as a general work of reference. Skylitzes provides an often very closely parallel text from AD 811 and, even for a reader of the Chronicle of the Logothete, Wortley's commentary is extremely useful. In my commentary, some prominence is given to Mango/Scott and Wortley.

Also useful are the notes and commentaries accompanying the *Short History* of patriarch Nikephoros (Mango 1990), the *Chronicon Paschale* (Whitby/Whitby 1989), and the *Chronography* of George Synkellos (Adler/Tuffin 2002). The introduction to the translation of George Synkellos, with an extensive treatment of the beginnings of the genre and matters of chronology, deserves special mention.

The papers by Jenkins 1965 (covering the years AD 867–913) and Treadgold 1979 (covering the years AD 813–845) provide a partial running commentary to the Chronicle of the Logothete.

Here, some words on the future of translating and commenting upon Byzantine texts may be permitted. The need for referencing to physical books is diminishing; there is a much less obvious need for this today than just a few years ago. We may still be wary of saying so, but, on a wide range of topics (from the history of various heresies and Arab–Byzantine relations to prosopographical data on individual Byzantines and foreigners), openly available electronic resources provide excellent help. In addition, future readers will do more of their reading in an electronic form, and they will be constantly accessing web resources when doing so. As commentators, we are well advised to consider how our trade is evolving and (as some already do) to take steps accordingly. Already, if we provide online versions of our conventional books, we can enrich our commentary with GPS coordinates, hyperlinks and disambiguations. It is a matter of some regret to me that I am not able to do my bit to this end.

Finally: why read the Chronicle of the Logothete? Hopefully, some reasons have emerged in this Introduction. In sum, the Chronicle is one of the most important witnesses to the hundred years of Byzantine history after Theophanes (who wrote into the early ninth century). Even more importantly, by the construction of a chain of events since Adam and Eve it tells us something about what the Byzantines saw as their history and why, in their opinion, things had occurred as they had. Considering the text's popularity, we may think that this is history as the Byzantines themselves liked to read it.

Contents of the Chronicle

95 (pp. 91–93): Theodosios I;
96 (pp. 94–95): Arkadios;
97 (pp. 95–98): Theodosios II;
98 (pp. 98–99): Marcian;
99 (pp. 99–100): Leo I;
100 (p. 101): Leo II;
101 (pp. 101–102): Zeno;
102 (pp. 102–105): Anastasios
Dikoros;
103 (pp. 105–107): Justin I;
104 (pp. 107–111): Justinian I;
105 (pp. 111–113): Justin II;
106 (p. 113): Tiberios I;
107 (pp. 114–117): Maurice;
108 (pp. 117–119): Phokas;
109 (pp. 119–123): Herakleios;
110 (p. 123): Constantine III;
111 (p. 124): Heraklonas;
112 (pp. 124–125): Constans II;
113 (pp. 125–127): Constantine IV;
114 (pp. 128–130): Justinian II;
115 (pp. 130–131): Leontios;
116 (pp. 131–132): Tiberios II
(Apsimaros);
117 (pp. 132–133): Justinian II
(second period as ruler);

118 (pp. 133–134): Philippikos
(Bardanes);
119 (pp. 134–135): Anastasios II
(Artemios);
120 (pp. 135–136): Theodosios III;
121 (pp. 136–141): Leo III;
122 (pp. 141–147): Constantine V;
123 (pp. 147–149): Leon IV;
124 (pp. 149–154): Constantine VI;
125 (pp. 155–157): Nikephoros;
126 (p. 158): Staurakios;
127 (pp. 158–159): Michael I;
128 (pp. 159–162): Leo V;
129 (pp. 162–163): Michael II;
130 (pp. 163–175): Theophilos;
131 (pp. 175–194): Michael III and
Theodora;
132 (pp. 195–202): Basil I;
133 (pp. 202–218): Leo VI;
134 (pp. 219–221): Alexander;
135 (pp. 221–229): Constantine VII;
136 (pp. 229–251): Romanos I;
137 (pp. 251–253): Constantine VII
(as sole ruler)

SELECT BIBLIOGRAPHY

Adler, W./P. Tuffin (2002), *The Chronography of George Synkellos: A Byzantine Chronicle of Universal History from the Creation* (translated with introduction and notes by W. Adler and P. Tuffin), Oxford: Oxford University Press.

Featherstone, J.M./J. Signes-Codoñer (2015), *Chronographiae quae Theophanis Continuati nomine fertur Libri I–IV* (ed. & transl. J.M. Featherstone/J. Signes-Codoñer), Corpus Fontium Historiae Byzantinae 53, Berlin–New York: Walter de Gruyter.

Jeffreys, E./M. Jeffreys/R. Scott et al. (1986), *The Chronicle of John Malalas: A Translation*, Australian Association for Byzantine Studies: Byzantina Australiensia 4, Melbourne.

Jenkins, R.J.H. (1965), 'The Chronological Accuracy of the "Logothete" for the Years A.D. 867–913,' *Dumbarton Oaks Papers* 19, pp. 91–112.

Kaldellis, A. (1998), *Joseph Genesios: On the Reigns of the Emperors* (translation), Australian Association for Byzantine Studies: Byzantina Australiensia 11, Canberra.

Mango, C. (1990), *Nikephoros, Patriarch of Constantinople: Short History* (text, translation, and commentary), Corpus Fontium Historiae Byzantinae 13 (Series Washingtonensis), Dumbarton Oaks Texts 10, Washington.

Mango, C./R. Scott (1997), *The Chronicles of Theophanes Confessor: Byzantine and Near Eastern History, A.D. 284–813* (translated with introduction and commentary by Cyril Mango and Roger Scott with the assistance of Geoffrey Greatrex), Oxford: Clarendon Press.

Neville, L. (2018), *Guide to Byzantine Historical writing*, Cambridge–New York: Cambridge University Press.

Ševčenko, I. (2011), *Chronographiae Quae Theophanis Continuati Nomine Fertur Liber Quo Vita Basilii Imperatoris Amplectitur* (ed. & transl. I. Ševčenko), Corpus Fontium Historiae Byzantinae 42, Berlin–New York: Walter de Gruyter.

Treadgold, W. (1979), 'The Chronological Accuracy of the Chronicle of Symeon the Logothete for the Years 813–845,' *Dumbarton Oaks Papers* 33, pp. 157–197.

Wahlgren, S. (2006), *Symeonis Magistri et Logothetae Chronicon* (ed. S. Wahlgren), Corpus Fontium Historiae Byzantinae 44:1, Berlin–New York: Walter de Gruyter.

Wallraff, M. (2007), *Iulius Africanus: Chronographiae. The Extant Fragments. In collaboration with Umberto Roberto and Karl Pinggéra* (translated by W. Adler), Die griechischen christlichen Schriftsteller der ersten Jahrhunderte NF 15, Berlin–New York: Walter de Gruyter.

Whitby, M./M. Whitby (1986), *The History of Theophylact Simocatta* (an English translation with introduction and notes), Oxford: Clarendon Press.

Whitby, M./M. Whitby (1989), *Chronicon Paschale 284–628* (translated with notes and introduction), Translated Texts for Historians 7, Liverpool: Liverpool University Press.

Wortley, J. (2010), *John Skylitzes: A Synopsis of Byzantine History, 811–1057* (introduction, text and notes; translated by John Wortley), Cambridge: Cambridge University Press.

THE CHRONICLE OF THE LOGOTHETE

1 When God, the Timeless, brought this world, which did not earlier exist, into time, He created heaven and earth in the beginning.[1] Water came into being at the same time as earth, and so did fire. And a clear proof of this is that abundant fire comes forth from stone and iron, which are from earth, and that water pours richly from springs and wells. For since earth came into being from non-existing components, so obviously is the case also with that which is in earth. **2** Thus everything was done according to God's will. But since heaven was like a tent and was strung around the rest of the material world and darkened the region within, God said: 'Let there be light.' And as soon as the word was pronounced, light, this most beneficial natural phenomenon, was brought into being, and it dispelled the darkness which was a consequence of the interposition of the bulk of heaven, and at once it transformed the air, which because of the heaven had been lightless, into exceeding radiance. **3** But it is obvious that everything that existed before the creation of this world was in light. For neither the choirs of the angels nor the whole heavenly host lived in darkness. Rather they fulfilled the duty befitting them in light and every spiritual joy, from the time when they, too, had been brought from nothing into being. **4** Since this light, for the reason mentioned, had been enclosed in the upper region, again God created the light that now shines over and brightens the area between heaven and earth. **5** This is what happened on the first day of Creation. On this day the heavenly powers were created, according to Moses in the *Lesser Genesis.*[2]

---

1 For Chapter 1, cf. Genesis 1.1–5.

2 The *Lesser (Lepte) Genesis* is the *Liber Jubilaeorum*, known from a translation into Ge'ez as well as from fragments in several other languages, including Greek. See J.C. VanderKam, *The Book of Jubilees. A Critical Text*, Leuven: Peeters Publishers, 1989, and J. VanderKam, *The Book of Jubilees* (Guides to the Apocrypha and Pseudepigrapha), London etc.: Sheffield Academic Press (Bloomsbury), 2001. Some excerpts from the same work are also present in George Synkellos (see Adler/Tuffin 2002, pp. 8–9).

2 On the Firmament[1]

Again, on the second day, when the abyss was spread around the earth without limit and boundary, God ordered that a firmament should come out of the waters and in between them, and this He then called the 'vault.'[2] And at once, upon the command, the work was finished. **2** This creation was called 'firmament' because of the fine and thin nature of the waters above and below. And it was called 'vault of heaven' since it could be seen through,[3] being stretched above our heads as a hide.

3 On the Sea[4]

Again, on the third day, God ordered the waters that were enclosed under the firmament to gather in one place, which He called sea, so that the dry land should become visible, and thus deep hollow spaces in the earth received the waters.

4 On the Dry Land and What Grows out of the Earth[5]

The earth was called dry since this designation is in accordance with its nature. For earth is what has dryness as its principal property. **2** When the earth had shed the waters lying on it, it was ordered to bring forth plants and seeds of different kinds and fruit-bearing trees. **3** And at once the earth was stirred into bearing fruit, and it produced countless kinds of shoots and plants, and it took on a worthy and pleasing appearance. For it was not only brightened by the sprouting of cornfields, but it was also well adorned with the spontaneous growth of cedars and cypresses and all other kinds of trees.

---

1 For Chapter 2, cf. Genesis 1.6–8.
2 Greek οὐρανός.
3 Οὐρανός is here associated with ὁράω, 'to see,' with a kind of popular etymology.
4 For Chapter 3, cf. Genesis 1.9–10.
5 For Chapter 4, cf. Genesis 1.11–13.

5 On the Lights of Heaven[1]

Again, on the fourth day, God said that there should be lights, and the sun and the moon and the stars came into being, just as He Who ordered it had willed. **2** And that most pure light which had existed on the first day of Creation,[2] He divided between these, and He gave manifold benefit from these to everyone.[3] **3** One benefit was to shine and by their light richly illuminate the world; another was, by rising and setting, to provide a basis for the measurement of time; and yet another, to benefit by some signs and in different ways those who inquire piously and do not ask beyond what is proper.[4] **4** Similar signs are also often given by the moon. For when its light is thin and clear by day, it promises stable fair weather. But when its beams are blurred and it appears somewhat red, it announces that there will be violent rain from the clouds or a storm. **5** In the same way too the sun indicates that there will be violent atmospheric conditions when, by its rays or its effulgence, it assumes the colour of coal and almost the colour of blood. Many seafarers, farmers and travellers on the road have been helped by these kinds of signs on many occasions.

6 On Fishes and Birds[5]

On the fifth day, God ordered that the waters should bring forth crawling animals[6] and also winged creatures to fly in the firmament of heaven. And with the command, the work was completed. The ability to engender life was inherent in the waters and, at once, the sea gave birth to manifold kinds of animals, and rivers and seas were filled with fish of appropriate kinds. **2** The waters also brought forth the winged creatures,[7] which in some way have a kinship with the water animals. For in the same way as the fishes go forward in the water by moving their fins (and they steer a straight course by frequently changing the direction of the tail), so also the birds swim through the air and cut it, and arrive where they want to.

---

1 For Chapter 5, cf. Genesis 1.14–19.
2 The text is here corrupt, but the approximate meaning seems clear.
3 Or: 'everything.'
4 An improper use of the signs would be to engage in magic on the basis of astrology.
5 For Chapter 6, cf. Genesis 1.20–23.
6 ἑρπετὰ ψυχῶν ζωσῶν.
7 Or: 'birds' (πετεινά).

7 On Tame and Wild Animals[1]

Again, on the sixth day, the earth was bidden to bring forth living animals according to their kind: four-legged animals, crawling animals and wild. And at once it brought forth both savage and tame animals. God ordered the earth to bring forth living animals, in order that, from this, the difference between the soul of the irrational animal and the human soul should be known. For the soul of the irrational animals was born from the earth, whereas the soul of humankind was created by the divine inbreathing. **2** And, further, that the soul of irrational animals is of earth can be understood from Scripture itself. For it is said: 'The soul of every animal is its blood.'[2] When blood coagulates, it becomes flesh, and when flesh decays, it is dissolved into earth. Therefore, it is logical that the soul of the irrational animal should be of an earthy nature. **3** When, then, everything had been adorned with appropriate beauty (the heaven with the rays of the lights; the sea and the air with the swimming and flying animals; the earth with the manifold varieties of plants and grazing animals), the Creator of everything introduces man into the world as a kind of king, and it is not as the last and most worthless thing that He creates man, but as destined to rule from his very creation.

8 On the Creation of Man

For what does Scripture say? 'And God said: Let Us make man in Our image and likeness, and let them rule over the fishes of the sea and the birds of heaven and the wild animals and all earth.'[3] **2** All other parts of Creation were brought into being by command alone. But man was marked out by a special distinction besides this at his creation. For he was created following deliberation, in order to show that he is of particular worth. **3** For the words 'Let Us make man in Our image and likeness' mean nothing other than that the Father, when He Created man, had recourse in counsel to His only begotten Son: the Son Who, according to the apostle, is the 'effulgence of His glory' and 'the very imprint of His substance.'[4]

---

1 For Chapter 7, cf. Genesis 1.24–25.
2 Leviticus 17.11; cf. Deuteronomy 12.23 and Genesis 9.4.
3 Genesis 1.26.
4 For these expressions see Hebrews 1.3. The apostle referred to is Paul who the Byzantines considered to be the author of the (Letter to the) Hebrews (an opinion not shared by modern scholarship).

For it would not have been possible for him to have recourse to any counsellor other than his living, enhypostatic Word, indistinguishable in form and of the same substance and the same power. **4** The works which, as Moses says, God made in the six days, were twenty-two in number. Therefore, there are twenty-two letters in the alphabet,[1] and the same number of books of the Hebrews, and twenty-two generations from Adam to Jacob.

9 On 'in Our Image'

Now, since, as has been said, man was brought into the world like a king, it is only fitting that he was created in God's image. For it was necessary that he who was to rule over the rest should be in the likeness of the King,[2] not showing his worth by a purple garment or a sceptre or a crown, since the correspondence with the original does not lie in this, but in being adorned with incorruptibility, immortality and virtue. **2** Honoured by these properties, man preserves his similarity to the prototype.[3] Further, it is free will that most clearly shows the royal and elevated nature of man and his similarity to the divine image, and in this sense too, man is the work of God's hands, because of the distinction of his creation.[4] For everything is the consequence of God's will. **3** Then, after man's creation, what does Scripture say? 'And on the sixth day, God completed His works, which He did, and on the seventh day, He ceased from all His works, which He had done, and He blessed the seventh day and consecrated it, since on that day God ceased from all His works which He had begun to do.'[5]

---

1 I.e. letters of the Aramaic/Hebrew alphabet.

2 'should be ... King': the Greek is somewhat odd (ὥσπερ τινὰ εἰκόνα εἶναι ἔμψυχον τῆς τοῦ βασιλέως ὁμοιότητος).

3 Here, too, there seems to be a slight corruption of the text, although the meaning appears to be clear.

4 'because ... creation' (διὰ τὸ τίμιον τῆς κατασκευῆς): this is vague; perhaps 'so as to give honour to what had been created.'

5 Genesis 2.2–3.

10 On the Sabbath

Why did God bless the seventh day only and not all days? This is because each of the others had its blessing from the act of creation taking place in it. But since this day was in danger of remaining without honour, as no act of creation took place then, therefore it, too, was blessed by God. **2** Again Scripture says: 'And the Lord God planted a garden in Eden, in the East, and He placed the man there, whom He had formed. And, further, God sent forth from the earth every kind of tree which was beautiful to look at and good to eat, and He placed the tree of life in the middle of paradise and the tree of the knowledge of good and evil.'[1]

11 On Paradise

Since God planned to honour his rational creation, He also prepares a glorious place for it to live in, full of every joy, and He places Adam there. **2** Having come so far in the story, one should marvel at God's ineffable love for humankind, since He, who had absolute and eternal power over everything, even offered Himself to till the soil for the sake of it. For He Who by his Word had created such an extent of heaven and earth and sea, was more than capable to plant a garden by His utterance alone, and to establish the most blessed place by His word. However, as has been said, in order to honour humankind, He who effortlessly, and by His will alone, brought this world from not being into being, even becomes a gardener for some mystic reason. **3** Scripture says further: 'And God brought all the wild and tame animals and the crawling animals to Adam, in order to see what he would call them. And whatever Adam called it became an animal's name.'[2]

12 On the Naming of the Animals[3]

Now, from this it could be seen what great honour was in store for man, paid to him by Creation itself. For Adam sat as a kind of leader in front of the animals, and God brought the countless wild and tame animals and the

---

1 Genesis 2.8–9.
2 Genesis 2.19.
3 For Chapter 12, cf. Genesis 2.19–20.

different kinds of birds to him, in order that they should acclaim as leader him whom He had made in His own image. **2** And Adam was inspired by a divine and prophetic spirit, and he gave names to every kind of irrational animal. And the animals, as if they received a great honour from this pronouncement, went away in pairs.

13 On the Creation of Woman

Since among all these species there was no one similar to Adam, again God, according to what Scripture tells, said: 'It is not good for the man to be alone. Let Us make a helper to him of his own kind,'[1] calling the female a 'helper' with regard to the begetting of children. For she was to work together with the male to increase the species and ensure its survival. **2** Then Scripture adds: 'And God cast a distraction on Adam and put him to sleep and took one of his ribs and filled up with flesh instead of it, and He built the rib, which He had taken from Adam, into a woman.'[2] **3** The meaning of the Scripture is: having decided, as He had also promised, to give Adam a helper of his own kind, God, Who made everything with wisdom, does not shape the female from earth, as He had done with the male, but He puts the male to sleep, and He subjects his mind to visions by the descent of the Spirit, and He invites his soul's eye to the sight of limitless light, in order that the man, being stunned by the vision of such beauty, should not perceive what was happening. Then He takes one of Adam's ribs, effortlessly not inflicting any feeling of pain on him, and at once, like a craftsman or a quick doctor, He filled the hole with flesh. **4** While He distracted Adam's soul by the insatiate pleasure of the sight,[3] He built the rib, which He had taken, into a woman, mystically shaping her into a rational creature, adorned with irresistible beauty and the most comely form. And He brings this creature to Adam. **5** Adam, who participated in divine inspiration, realised that she came from him, and he said: 'This is bone from my bones and flesh from my flesh. She will be called woman, since she has been taken from her man.'[4] **6** Now, when

---

1 Genesis 2.18.
2 Genesis 2.21–22.
3 'insatiate (or 'unceasing') pleasure of the sight': or 'the insatiate/unceasing divine pleasure.' The Greek text is corrupt at this point.
4 Genesis 2.23.

Adam was looking at the woman he did not respond to her as to a woman, but he was experiencing joy in his soul as if he beheld himself, for he saw that also she was of similar design. Likewise, the woman was very glad on seeing the man, realising that she was of his kind.[1] 7 When they thus were in the paradise of luxury, God gave them a law as a benefaction, so as to show that, by their nature, the humans possessed their own free will, but also to indicate that they are subject to a lord and guardian. This He did by saying thus: 'You may eat from every tree in the paradise. But from the tree of knowledge of good and evil, you must not eat from that, you two. The day you eat from it, you will suffer death.'[2] That is, 'you will be mortals.' For this is also Symmachus' interpretation:[3] 'The day when you eat from the tree, you will be mortal.'

14 On the Tree of Knowledge of Good and Evil

But no one should suppose that the tree was of such nature that it gave knowledge of good and bad. For there was nothing harmful in paradise. But a restriction was placed on the plant as an exercise in the use of free will. And it is evident that the tree was not the cause of knowledge to Adam. For the command was given as if to someone who already knew both, good as well as evil, obedience and disobedience, and therefore knowledge preceded the command. 2 This command was given so that, as has been said, humankind, who, moved by its own will, over which it had control, had been allowed to take from every other tree but had been commanded to abstain from this one only, should realise that it is subject to a lord, who gave the command. 3 Thus Adam and Eve lived in this most pure place, and they abundantly enjoyed the diversity of the immortal blossoms.

15 On the Devil and the Serpent

But the enemy of our nature became angry and envious at the great honour accorded to the man and started a war against him, and he assumed the

---

1 For § 6, cf. Genesis 2.26.
2 Genesis 2.16–17.
3 This Symmachus, one of the translators of the Old Testament, is also mentioned below, Chapter 67, § 2.

shape of a serpent and came to the woman (this was while Adam was absent), and cunningly and by lies he diverted her from what is right, and he deceived Adam together with her and made them become transgressors of the divine law. **2** For Scripture says the following about these things: 'The serpent was more sagacious than all the other animals on earth which the Lord God had made.'[1] The serpent is called sagacious since he was to deceive the rational animal, the human, who differed from the others with regard to intelligence. **3** Then it adds: 'And the serpent said to the woman: "Did God say to you: Do not eat from any tree in paradise?" And the woman said to the serpent: "We may eat from the fruit of paradise, but with regard to the fruit of the tree which stands in the middle of paradise, God said: Do not eat from it or even touch it, lest you die."'[2] **4** Did the serpent also use human speech? Not at all, but the first humans,[3] since they were untainted by evil, had the most acute senses, very much different from ours, and thus their ears could hear and interpret any sound. And Scripture[4] says that the wild and the tame animals once spoke with one tongue. However, when Adam was condemned, they too were silenced, and the serpent was deprived of his legs and had to creep on the earth, and poison was put on his tongue. **5** Then Scripture adds: 'And the serpent said to the woman: "You will not die. It is simply that God knew that the day that you eat from it, your eyes will be opened and you will be like gods and understand what is good and what is evil." And the woman saw that the tree was good for eating and pleasant to look at and beautiful to perceive, and she took of its fruit and ate and gave to her man. And they ate, and the eyes of the two were opened, and they realised that they were naked.'[5]

16 On 'the Eyes of the Two Were Opened'

It is not because the first humans then for the first time literally opened their eyes that it is said that 'the eyes of the two were opened.' For they are shown to have been able to see even before eating, since it is said: 'And the woman saw that the tree was good for eating and pleasant to look at.'[6] That their eyes

1 Genesis 3.1.
2 Genesis 3.1–3.
3 Or: 'first created beings' (πρωτόπλαστοι).
4 'Scripture': here, as in § 5, this is my addition.
5 Genesis 3.4–7.
6 Cf. above, Chapter 15, § 5.

were opened is rather said in the sense that, through the transgression, they lost their ignorance of evil, an ignorance which also made the nakedness of no consequence. **2** For it is in the nature of any eye to be awakened only by the mind to what it sees (for the eye has no understanding of its own), and therefore, when the mind is occupied with something else, we are often able to pass by even a person we know very well, as a blind person would do; and, if we are accused of this, we excuse ourselves by explaining that we were preoccupied with our thoughts.[1] **3** Thus Adam and Eve are awakened to seeing by the perception of the mind. For the words 'they realised that they were naked' indicate the revelation that came to the mind, not the actual opening of the eyes. **4** It should also be said that, prior to their disobedience, when it was not the time for the begetting of children, God had not given it to humans to pay heed to nakedness, but they lived as if without a body, for the time had not come for them to live in the flesh.[2] But when the disobedience took place and gave rise to mortality, the feeling of shame before each other was rightly given to them. And they noticed at last the difference of their physical forms, a difference envisaged in advance by the Creator for the needs of the continuation of the species.

17 On the Leaves of the Fig Tree

Thus, realising that they were naked, Adam and Eve, after the transgression, made themselves girdles from fig leaves, alluding by this tree to the nature of their crime. For just as the fruit of the fig is sweet but its leaf most harsh and bitter, so too every sin seems sweet when committed, but afterwards it brings pain to the perpetrator. **2** What does Scripture say then? 'And they heard the voice of Lord God walking in paradise in the evening, and Adam and his wife hid themselves in the middle of the wood of paradise.'[3] **3** Having come to understand their sin after the daring act, they are paralysed by fear of the Judge, and they attempt to hide from the eye from which nothing escapes, and they avoid appearing and shrink from showing themselves. On seeing them in such confusion because of their

---

1 This is a very interesting commentary—a personal aside reflecting an interest in the problem of human perception as in the ancient Greek tradition.

2 'for ... flesh': this is a free translation of the Greek (σαρκικῆς διαθέσεως οὔπω καιρὸν ἔχοντες).

3 Genesis 3.8.

fear, God calls upon them like a loving father and says: 'Adam, where are you?' And Adam said to Him: 'I heard Your voice when You were walking in paradise, and I was frightened since I am naked, and I hid myself.'[1]

18 On the Judgement Against the First Humans and the Serpent

Then it could be seen how the luxuriant place that was paradise became a tribunal and a severe and fearful court. For God brought forward those who had been harmed, and the one who had done the harm and, having found that the serpent was guilty of sinning, and that Eve had been sinned against, He pronounced the punishment appropriate to each of them.[2] **2** For, having declared the serpent cursed, He condemned it to drag along on its breast and belly and to eat earth instead of edible food. And He pronounced that Eve should have sorrow as her companion and give birth in pain. And He judged that Adam should eat bread by the sweat of his brow until he returned to the earth from which he had been taken. **3** Then Scripture says: 'And God made garments[3] of skin for Adam and his wife, and He dressed them in these. And God said: "Behold, Adam has become Our equal and is able to distinguish between good and evil. And let him not now extend his hand and take of the tree of life and eat of it and live eternally."'[4]

19 Why Man is Exiled from Paradise, and on the Garments of Skin

It can be understood from what has been said that man, had he tasted the tree of life, could have lived eternally even after the transgression. Therefore, in order that man should not become an immortal evil, God declared him mortal by girding him with mortality.[5] For this is the significance of the garments of skin, because the animals are dead, so that, through the dissolution of the body and of the binding [of body and soul],[6] all sin should be destroyed completely.

---

1 Genesis 3.14–16.
2 For Chapter 18, §§ 1–2, cf. Genesis 3.11–19.
3 Or: 'shirts' (χιτῶνας).
4 Genesis 3.21–22.
5 'girding him with mortality' (νεκρότητι περιβαλών): or 'dressing him in something dead' (i.e. in the skin of dead animals).
6 ['of body and soul']: added here by me.

20 On 'Behold, Adam has Become Our Equal'

It is said by God: 'Behold, Adam has become Our equal and is able to distinguish between good and evil.' This is not said as if man, through his disobedience, progressed to the understanding of virtue and evil, but because he had been created in this way from the beginning. For earlier, Scripture said: 'God made man; in God's image did He make him.'[1] It is clear that the one made according to God's image already had the ability laid down in his nature to discern between good and evil. 2 Therefore, in order that he should not decide of his own free will to take from the tree of life and become an immortal evil, he and Eve were cast out onto the earth from which he had been created. 3 For, what does Holy Scripture say after all this? 'And the Lord God sent him out of the luxuriant paradise to work the earth from which he had been taken. And He cast Adam out and settled him opposite the luxuriant paradise, and He placed the cherubim and the flaming sword, the one which turns, to guard the road to the tree of life.'[2]

21 On the Cherubim and the Flaming Sword

When man had been cast out from the blessed place, unconquerable and most haughty guards were put into place to protect the road to the Tree of Life, so that no one henceforth should be able to approach this place with impure[3] feet. 2 A flaming sword was also placed there, so that anyone who approached should, being composed of matter, be consumed by fire there and be destroyed. 3 The sword turns, so that in the new life,[4] when man becomes the inhabitant of paradise again, it will shine for the righteous who come to the divine place of immortality, while it will burn the unjust if they come close. 4 Prior to Adam's transgression, the earth brought everything forth of its own accord but, after this, even earth itself was ordered not to bring forth anything without toil.

22 Thus Adam left paradise together with Eve, and he had intercourse with her and begot Cain, and after him Abel.[5] Cain was a farmer, whereas

---

1 Genesis 1.27.
2 Genesis 3.23–24.
3 'impure': or 'unhallowed/profane' (βεβήλοις).
4 'new life': or 'regeneration' (παλιγγενεσίᾳ).
5 For Chapters 22–23, cf. Genesis 4.1–15.

Abel was a shepherd. **2** Abel offered a gift to God from his first-born lambs, and God accepted his offering. Cain, however, did not offer from the first-born but brought his offering to God only after having enjoyed the fruits himself and with other people. Therefore, God did not accept them [not only these; there are also other examples, taken from the *Lesser Genesis*, of the extreme wickedness of Cain][1] (this became obvious through the fire sent from heaven to consume the offerings), and Cain envied Abel. **3** It should first be investigated why God did not accept Cain's offering. Scripture answers this question itself, saying: 'And it happened that, after some days, Cain made an offering of the fruits of the earth.'[2] By this, Cain is put to shame. For he did not offer the best of the produce, nor the first, to God, but reserved this for himself, while he tried to honour God in an impious way with the second best. **4** Further: why does Scripture call the offering of Abel's victims *gifts*, but the gifts of Cain's fruits a *sacrifice*? With regard to this question it can be said, following a correct method of reasoning: Abel's sacrifice was called a gift because he imitates those who give gifts when he brings the victim to God. **5** For Abel sacrifices the first-born of the animals and offers the fattest of the meat in the manner of those who, when giving a gift, want to please the recipients, and select the very best and give everything in its entirety, and bring the gift to the people they love without taking anything away from it. **6** For, the one who makes a sacrifice is likely to make a division so that he pours the blood over the altar but takes the meat home. But he who gives a gift surrenders the gift in its entirety to the recipient.[3] I think that it was in this manner that Abel dedicated the first-born, and he demonstrates that his purpose is love of God rather than love of self. By contrast, Cain accords the first produce to himself and he impiously deigns to offer to God the second best, after days had passed rather than at once, and he demonstrates that he loves himself rather than God. And, as is reasonable, he gives offence, and his gift is thrown back at him as unworthy.

   23 Cain was the first to devise a plough and to feel greed, whereas Abel was concerned for justice. Having killed Abel, Cain concealed the body, thinking that he would escape notice in this way. But God hears

---

1 The text included in square brackets is certainly a gloss added in the margin and then incorporated by a scribe into the text.

2 Genesis 4.3.

3 'in its entirety to the recipient': the Greek (παντὶ τῷ λαμβάνοντι) is slightly awkward and probably corrupt.

the blood crying out to Him. For God hears the righteous even if they are dead, but He turns away even the prayers of the unrighteous. For He has decided that the former should live though they are dead, and the latter He has condemned to death from any true life even if they are still alive. **2** God punishes Cain by not killing him at once, but He curses him with fear and sorrow for his whole life. Therefore, when Cain fears that he will be killed because he is a murderer, God says: 'Not so: whoever kills Cain will be punished sevenfold.'[1] This is as if to say: 'You should not think that your punishment will be small or negligible, nor should you have great hopes that you will escape the hardships of life by the swiftness of death. Rather you will have to suffer punishment commensurate with your sin. Therefore, you who have introduced the greatest of evil to the rest of mankind will be punished sevenfold. Thus you will not be killed now, as anyone who dares to kill you now and deliver you from the hardships of life will annul your sevenfold punishment.' Another version: 'Not so: whoever kills Cain will annul a sevenfold punishment. Every person[2] will die because of his own sin. But you, who introduced murder and became the guide for others to this sin, will pay a sevenfold punishment, that is, you will be punished sevenfold. For, to die brings an end to the evils of life, but a life in fear and sorrow brings limitless deaths, which are felt.' **3** Thus, trembling and wailing, Cain lived out the rest of his life as if possessed by a demon and suffering from seizures; this was the sign given from God that he should not be killed. After the condemnation he lived a more despicable life, and became greedy and rapacious. And he was the first to devise measures and weights and boundaries for land, and he built a city and forced all his people to gather at one place and to devote their time to war.

24 Cain took his sister Sauas for wife[3] and had a son, Enos.[4] From him was born Gaidad, and from him, Maouel,[5] and from him, Methuselah. Methuselah begets Lamech. Lamech took two wives, Adda and Sela, and by Adda he had as sons Jubal, who was a kithara player, and Jobel, who was a cattle keeper; and by Sela he had Thobel, who was a copper- and ironsmith, and a daughter, Noema. **2** And up to this point, the family

---

1 Genesis 4.15.

2 'Every person' (ἐκείνων μὲν γὰρ ἕκαστος): freely translated and somewhat uncertain.

3 Or: 'Awan.' The name and identity of Cain's wife are not given in Genesis; this information derives from Jubilees 4.9.

4 For Chapter 24, cf. Genesis 4.17–5.32.

5 Or: 'Maiel.'

of Cain is considered worthy of being remembered in books. But he is banned from the line of patriarchs, that he should neither be considered one of the first, nor the beginner of a line.[1] Because of the brutality of his character, he is in a way exiled from rational nature to the irrational.[2] As Moses says, Cain died when his house collapsed on him. 3 At the age of 230 Adam begot Seth and, having lived for an additional 700 years, he dies on the very day of the anniversary of the transgression. For, while God's day has a span of a thousand years, Adam lived for a mere 930 years and then died. 4 It is said that Adam was the first to be buried in the earth from which he was taken, and a Hebrew tradition tells that there is a monument to him in the region of Jerusalem. It was as it should be that Adam should be buried in the earth before anyone else, for he was the first to hear from God: 'You are earth, and to earth you will return.'[3] It is said[4] that Abel's body disappeared, indicating good hopes for righteous people in the future. 5 Seth took his sister Azouran for wife[5] and begot Enos at the age of 205 years. He was the first who had the confidence to[6] invoke the name of the Lord God; that is, to address God with His name. 6 This Seth gave names to the five planets: Kronos, Zeus, Ares, Aphrodite, and Hermes (for, God had named the two lights Sun and Moon); for, Seth was the first to understand the wisdom of the heavenly motions. 7 For, since Adam had predicted that there would be a destruction of the whole world, either by water or by fire, the descendants of Seth devised two stelae, one of clay and the other of stone, and they engraved learning on these. This Seth invented the Hebrew script and became the first writer. 8 Enos married his sister Emma.[7] At the age of 190 he begets Kainan. At the age of 170 Kainan begot Maleleel. At the age of 165 Maleleel begot Jared. At the age of 162 Jared begot Enoch. He is the first to learn and to teach reading and writing, and he is deemed worthy of revelations concerning the divine mysteries. At the age of 165 Enoch begot Methuselah and, having lived for a further 200 years and

1 Because Cain is excluded from the line of patriarchs, the narrative continues with Seth, the third son of Adam and Eve, and his offspring.
2 'exiled ... irrational': or 'classed with irrational rather than rational nature.'
3 Genesis 3.19.
4 Or: 'tradition/Moses/Scripture says' (φησί); cf. above, Chapter 15, § 4, etc.
5 So Jubilees 4.11 (Genesis 4.26 does not mention Seth's wife specifically).
6 ἤλπισεν.
7 Noam according to Jubilees 4.13 (Genesis 5.9 does not mention the name of his wife).

having borne witness to the *egregoroi*[1] concerning the punishment for the transgression, he is removed to Eden where paradise is. **9** It[2] should be noted that, whenever angels falter and turn to vile behaviour, then man is deemed worthy to experience a change for the better. For it is said that it was in his[3] days that those angels who are also called *egregoroi* came down to earth. **10** At the age of 187 Methuselah begot Lamech. At the age of 188 Lamech begot Noah. At the age of 500 Noah begot Shem and, after him, Ham and, after him, Japheth. **11** The *egregoroi* have intercourse with the daughters of men and become fathers of the giants, and they introduce divination and magic to the humans as well as astronomy and astrology and the knowledge of all heavenly motions,[4] and they gave the women the knowledge of all this, and they made humans attain the utmost of evil. [He says that the children of the *egregoroi* are evil spirits who are lusty and cherish the body][5] By this, the *egregoroi* provoked God to anger against them, and they are thrown into the depths of the earth.

25 God, wishing to destroy everyone by a flood, commanded Noah alone (Noah had won His liking because of his righteousness) to build an ark in order to preserve himself and his kin.[6] **2** And the ark is prepared by him over the course of a total of one hundred years, but the years are made longer during its construction[7] because of his great goodness. For, through his magnanimity, he caused the impending destruction to be delayed, and he brought it about that there was sufficient time for his household[8] to repent. **3** Having entered the ark, Noah and his three sons, in accordance with the divine guidance, brought in seven of each of the clean animals and two of each unclean, to preserve the best for the continuation of every species. When this had been done, the flood came over the earth. This was

---

1 Or: 'Watchers,' descended from Heaven (see below, §§ 9 and 11). This derives from the Book of Jubilees or the Book of Enoch (see Adler/Tuffin 2002, p. 12ff.). Cf. also Genesis 5.24 and 6.4.

2 The whole of § 9 is likely to be a marginal gloss that has entered the text at a secondary stage.

3 I.e. Enoch's.

4 ὑψηλῆς καὶ μετεώρου κινήσεως.

5 'He says ... body' is most certainly a marginal gloss that has entered the text at a secondary stage.

6 On Noah and the flood, cf. Genesis 6–9.

7 μηκύνονται δὲ οἱ χρόνοι τῆς κατασκευῆς.

8 'his household' (τοῖς συνιοῦσιν): or 'people conversing with him.' From 'his great goodness' and onwards it could be that God is the intended subject (here I have taken it for granted that it is Noah and that there is no change of subject).

in the 600th year of Noah, and the water descended for a total of forty days and as many nights. **4** When the water was already receding and the ark had come to rest on the mountains of Armenia, Noah and his three sons leave the ark together with their wives and their whole household, and he drives the animals out from it. Noah offers a sacrifice to God and beseeches Him not to make another flood. God showed His appreciation of the man's virtue and promised this, putting up the rainbow as a sign. **5** The flood took place in Noah's 600th year. There are 2,242 years from Adam until Noah and the flood.[1]

26 In the second year after the flood, Shem, who was a hundred years old, begot Arphaxad. **2** At the age of 135 Arphaxad begot Sala. **3** When he grew up, his father taught him letters. And when Sala once had set out on his own, thinking about founding a colony, he comes to the land of the Chaldeans, where he finds letters carved into rocks. This was the tradition stemming from the *egregoroi*. Sala wrote it down, and he himself sinned because of it and also taught others the absurdities contained in it. **4** At the age of 130 Sala begot Eber. During his time humans once again multiply into a countless multitude and, having reached a height of evil, they decide to build a tower[2] as high as the heaven, so as to be able to ascend to heaven through it. **5** They built this tower at the behest of Nebrod and in order to escape inundations, supposing that God was laying plans against them with water. The total number of peoples engaged in the building was seventy, and they had all the same language. Nebrod, the giant, the son of Chouse the Ethiopian, hunted for food and gave them animals to eat. It was the task of Eber, the son of Sala, to ensure the progress of the construction work. **6** When it seemed to them that the project was prospering, God confused their tongues, dividing them into different kinds of languages. It is said that only Eber kept the ancient language, and his descendants, who inherited this language, called themselves 'Hebrews' from their founding father, and they called the language 'Hebrew.' **7** Proof that this was the language before the confusion are the ancient names.[3] Where it is not possible to produce an etymology from any other language, it is possible to make an interpretation according to this language. There is, for example, no explanation

---

1 From the information given above, the expected sum should be 2,262 years (230+205+190+170+165+162+165+187+188+500+100 = 2,262). Cf. also below, Chapter 33, § 5, with note.

2 On the Tower of Babel, cf. Genesis 11.1–9.

3 Or: 'names of the ancients': i.e. of people before the flood.

to be found in any other language of the name of Adam, but in Hebrew it means 'human being.' And the name of Noah cannot be explained in any other idiom, but in Hebrew it means 'righteousness'; and Chous means 'Ethiopian,' and Mesraeim 'Egypt,' and Phalek 'division.' **8** The tower, work upon which had gone on for forty-three years, remained half-finished, due to the discord following the confusion of the tongues. The city at the place was named Confusion, after the event. This is Babylon, which is built there. For the Hebrews call confusion 'babylon.' Later, God overturns the tower completely by a storm, but there are still[1] traces left of the tower between Asour and Babylon.

27 At the age of 134 Eber begot Phalek. It is at the beginning of Phalek's days that Noah's sons quarrel and divide the earth between themselves. [At the age of 130 years Phalek begot Ragau and, having lived for a further 209 years, he died. **2** There are a total of 3,000 years from Adam until the death of Phalek.][2] Therefore, Phalek's name is appropriate. For it translates as 'division,' alluding to both the partitions: first, the allotment of the earth is made by Noah's sons during his reign; further, the division[3] of the supposed time of 6,000 years happens at the end of his days; the first division[4] takes place at the beginning, the second at the end of his life. **3** Then the three sons of Noah send for all their descendants, and Noah gives them a written document defining the division of the land, and everyone, together with their tribes and their families, receives lands[5] and regions and villages and islands and rivers according to the exposition below. **4** Shem, Noah's first-born son, receives the land from Persia and Bactria as far as India and Rinokorourai; Ham, Noah's second son, receives the land from Rinokorourai as far as Gadeira, everything towards the south; Japheth, Noah's third son, receives the land from Media as far as Gadeira, everything towards the north.

28 The lands allotted to Shem, the first-born son of Noah, are the following by name: Persia, Bactria, Hyrcania, Babylonia, Cordyne, Assyria, Mesopotamia, Old Arabia, Elymais, India, Arabia Felix, Coele-Syria,

---

1 'still': we may ask to what age this 'still' refers, and when someone was able to check that traces of the tower remained.
2 The text within square brackets is certainly a marginal gloss that has entered the text at a secondary stage. The following 'Therefore etc.' belongs as a direct continuation to the preceding 'earth between themselves.'
3 'division': i.e. into two, or in the middle (6,000/2 = 3,000).
4 There is a textual problem here, but the meaning seems clear.
5 'lands ... villages': τόποι καὶ κλίματα καὶ χῶραι.

Commagene and the whole of Phoenicia. In his part there is the river Euphrates. **2** Out of Shem's tribe there appeared a man of the race of giants, named Kronos (after the planet) by his father.[1] Kronos was the first to rule over the Assyrians. He had a wife, Semiramis, who was also called Rhea, and by her he had a son called Zeus, or Pikos, who married his own sister, Hera. Kronos had another son, too, by the name of Afros, and to him he gave the land in the direction of Libya[2] as his lot by inheritance. Afros married Astynome and had a daughter by her whom he called Aphrodite. **3** On being ousted from power by Zeus, his own son, Kronos left his sons, Zeus and Ninos, to rule over the Assyrians together with their mother, Rhea. He himself goes to the West, assumes power there and becomes the king of all Italy. However, Zeus left the Assyrians and came to his father who accords him all Italy to rule over. And having reigned for many years, he[3] dies and is buried in Crete. **4** After Ninos, Thourras became king of the Assyrians. He was renamed Ares, for he was most warlike and valiant. Renaming him Baal the god, the Assyrians erect a statue to him and worship him. **5** After Zeus' death, his son Faunus reigned. He was renamed Hermes, for he was most intelligent and fond of learning. It was he who taught mankind how to extract gold from ore.

29 To Ham, Noah's second son, the lands named as follows were allotted: Egypt, Ethiopia (the part which looks towards India), the other Ethiopia (from which the river of the Ethiopians flows out), Erythra[4] (which stretches towards the East), Thebais, Libya (as far as Cyrene), Marmaris, Syrtis, Libya (the part stretching from the Delta as far as the end of Syrtis), Numidia, Massyris, Mauritania (which stretches as far as to the Pillars of Hercules, opposite Gadeira). **2** To him belong in the north, along the sea, Cilicia, Pamphylia, Pisidia, Moesia, Lycaonia, Phrygia, Camalia, Lycia, Caria, Lydia, the other[5] Moesia, Troas, Aiolis, Bithynia, the old Phrygia. He also possesses the islands of Sardinia, Crete and Cyprus, and the river Geon, called the Nile.

---

1 The following has parallels in the Chronicle of George the Monk. In the MS Vat. gr. 163 (of the Logothete) it is hinted that at least some of it stems from Julius Africanus (cf. Introduction). It is a case of the incorporation of Hellenic deities into the biblical schema, well known also from other chronicles (cf. Introduction).

2 'land in the direction of Libya' (τὴν πρὸς Λιβύην γῆν), i.e. Africa.

3 This should refer to Zeus.

4 'the other (or 'another') Ethiopia ... Erythra': or 'another Ethiopia ... called Erythra [the Red].'

5 Or: 'another.'

30 To Japheth, Noah's third son, the lands named as follows were allotted: Media, Albania, Amazonis, Greater and Lesser Armenia, Cappadocia, Paphlagonia, Galatia, Colchis, Bosporania, Maiotis, Dervis, Sarmatia, Taurianis, Bastranis, Scythia, Thrace, Macedonia, Dalmatia, Molossia, Thessaly, Locris, Boeotia, Aetolia, Attica, Achaea, Pellene which is called Peloponnese, Arcadia, Epirus, Illyria, Lychnitis, Adria, from which [is named] the Adriatic sea. **2** To him belong also the following islands: Britain, Sicily, Euboea, Rhodes, Chios, Lesbos, Cythera, Zakynthos, Cephalonia, Ithaca, Corfu and the Cyclades, and the part of Asia, which is called Ionia. There is in his territories the river Tigris, which divides Media from Babylon. **3** From the sons of Japheth, through Gamer, stem the Gomareis, now called Galatians, and from Magoth, the people now called Scythians, and from Mados, the Medians. From Ion stem the Ionians and the other Greeks, and from Thobel, the Thobelians, now called Iberians, and from Mesoch, the Meschenians, now called Cappadocians (therefore, their capital is called Mazaka), and from Thera, the Thracians, and from Tharron, the Tharseis, now called Cilicians (from him comes the name of Tarsos, the most important city of the Cilicians).

31 When the afore-mentioned distribution had been accomplished, Shem, who had settled at the same place as his father had done, divides his part of the inheritance amongst his children. However, Ham's son, Canaan, seeing that the land that lies up to Mount Lebanon was good and productive and very much different from his own, takes up his quarters there and cuts off this land from the land allotted to the descendants of Shem. This he did although his father and his brothers tried to stop him and reminded him of the curses their father Noah had called down upon those who did not respect his decision. From this point, that whole land was called Canaan.

32 So when Noah's three sons had, as has been said, divided the world into three parts and, since the part given to each of them has been indicated, it is now time to return to our main subject. Since we ended with the birth of Ragau from Phalek, let us start again from him. **2** At the age of 132 Ragau begot Serouch. During his time, humans became more arrogant in their dealings with each other, and they appointed themselves generals and kings and then, for the first time, they constructed instruments of war and started to fight each other. And at once, the descendants of Canaan are defeated, and they are the first to fall under the yoke of slavery, in accordance with Noah's curse. **3** At the age of 130 Serouch begot Nachor. Serouch lived in the land of the Chaldeans and in the city of Ur. When

Nachor grew up, he was taught by his father to interpret every kind of omen and to distinguish all signs in heaven and on earth and every kind of Chaldean divination. 4 And at the age of seventy-nine Nachor begot Tharra. In the forty-third year of the reign of Ninos, the first king of the Assyrians, Abraham is born. He [Ninos] married his mother, Semiramis, also called Rhea, and he founds the city of Nineveh and calls it Ninos. From him the custom has prevailed among the Persians to marry their own mothers and sisters—just as Zeus had also married his sister, Hera. After Ninos, his wife, Semiramis, reigned over the Assyrians. It was she who had the mounds built to prevent flooding. At the same time, the sixteenth dynasty ruled in Egypt, during which the Thebans possessed the power. 5 At the age of seventy Tharra begot Abraham by his wife Edna, the daughter of his paternal uncle, Abraham.[1] Abraham's mother named him after her father, who had died before Abraham's birth. Tharra also begot Arran and Nachor. Abraham receives Sarah as his wife from his father. Abraham was the only one anywhere to recognise the true God, whereas everyone else suffered under the deception of the idols. Arran also received a wife, and he got a son, Lot, and a daughter, Melcham. Nachor takes Melcham as his wife.

33 Abraham was already in his sixtieth year and, since he did not think that he would ever be able to persuade his father and the rest of the household to abandon the superstition of the idols, at night, he secretly set fire to the house with the idols. When these were beginning to be destroyed, his brothers realised what was happening and jumped up from their beds, and they tried to extract the idols from the fire. 2 Arran engages with particular zeal in the matter, and perishes in the fire, and his father buries him in Ur, the city of the Chaldeans, and then moves with his complete household to Harran in Mesopotamia. 3 Having lived there together with his father for fifteen years, one night, Abraham considers predicting the coming time from the movement of the stars. For he had been well trained by his father in all science of this kind. Yet, having thought about every aspect of the matter, he comes to the conclusion that all this searching is in vain. For, he thought, God could, if He wanted to, change His prior decisions at will. 4 Having renounced all such matters out of a complete conviction, Abraham, who had given perfect proof of his piety with regard to the divine, hears a voice from God, saying: 'Leave your country and the house of your father.'[2] And Abraham leaves together with his wife, Sarah,

1 Or: 'Abram.'
2 Genesis 12.1.

and his nephew, Lot, and he moves to the portion belonging to his father, Arphaxad, which the Canaanites had occupied and renamed Canaan. Abraham was seventy-five years of age at that time. 5 The following is the total of years up to Abraham's migration: the division of the earth took place in the beginning of the days of Phalek. From the division of the earth, there are 616 years; from the flood, there are 1,015 years; from Adam, there are 3,277 years.[1] 6 Having lived in the land of the Canaanites for twenty-five years after his departure, Abraham begets Isaac. Before Isaac, Ishmael is born to Abraham from Hagar; from Ishmael stems the Ishmaelite tribe (these are the same as the Hagarenes, who are also called Saracens). 7 At this time, God lets fire rain over Pentapolis, and He destroys all mankind there. He also lays waste all this stretch of land, and the waters of the adjacent sea are deprived of all life. 8 Shortly afterwards, Abraham moves from the Oak of Mamre to the Well of the Oath and, having set up tents for himself privately and for the members of his clan according to their family connections, he then for the first time celebrates the Feast of Tabernacles for seven days. This festival is still celebrated by Israel through the pitching of tents.

34 It is said that Isaac was twenty-five years of age when he was brought to be sacrificed.[2] Abraham built the altar at the same spot where later David founded the temple. At the age of sixty, Isaac begets Esau and Jacob. 2 When Jacob was already in his seventy-fifth year, he flees from Esau, his brother, and encounters Laban in Harran, in Mesopotamia. Laban was the brother of Rebecca, the mother of Jacob. 3 Jacob guards Laban's sheep for a total of twenty years. He receives Leah and Rachel, Laban's daughters, in marriage in return for fourteen years of service, and an agreed salary for the remaining six years. Later, he receives Bilhah and Zilpah, the maidservants,[3] as gifts from his wives and, during the thirteen years he spent in Mesopotamia after the first seven years, he begets children with the four women: eleven sons and one daughter. From Leah, he gets Reuben and Simeon and Levi and Judah and Issachar and Zebulun and Dinah; from Rachel, he gets Joseph; from Bilhah, he gets Dan and Naphthali; from Zilpah, he gets Gad and Asher. 4 In the

---

1 Cf. above, Chapter 25, § 5.

2 For the Sacrifice of Isaac see Genesis 22:1–19. Nothing is said in the Bible about Isaac's age, but he is obviously depicted as a child. That he was twenty-five years old (a claim here introduced by 'It is said,' Greek φησί) is an Orthodox tradition.

3 'maidservants' (παιδίσκας): or 'slave girls.' Greek forms of their names are Βάλλα and Ζελφά.

twentieth year, Jacob fled from Laban, but he is apprehended by him on the seventh day on Mount Galaad.[1] There they make an agreement under oath and then depart from each other, Laban to Harran, and Jacob to the city of Salem, close to Sikima.[2] **5** This is where Dinah is raped by Shechem.[3] Rachel bears one more son to Jacob, Benjamin, and on dying, she is buried in the Ephratha region where Bethlehem is now.[4] Simeon and Levi take revenge for the outrage suffered by their sister, and they kill Shechem and his men by the use of every kind of guile.[5] **6** Remembering the vision he had seen on his arrival in Mesopotamia, Jacob goes up to Bethel (this was the name of the place where he had gone to sleep and had the vision), and he gives a tenth of all his possessions to God. Last of all, he does the same with his sons and subjects them to the casting of lots and, when Levi is chosen, Jacob dedicates him to God and makes him the priest of God. Levi offers up his father's tithe as the first sacrifice to God. **7** Now, since the Levitic tribe continues to Aaron and Moses, of whom the one serves as high priest and the other as military commander to Israel, it is reasonable to trace the lineage after Jacob through Levi. **8** When Jacob was eighty-seven years old, he begot Levi. Rebecca demanded that Isaac should bring Esau and Jacob and reconcile them to each other and exhort them and make them swear that they will keep peace with each other and cherish a disposition of brotherly love. This Isaac did, and he forewarned Esau, that 'if you rebel against Jacob, you will fall into his hands.' **9** Rebecca dies first, and Isaac shortly after. They had left the privileges of primogeniture to Jacob. **10** Esau's sons incited their father against Jacob and his sons, and they armed themselves together with Gentiles and went to war. But Jacob closed the city gates and entreated Esau to remember the commandments and exhortations of their parents. But Esau did not accept this, and he treated Jacob with derision, at which, being asked by Judah to do so, Jacob stretched his bow tight and hit Esau in the breast on the right side and struck him down. And, when Esau had died in this way, the sons of Jacob opened the city gates and came out to attack, killing almost everyone.

1 Or: 'Gilead': see Genesis 31:49.
2 Or: 'Shechem.' Septuagint Genesis 33.18 has Σαλὴμ πόλιν Σικίμων. It is an open question whether the chronicler is thinking of a people or a place.
3 Or: 'Sychem.'
4 On Rachel's death, cf. Genesis 35:16–20.
5 Cf. Genesis 34.

35 In the second year of Israel's sojourn in Egypt [it is said[1] that a fearsome[2] sacred scribe[3] had predicted that a child born[4] to the Hebrews in that year would dissolve the kingdom of the Egyptians; and for that reason, the Pharaoh ordered that all children born to the Hebrews should be killed],[5] **2** Levi, who was forty-five years old, begets Kaath. At the age of sixty-three years, Kaath begets Ambram. At the age of seventy years, Ambram begets Moses. **3** Ambram, the father of Moses, so Scripture tells, prayed to God not to allow the Hebrew people to be destroyed. Also, he is said to have received a divine revelation in a dream about the birth and the power of the child Moses. **4** When Moses had been born and had been exposed, he was taken care of by Thermouthis, Pharaoh's daughter. The child was of such charming beauty that all who saw him watched him in constant admiration. **5** From Abraham and Chettoura, Jexan is born, and from Jexan, Dadam, and from Dadam, Ragouel and Jothor, also called Jobab, and from Jothor, Sepphora whom Moses married. As Demetrios tells, according to what Eusebios claims in the *Chronicle*,[6] Moses is the seventh from Abraham and Sepphora the sixth. At the age of eighty, Moses leads the exodus from Egypt after the 430 years of exile.[7]

36 It should be noted that the 430 years of the people's exile should be counted until the return.[8] **2** In his thirtieth year, Joseph is entrusted with the power of the Egyptians. When seven years of plenty and two years of famine had passed, Jacob came down with his children to Egypt. It is said[9] that the Nile did not rise during all of the seven years of famine in Egypt. Thus Joseph was thirty-nine years of age then, and he lived for a total of 110 years. **3** After Joseph's death, the Hebrews serve as slaves to the Egyptians for 144 years. **4** The total of years of the exile in Egypt

1 Or: 'Scripture says' (φησί).
2 Or: 'powerful' (δεινόν).
3 'sacred scribe' (ἱερογραμματέα): i.e. a high-ranking Egyptian official.
4 Or rather: 'the child born' (τὸ τικτόμενον παιδίον).
5 The text within square brackets is certainly a gloss incorporated into the text at a secondary stage. The text before the brackets ('In ... Egypt') is continued by the text after the brackets ('Levi,' etc.).
6 Eusebios' *Chronicle* (or *Chronographia*) has been lost in the original Greek but was used extensively by chronographers (cf. Introduction). Cf., however, in this case also the *Praeparatio Evangelica* 9.29.1–3 (frg. of Demetrios, a Jewish chronicler of the third c. BC).
7 The text is problematic here and the translation hypothetical.
8 'return' (ἀνάβασις): or 'ascent.'
9 Or: 'Scripture says' (φησί).

is therefore 215,[1] and it lasted from the departure from Harran until the exodus towards the land of the Canaanites.[2] Moses is shown to have organised this exodus in his eightieth year. For the [total] exile was not only spent in Egypt, but also in the land of Canaan. This is also presented to us by Scripture itself which says: 'The sojourning of the sons of Israel, which they spent in the land of Egypt and the land of Canaan, 430 years.'[3] 5 In Abraham's days there was Melchizedek, a pious man, the son of the king Sidos, son of Aegyptus. It was Melchizedek who founded the city of Sidon. 6 And Abraham lived twenty-five years from the march up from Harran until the birth of Isaac; and Isaac lived sixty years until Jacob [was born]; and Jacob lived eighty-seven years until Levi (when Levi was forty-three years of age, Jacob, being himself 130 years of age then, went down with all his household to Egypt). Levi lived forty-five years until Kaath, and Kaath lived sixty-three years until Abraham,[4] and Abraham lived seventy years until Moses, and Moses lived eighty years before the exodus.[5] 7 During this time Inachos ruled as first king of Argos, and after these years, the people spend forty years in the desert. Phoroneus ruled the Argives, and it is during his reign that the Greeks say that the Ogygian flood took place.[6] And after their first king, Pikos, who died in Crete and who at that time had been renamed Zeus, Ninos' [wife] Semiramis became queen of the Assyrians.[7] 8 On assuming the leadership Joshua son of Nun[8] crosses the river Jordan and reigns over the people for twenty-five years after Moses. He destroyed seven provinces and dethroned twenty-nine kings. 9 Thus there are 2,263 years from Adam until the flood, and from the flood to the division of the earth 399 years, and from the division until Abraham's emigration 616 years, and from the emigration until the death of Joshua son of Nun 495 years. In sum, there are 3,774[9] years from Adam.

1 I.e. 110–39+144 = 215.
2 The text of this sentence is possibly corrupt and the translation therefore hypothetical.
3 Exodus 12.40.
4 I.e. Ambram (cf. above, Chapter 35, §§ 2–3).
5 Thus, a total of 430 years are accounted for in this paragraph (25+60+87+45+63+70+80 = 430).
6 Ogyges was a mythical king of Attica during whose reign a great flood is said to have taken place.
7 Cf. Chapter 28 for people mentioned here.
8 Or: 'Jesus son of Naue.'
9 Strictly speaking, this gives 3,773 years (2,263+399+616+495 = 3,773). However, the years from Adam until the flood should be 2,262, not 2,263.

37 After Joshua, elders[1] from the tribes of Judah and Simeon in turn are said to have ruled over the people for thirty years while favouring each other's parties.[2] **2** After this, the people turn to idolatry and are delivered into the hands of Chousarsasthon,[3] the king of Mesopotamia, who ruled over them for eight years. It is said that Prometheus lived at this time. He was a wise and well-educated man, and by this he formed mankind so as to liberate them from their uncouthness. When now the people returned to God, He elevates Gothoniel, who acted as the people's judge for fifty years. Gothoniel was the brother of Chaleb.[4] **3** During these years, it is said that the flood under Deucalion took place.[5] It seems that also the Egyptians make reference to this, when they say that their country was not flooded and that this flood was local only. The earlier flood[6] they do not know about either, since their patriarch[7] had not been born yet. For Ham, the son of Noah, was the father of Mesraeim[8] from whom the Egyptians descend. **4** The sons of Israel sin again and are delivered into the hands of Eglom,[9] the king of the Moabites, and they serve him as slaves for eighteen years. When they once again return to God, they are saved through Aod the Ambidextrous (he received the nickname Ambidextrous since he was able to use his left hand with the same skill as his right in every matter). He led the people for eighty years. In the twenty-seventh year of his reign, Cecrops Diphyes became king of Attica (he was so called because he spoke two languages[10]). In the seventy-seventh year, the flood in Thessaly[11] and in Ethiopia is recorded by them.[12] **5** The people sin

---

1 Greek πρεσβύτεροι, later on a term for a person of influence, and with office, within the Church (cf. Index of terms and concepts).

2 'favouring ... parties' (τοῖς ἀλλήλων σχοινίσμασιν ἀνὰ μέρος βοηθοῦντες): this is vague. σχοίνισμα may refer either to a portion of a people or a piece of land.

3 Or: 'Chousarsathaim.'

4 Or: 'Caleb.'

5 Cf. the Ogygian flood (above, Chapter 36, § 7) and, of course, that of Noah.

6 I.e. that of Noah (see above, Chapter 25).

7 'patriarch': or 'chief of kin' or 'ancestor.'

8 Or: 'Mizraim.'

9 Or: 'Eglon.'

10 Literally 'with two tongues.' Cecrops was the mythical founder of Athens. 'Diphyes' means 'of two natures' and is in other accounts interpreted as referring to his body, with a human head and torso, and a fish-tail or snake below.

11 The flood associated with Deucalion (see above, § 3) is also located in Thessaly, and perhaps this is a reference to the same event.

12 'them': presumably in reference to Greek pagan tradition.

again and come, for twenty years, under the power of Jabe, the king of the Canaanites. During his reign Deborah, the wife of Laphidoth,[1] of the tribe of Ephraim, acts as prophetess. By her agency, Barak, son of Abithem from the tribe of Naphthali, came to lead the people for forty years. During this time Cadmus became king in Thebes. It was he who brought Tiresias, the philosopher and seer, to Thebes. It is about Tiresias that Sophocles says that 'having seen Pallas bathing, Tiresias was changed from being a man into a woman by nature.'[2] 6 After Deborah's death, the people sinned again, and they are enslaved to the Midianites for seven years. But by divine signs Gideon, of the tribe of Manasseh, gains a belief in victory, and he organises a rebellion and, having slaughtered 120,000 men with the help of 300, he ruled the people for forty years; and Abimelech, his son, ruled for three years; and Thola, son of Phoua, from the tribe of Ephraim, ruled for twenty-three years; and Jaeir the Galaadite, from the tribe of Manasseh, ruled for twenty-two years. 7 After him, the people sinned and were delivered into the hands of the Ammonites for eighteen years. Then they return to God, and He saves them through Jephtha the Galaadite, born from a mother of different origin but belonging himself to the tribe of Manasses. Jephtha rules the people for six years. 8 After him, Esebon, of the tribe of Judah, from Bethlehem, ruled for seven years. During this time, Ilium was built, and Asclepius pursued the science of medicine. 9 Eglom the Zaboulonite acted as the judge of Israel for ten years, and Abdon the Marathonite,[3] son of Eleim, for eight years. During this time, Orpheus, the poet, became famous. 10 Having sinned again, the people are delivered into the hands of foreigners for forty years. When they have returned to God, He elevates Samson. Samson was the son of Manoe and of the tribe of Dan. He, having defeated the foreigners, rules for twenty years. During this time Herakles, who accomplished the twelve labours, became famous. 11 For[4] Samanei led the people for one year and, according to Hebrew tradition, there was anarchy and everyone did what he wanted to, as is wont to happen during anarchy. The people had forty

---

1 Or: 'Lapidoth.'

2 Variations of this (which is not known from any of Sophocles' preserved plays) are told in several Byzantine sources, e.g. Eustathios' *Commentary on Homer's Odyssey* I.390.6–7 (who attributes it to Kallimachos); see also Malalas (see Jeffreys/Jeffreys/Scott et al. 1986, p. 20).

3 Or: 'Labdon the Pharathonite/Phraathonite' (Septuagint Judges 12.14: Λάβδων ὁ Φρααθωνίτης).

4 'For' (Greek γάρ): this is not clear.

years of peace with the foreigners, and Samanei[1] led them during thirty of these years. **12** The high priest Eli ruled the people for twenty years. During this time, the Trojan war was fought for ten years, and Ilium was captured. **13** Samuel succeeded Eli as high priest and leader, and he takes control over the people. It is said that he was twelve years of age when God first appeared to him and talked to him. During this time[2] the ark stood in the house of Aminadam. And Eli was responsible for the anointing of kings for seventy years. **14** There are 610 years from the death of Joshua until the death of Samuel, 2,120 years from Noah and the flood, and 4,382 years from Adam.[3]

38 When Samuel had himself already grown old and only reluctantly acted as the overseer of the people, and when his children were continually compromising with the rule of law by accepting gifts, he anoints as king Saul, son of Kis, from the tribe of Benjamin. He did this under compulsion from the people and with God's consent. **2** For Saul and his boy,[4] who were looking for their donkeys, went in to Samuel, and Samuel told Saul about the kingship and what he sought. And Saul went out to his relative and friend and told him all of this except about the kingship, indicating by this that one should not trust friends nor relatives[5] when it comes to great matters, because of the ease with which one becomes the victim of human malignity. **3** This Saul reigns for twenty years with the support of Samuel, and twenty years on his own. During his[6] reign, Samuel acted as a prophet as well as a high priest, and Abener, the son of Ner, led the military forces for him.

39 Since Saul had offended God, Samuel anoints a new king, David, son of Jesse, from the tribe of Judah. And Samuel dies two years before Saul. David reigns for seven years while Saul is still alive, and for thirty-three years after Saul's death. **2** During his reign Abiathar, son of Abimelech,

---

1 Presumably, this is not the same man as the one mentioned at the beginning of the paragraph.

2 'During this time': the text is problematic and the translation uncertain.

3 Here, too, the calculation is almost correct: adding 610 to the previous 3,774 (see Chapter 36, § 9) we should arrive at 4,384 and, adding 2,262 years (cf. here, too, Chapter 36, § 9, in which the text has 2,263 years) to 2,120, we arrive at 4,382.

4 I.e. 'servant' (παῖδα). In our chronicle, a long biblical story is abbreviated and separate episodes conflated (see 1 Sam. 9–10:). The 'relative and friend' mentioned in the chronicle (see the following), who appears rather suddenly to the reader, is the one referred to in 1 Sam. 10.14.

5 'one … relatives': this is slightly reminiscent of Jeremiah 9.4.

6 Presumably Saul.

held the office of high priest; he was related to Eli, but from another family,[1] namely that of Sadok. David himself, Gad, Nathan, Asaf and Idithoum acted as prophets, and Joab was David's military commander. **3** Forty years of Saul should be counted in the overall chronology, and forty years of David, since, as has been said, David reigned seven of his years while Saul was still alive. **4** It is said that, because of the marriage to Melchol, Saul asked for and received from David not a hundred foreskins, but 600 heads of foreign men.[2] **5** During his reign Joab, the commander of the military forces, made a census of Israel's tribes, and he arrived at a number of 1,100,000; the sons of Judah were 470,000.[3] But he did not count the tribes of Levi and Benjamin. Because of this, 70,000 fell out of the people.[4] **6** It is said that David composed an immeasurable number of songs and hymns to God, to be performed with many kinds of musical instruments. It is also said that Solomon buried a lot of gold together with David. The Hebrew kings of different times used, when they were besieged, to open his grave and to take gold to the amount of many talents.[5] But no one laid hands on the coffins of the kings, for these had been hidden by Solomon and could not be found.

40 Solomon, the son of David, succeeded his father and reigned for forty years. **2** He, having laid the foundation of God's temple in the fourth year of his reign, and having worked upon it over a period of seven years, dedicates it in the eleventh year of his reign. **3** Under Solomon, Sadok was high priest, and Nathan, who also had encouraged him to build the temple, acted as prophet together with Achiam the Silonite, and Sameas, son of Salame, and Addo; and the armed forces are entrusted to Baneas, son of Jodae. **4** From such a multitude of wives Solomon had only one son, Rehoboam.[6] **5** Solomon laid down many works in writing, and he also contrived many incantations and oaths to exorcise demons.[7] Some Jews

---

1 'family': Greek πατριᾶς.

2 On the foreskins see 1 Sam. 18.25–27. The version with the 600 heads is known from Josephus' *Jewish Antiquities* 6.10.3.

3 Cf. 1 Chr. 21.5–6.

4 I.e. because of the apparently sinful act of organising a census David was punished, and 70,000 people had to die.

5 See Chapter 48, § 4, with note.

6 Or: 'Roboam.'

7 The material of this paragraph belongs to the tradition of the *Testament of Solomon* and, as far as its use in Byzantine chronicles is concerned, it would seem to be derived from Josephus' *Jewish Antiquities* 8.2.5.

used these and, according to the instructions of Solomon, they put a ring with a seal together with a root in the nose of the sufferer, in order that the demon should smell this and be drawn out. And they used a glass full of water or some other kind of vessel as a sign of this; for on escaping the demon always crushed this. **6** During this time Homer became famous, as well as Hesiod.

41 Rehoboam, son of Solomon, reigns for eighteen years. During his reign the entire people is divided into two groups, and the tribe of Judah remains with him as well as that of Benjamin, whereas the remaining ten tribes appointed as their king Jeroboam, the son of Nabat, from the tribe of Ephraim, a man who belonged to the household of Solomon. **2** Rehoboam's palace was situated in Jerusalem, and the population under his rule was called Judah, and the house [was called] David, taking its name from the most powerful tribe. **3** Jeroboam's main city was Samaria, and his palace was in Thersa, and there were two altars, one in Bethel (for he places one of the calves there), and the other in Samaria, in the tribe of Dan (for he had the other calf consecrated there[1]). The name of his people was Israel, because of its quantity, and Ephraim, because of the tribe to which the king belonged. **4** During this time Sameas, the son of Salame, still acted as prophet, as did also the man who had come from Judah to Samaria and prophesied to Jeroboam in front of the altar.[2] Having transgressed God's command, this man was killed by a lion who happened to encounter him on the road as he travelled back home.

42 Abia takes over the rule after his father and reigns for three years. **2** After him, his son, Asa, reigns for forty-one years. When he was already old, he was struck by arthritis in the feet. During his reign Ananias[3] acts as prophet. **3** After him, his son, Josaphat, reigns for twenty-five years. During his reign Micah,[4] the son of Jembla, acted as prophet as well as Abdioum, the son of Ananias, and Eleazar and Ananias. There was also the false prophet Sedekias, the son of Canaan.[5] During this time Elijah also acted as prophet in Israel, and after him, Elisha. **4** Having succeeded his father, Josaphat, Joram[6] reigns for eight years. He was a man who surpassed most with regard to impiety. He was the son-in-law of Ahab, the king of

---

1 Cf. 1 Kgs 12.26–30.
2 For this unnamed prophet see 1 Kgs 13.
3 Or: 'Hananiah.'
4 Or: 'Michaias' (of Moresheth).
5 Or: 'Zedekiah son of Chenaanah.'
6 Or: 'Jehoram.'

the Israelites, and he also came to be an admirer of his way of life. There were the same prophets during his reign, and Jodae served as high priest. **5** Ochozias,[1] having succeeded him, reigns for one year. He was killed by Jehu, the king of Israel, when he annihilated Ahab's kin.[2] **6** After him, Gotholia,[3] daughter of Zambre, the king of the Israelites, wife of Joram, and mother of Ochozias, reigns over Jerusalem for eight years. Being the most impious of women, she, in an act of vengeance against Ahab, the king of the Israelites, destroys all of Ochozias' children. For, Ochozias seemed to be of Ahab's kin.[4] But Josabed, the sister of Ozias, the wife of the high priest Jodae, having stolen away Joas, the son of Ochozias, still an infant, brings him up.[5] During her [Gotholia's] reign Jodae served as high priest, and his son Zacharias acted as prophet. **7** When Joas,[6] the son of Ochozias, was eight years old, the high priest, Jodae, anointed him and proclaimed him king. This he did after having killed Gotholia.[7] Having been pious at the beginning, Joas tears down all idols except those in high places.[8] During his reign the high priest Jodae died after having lived for 130 years. It should be noted that he seems to be the only person after Moses to have lived for such a long time. Towards the end of his life Joas starts to worship the idols, and he had Zacharias, the son of Jodae, who accused him of erring, killed by stoning.[9] Joas reigns for forty years. **8** His son Amesias succeeds him and reigns for twenty-nine years. During his reign the Cumaean Sibyl became famous. **9** Ozias,[10] also named Zacharias, the son of Amesias, reigned for fifty-two years; he was a pious man. But later he tried to enter the holy places[11] and was struck with leprosy, and his son had to act as judge in his stead. During his reign Azarias was high priest. Amos and Isaiah, his son, acted as prophets, as did also Hosea[12] the son of Bekrei[13] and Jonas the

1 Or: 'Ahaziah.'
2 Cf. 2 Chron. 22; 2 Kgs 9.14–29.
3 Or: 'Athaliah.'
4 I.e. because of the true or believed relationship of Ochozias to Ahab, Gotholia had Ochozias' children, her own grandchildren, killed.
5 Cf. 2 Chron 22.10–12; 2 Kgs 11.1–3.
6 Or: 'Joash'/'Jehoash.'
7 Cf. 2 Kgs 11.4–16; 2 Chron 23.1–11.
8 Cf. 2 Kgs 12.1–3.
9 Cf. 2 Chron 24.17–21.
10 Or: 'Uzziah.'
11 Cf. 2 Chron 15.1–7; 26.16–21.
12 Or: 'Osee.'
13 Or: 'son of Beeri' (cf. Hosea 1.1).

son of Amathei, from Gopher. At this time, Lycurgus the Lacedaemonian issued his laws. **10** Joatham, the son of Ozias, reigned for sixteen years after the death of his father. And during his reign Elijah, Hosea, Micah[1] the Morathite,[2] and Joel, the son of Bathouel,[3] acted as prophets. **11** After him, his son Ahaz reigned for sixteen years. Also during his reign Isaiah, Hosea, and Micah acted as prophets, and Uriah[4] was high priest.[5] In the first year of his reign Iphitos established the celebration of the Olympic Games. In the same first Olympiad, Romos[6] and Romulus were born, and in the seventh Olympiad they started to build Rome. From Romulus and the consuls they ended with Julius Caesar, having had monarchy for 245 years.[7] **12** Hezekiah,[8] a most pious man, having succeeded his father Ahaz, reigns for twenty-nine years. During his reign Isaiah, Hosea, and Micah still acted as prophets. During his reign Salmanasar, the king of the Assyrians, moved the inhabitants of Samaria to Media and Babylonia to be kept under surveillance; their king at this time was the prophet Hosea.[9] This was in the sixth year of the reign of Hezekiah. Since the people made offerings to it, Hezekiah tore down the snake that Moses had hung up.[10] He also erased the inscription of Solomon's book of remedies to all kinds of illnesses. At this time, Thales the Milesian died in Tenedos, and the Erythraean Sibyl became famous. **13** Manasses,[11] the son of Hezekiah, reigned for fifty-five years. He was a most abominable man who worshipped the idols no less than the Canaanites did. It is said, however, that he lived piously towards the end of his life. During his reign the prophet Isaiah departed from life. At this time Romulus was cut to pieces in the Senate house and carried out. This was in the sixteenth Olympiad, when he had reigned for

---

1 Or: 'Michaias.'
2 Or: 'of Moresheth' (cf. Micah 1.1).
3 Or: 'Joel, son of Pethuel' (or 'Bethuel,' cf. Joel 1.1).
4 Or: 'Ourias.'
5 Cf. 2 Kgs 16.10–16.
6 I.e. 'Remus.'
7 This sentence is obscure and possibly corrupt. It is, of course, more or less correct to calculate the duration of the monarchy in Rome as 245 years (753–509), and a lack of interest in the Republic is typical of Byzantine chronicles. However, the way in which it manifests itself here is odd.
8 Or: 'Ezekias.'
9 This is an error in the tradition of the Logothete: this king is not identical with the prophet (see 2 Kgs 17.1).
10 Cf. 2 Kgs 18.4.
11 Or: Manasseh.

thirty-eight years.[1] **14** Amos,[2] the son of Manasses, having succeeded his father, reigns for two years. At this time Midas, the king of Phrygia, died. It was said at the time that he had donkey's ears. **15** Josias, having succeeded his father Amos, takes over the rule at the age of eight, and he rules for thirty-one years. In the eighteenth year of his rule the high priest Chelkias finds a book in the temple (Chelkias was the father of Jeremiah, the prophet) and brings it to the king. He (for he was pious) was at the time celebrating Passover for the Lord, a celebration which had not taken place since the time of Joshua son of Nun. Also, he collected the bones of those who had died in a state of impiety and had them burnt on the altars of the idols, and he destroyed everything [of this kind] and gave by this an example of piety to the people. It is said that Chelkias died at once after having read the book. During the reign of Josias, Jeremiah, the son of Chelkias, and Sophonias and Heliba,[3] the wife of Seleim, keeper of the high priest's wardrobe, acted as prophets. There was also the false prophet Ananias. During this time the Sibyl in Samos became famous, and people from Megara founded Byzantium. **16** Joachas, the son of Josias, having succeeded his father, reigns for three months. Nechao, the king of Egypt, having attacked Jerusalem with an army and seized Joachas, brings him as a prisoner to Egypt, and appoints Joakeim, also known as Eliakeim, king over Jerusalem in his stead. **17** [Eliakeim], the brother of Joachas,[4] having succeeded to the throne, reigns for eleven years. During his reign Nebuchadnezzar, having set out from Babylon, takes control of all of the Egyptian land. By this, he deprived the Egyptians of the possession of the neighbouring regions, that is, the land from the Egyptian river valley as far as the river Euphrates. And he made the whole of Judaea liable to pay taxes to him, and Joakeim came to serve as a slave to Nebuchadnezzar for three years. During his[5] reign Jeremiah, Bouzi and Uriah, the son of Sameas, act as prophets; when Uriah flees to Egypt, he is apprehended by Joakeim and put to death. Nebuchadnezzar bound this Joakeim in fetters of copper

---

1 This is in line with conventional dates, according to which Romulus reigned 753–717. However, putting the first Olympic games at the conventional date of 776, the year 717 falls rather within the 15th Olympiad (776–15×4 = 716).

2 Or: 'Amon.'

3 Or: 'Olda.'

4 Eliakeim (i.e. Joakeim) in brackets has been added by me. The textual problem no doubt arose from the confusing fact that two different Eliakeims are mentioned so close to each other.

5 Presumably Joakeim (Eliakeim).

and brought him to Babylon, and Daniel, Ananias, Misael and Azarias went together with him as prisoners. During this time Epidamnos was founded, later renamed Dyrrhachium. **18** Joakeim, also called Jechonias, having succeeded his father Eliakeim, also called Joakeim, reigns for three months. When Nebuchadnezzar besieges Jerusalem in the eighth year of his reign,[1] Joakeim secretly leaves the city together with his mother Estha and all his kin, but falls into the hands of Nebuchadnezzar. The latter razes the city to the ground and also abducts these people as prisoners together with many others. Among the ones abducted was also the prophet Jezekiel. **19** He[2] appoints his[3] uncle Manthanias leader of the others instead of him, and he renames him[4] Sedekias, having received oaths from him in the name of God that he will not secede. **20** There are a total of 144 years from the first year of Ahaz and the first Olympiad until this deportation; and 406 years from Saul, the first king of the Hebrews; and 1,100 years from the death of Joshua son of Nun; and 2,610 years from Noah and the flood; and 4,872 years from Adam.[5]

    43 While keeping to the chronological scheme with help of the dynasty of David's descendants, I do not consider it out of place, as an excursus, to go over the dates of the rulers of Samaria. **2** On the death of King Solomon his son Rehoboam ascends to Sikima (for the people had gathered there), in order to be made king by them. **3** But when he was about to be anointed, the people came forward to him and begged him to be relieved from the many tax duties that his father Solomon had exacted from them. Having been accorded three days to think the matter over and to give a proper answer, and having been told by the elders that he should relieve the people, but by members of his own generation that he should burden them even more, he trusts to the latter and, on the third day, he gives the advice of the younger people as his answer. **4** At this, the people retreat and bid farewell to his

1 Presumably in the eighth year of Joakeim's reign.
2 Nebuchadnezzar, according to the story as told in 2 Kgs 24.17.
3 This is vaguely put but refers to Joakeim's uncle.
4 I.e. Manthanias.
5 This calculation presents some problems. If we subtract 144 from 776 (employing 776 as starting date for the first Olympiad) we arrive at 632 BC, which is not in keeping with the conventional date of 597 for the Babylonian captivity. On the other hand, to place the Babylonian captivity at 632 BC or thereabouts is reasonable if the years from Adam until this point are believed to be 4,872: we so arrive at 5,504 years from Adam until the birth of Christ. Calculating in yet another way: 144 years is a fairly plausible calculation of the time between Ahaz (possibly co-regent from 736/5 and sole ruler from 732/1) and the actual date of the Babylonian captivity.

rule. And ten of the tribes appoint Jeroboam as their king. He was the son of Nabat and Sarira, a second wife,[1] and he came from the tribe of Ephraim. The tribes of Judah and Benjamin stay with Rehoboam. Thus, as has been explained above, the people were divided at that time, and each part of the people acquired a name and a place for a royal palace of their own.

44 Jeroboam, the son of Nabat, reigns in Samaria for twenty-two years. During his reign the Silonite[2] acts as prophet. During his time, Sousakeim, the Egyptian, having attacked Jerusalem, takes away all the treasures of the temple as well as those belonging to their king Rehoboam. **2** Nabat, having succeeded Jeroboam, reigns for two years. **3** Baasa, the son of Achiam, having killed Nabat, reigns in Samaria for twenty-four years. During his reign Jous, the son of Ananias, acts as prophet. **4** Having succeeded his father, Baasa, Ila reigns for two years. **5** Zambre, to whom the command over the chariots has been entrusted by Ila, kills Ila and, having destroyed all his household, reigns for seven months. **6** Zambre, the commander of the military forces, rebels against Zambre, the king. Just as many thought that he was achieving complete victory, Zambre [the king] set fire to his belongings and perished with them. Then Israel was in a state of turmoil with regard to who should be their king, and some favoured Zambre, while some favoured Thamne, the son of Gonath. The supporters of Zambre were the ones to prevail, and he reigns over Samaria for twelve years. **7** Ahab, having succeeded his father Zambre, reigns for twenty-two years. His wife Jezebel (she was the daughter of Eisbaal, the king of the Sidonians) deceived him and made him disgrace himself and act impiously. Micah, the prophet, put a strap round his head and criticised Ahab because of Ader. At this time it happened that Jericho was founded. It is Achar from Bethel who founds this city, and he lost his first-born son Abeiron when the foundations were laid (this happened according to the prophecy of Joshua), and his younger son Segour when the city was completed. During his reign Elijah and Abdiou act as prophets. Abdiou lived in constant hiding, and he also kept the other prophets hidden; this he did for fear of Jezebel's plotting. Towards the end[3] Elijah anoints Elisha as prophet. Micah still acted as prophet at that time. **8** Ochozias, having

---

1 'a second wife': perhaps there is a textual problem and we should read 'a woman who was a widow' (the Greek text's γυναικὸς ἑτέρας should then be changed into γυναικὸς χήρας, cf. Regn. III.11.26).

2 I.e. Achiam, see above, Chapter 40, § 3.

3 I.e. of his life on earth.

succeeded his father Ahab, reigned for two years. Also during his reign Elijah and Elisha act as prophets. **9** Joran, the brother of Ochozias, having succeeded him on the throne, reigns for twelve years. During his reign Elijah was lifted up from the earth. During his reign the people of that region were struck by famine, and they slaughtered their own children and tasted the flesh and ate it, dipping it in dove dung instead of salt. **10** Jous, the son of Saphat,[1] son of Namese,[2] was anointed king of Samaria by Elisha, and he punished all the household of Ahaab. He kills the king Joran himself by an arrow, having found him when he was attending to his wounds. He disposes of Joran's mother Jezebel and Ahaab's seventy sons by pushing them off a cliff, and he puts up their heads at the main streets.[3] He then gathered all the prophets of Baal and the priests and the people[4] and, feigning that they were to make a public sacrifice, he has all of them killed and razes the sanctuary of the idol to the ground and builds a public toilet[5] there. He reigned for twenty-eight years. Also during his reign Elisha acted as prophet. **11** Joachas succeeds his father Jous and reigns for seventeen years. Also during his reign Elisha acted as prophet; he then died. **12** After him Joas, the son of Jachaz, reigns for sixteen years. **13** Jeroboam, having succeeded his father Joas, reigned for forty-one years. During his reign Jonas and Amos acted as prophets. **14** Zacharias succeeded his father Jeroboam and reigned for six months. **15** Seloum killed Zacharias and reigned for one month. **16** Manaeim, the son of Gades, rebelled against Seloum and reigned for ten years. He apprehends those in Thersa who did not accept him as king, and he kills them and dismembers their pregnant women. **17** Phalkias, the son of Manaeim, succeeded his father and reigned for two years. **18** Phakee, the son of Romelios, killed Phalkias and reigned for twenty years. During his reign Theglaphalasar, the king of the Assyrians, having marched into Judaea, seizes the greater part of their land. **19** After Phakee, Osee, the son of Ila, reigns for nine years. During his reign Salmanasar, the king of the Assyrians, having attacked Samaria, carries away the king as a prisoner and all of Israel with him, and he settles them in Alae and Abor (these are Median cities) and at the river Gozan. There they are maltreated

---

1 Read: 'Josaphat' (Jehoshaphat).
2 Or: 'Nimshi.'
3 Or: 'city gates' (διεξόδους).
4 δήμους.
5 λύτρωμα.

and pay the price for their transgressions of God's commands. But the Assyrian, having sent Babylonian men to Samaria—men who had lived shamefully and been breaking the laws—ordered them to settle there. God destroyed these men by sending lions against them. On learning this and understanding that in that country it was necessary for service to God to be fulfilled, the barbarian sent one of the priests there and ordered him to conduct the lawful rites. This priest stayed in Bethel and taught the law to the people and how to honour God. And so it happened that from this time the country had peace from lions. These people are still called Samaritans from the region in which they live, and[1] they are of strange habits. Because of their emphasis on the teaching of the law[2] they lay little stress on piety. They have not even found it fit to accept more than the Decalogue. **20** Here the times of the Israelitic kingdom ended after 303 years and seven months, starting with Jeroboam, the son of Nabat, and ending with Osee, the son of Ila, and the removal of Israel from Samaria to Media by Salmanasar. And the rule of David's kin flourished.[3] This took its beginning from the tenth [year] of Saul's reign and ended with that Joakeim who reigned for three months. And having ravaged the people of Judah, he[4] removed them to Babylon.

45 How the Seventy Years of the Captivity Are Counted

It is appropriate now to treat summarily the leaders during the seventy years of the captivity. Up to the time of this last Joakeim, there are a total of 4,872 years from Adam.[5] We should therefore now count the following years[6] from the first year of Sedekias. **2** When Nebuchadnezzar had destroyed Jerusalem and taken away Joakeim together with the others to Babylon, he appointed Joakeim's brother, Manthanias, king of the remaining population, and he renamed him Sedekias. And he allowed him to live in peace in his home country as long as he paid a yearly tribute to Nebuchadnezzar. **3** For nine years Sedekias sent the tax money, and Israel lived in peace. But in that

---

1 'and they are': Greek διὸ καί, etc., which would rather seem to mean 'and therefore they are also, etc.'
2 'Because ... law': this is a free translation of διὰ δὲ τὴν τοῦ νόμου διδασκαλίαν.
3 The Greek is somewhat uncertain here.
4 I.e. Nebuchadnezzar.
5 Cf. above, Chapter 42, § 20.
6 I.e. when making the chronology of subsequent world history.

year Sedekias rebelled, and with great arrogance he disregarded God and the king and so provokes another attack on Jerusalem by Nebuchadnezzar. **4** Nebuchadnezzar besieges the city and takes control of it in the second year and burns the temple. He killed Sedekias' children in front of their father. Then, having blinded and put him in fetters, he takes him away to Babylon together with all the people. Then he made Gotholias, the son of Achikan, the leader of the remaining. **5** But the powerful of those who were left there abandon Gotholias and then kill him and, out of fear of the Chaldeans, leave the country and go to Egypt. After a short time there they are corrupted and become zealous followers of the Egyptian superstition. **6** Sedekias is removed after a total reign of eleven years. During these,[1] Areas was high priest, and Jeremiah acted as prophet in Judaea, and Daniel in Babylon. In the second year of the exile and the reign of Sedekias, Daniel interpreted the dream of Nebuchadnezzar and announced its meaning. Jezekiel acted[2] as prophet in their fifth year. Thereafter, Naum acts as prophet as well as Malachias. **7** When Sedekias had died in Babylon, i.e. after the eleven years of Sedekias' reign, those who were subjected[3] reigned for the rest of the seventy years. **8** This Nebuchadnezzar destroyed Jerusalem three times. For the first time, when he came up in the third year of Eliakeim and seized that man Jechonias and his mother and the prophet Jezekiel and all the rest; this was in the first year of his reign. For the second time, when he came up in the third month of the reign of Jechonias, the one also called Joakeim, and took, among others, Daniel, Ananias, Misael and Azarias back with him; this was in the eighth year of his reign. For the third time, when he came up in the eleventh year of Sedekias and burnt the temple and blinded Sedekias and slaughtered his sons together with other people and carried off the rest of the people in captivity; this was in the nineteenth year of his reign. **9** In addition to the nineteen years which he had reigned so far, Nebuchadnezzar reigns for another twenty-five years. During his reign the afore-mentioned Daniel and Jezekiel acted as prophets. **10** Marodach, his son, having succeeded him, reigns for twelve years. **11** Marodach's brother Baltasar, the son of Nebuchadnezzar, reigned for four years. Also during his reign Daniel acts as prophet, and the vision, which he saw when he was dining and drinking from the liturgical vessels, is explained to

---

1 'During these' (ἐπ' αὐτούς): probably wrong for 'during him' (ἐπ' αὐτοῦ).

2 Or: 'began to act.'

3 'those ... subjected' (οἱ ὑποτεταγμένοι): this is vague (perhaps 'subjected to foreign rule').

him. In the following night Darius, the son of Asuerus,[1] killed Baltasar in accordance with the interpretation of the vision and achieved control of the state. **12** The said Darius, the son of Asuerus, who was called Astyages,[2] reigned for seventeen years. During his reign, Daniel is thrown into the lions' den. Having not suffered any harm from the lions, he is raised up by the king on the seventh day.[3] He then understands the significance of the seventy years of the exile, and the mystery of the weeks[4] is revealed to him. **13** And if someone should wish to study the matter of the weeks carefully and count the years through, he should start at the beginning of the return,[5] as described by the prophet,[6] and the rebuilding of Jerusalem, that is from Nehemiah, the son of Achele, chief cupbearer of Artaxerxes. It was he who asked for and received permission to go up to Jerusalem and rebuild it. Whoever studies this, will find that the seventy periods of seven, that is the 490 years, are completed at the time when the transgression is cancelled out, and the sin is brought to an end, and the vision is sealed and the prophets,[7] and the Holy of Holies is anointed—that is, at the coming of Christ and what follows.

46 Having ousted the Medes and Assyrians from power and having seized the whole of Asia, Cyrus the Persian reigned for thirty-one years. **2** In his first year the seventy years of the exile are fulfilled. In the following year he allows the powerful among the Hebrews to go up to Jerusalem and settle there, and he ordered that the temple should be rebuilt. Jesus, the son of Josedek, who was high priest, led the return together with Zorobabel, the son of Salathiel, and Angaios and Zechariah, son of Addo, acted as prophets. **3** When Jesus and his men had laid the foundations of the temple, they were prevented for as much as forty-two years from finishing the work. This went on until, in the second year of his reign, Darius, the son of Hystaspes, makes the completion of the temple possible by sending away those who hinder the project. It is

---

1 I.e. Ahasuerus.

2 I.e. Darius was called Astyages.

3 Greek ἑβδομαῖος: according to Daniel, Chapter 6, he only had to spend the night with the lions.

4 Or: 'periods of seven' (ἑβδομάδες). The following section is alluding to the vision in Daniel, Chapter 9.

5 'return, etc.' (ἐξόδου λόγου): the text is obscure at this point.

6 See Nehemiah, Chapter 2.

7 'prophets' (i.e. προφῆται: so pseudo-Julius Pollux, for which see Introduction): the Greek of our chronicle (προφητεύει, i.e. 'he prophecies'?) cannot be correct.

then finished after four more years. Thus it took in all forty-six years for it to be completed. This is made clear by the following. **4** Cambyses, also called Artaxerxes (he is the one called Arthasastha in Esdras), succeeded his father Cyrus and reigned for eight years. **5** Sphendatis and Kimerdios, who were *magi* of Median descent, attack him and then reign for seven months. **6** Darius, who was a descendant of Cyrus and the son of Hystaspes, attacked the *magi* and gained power and reigned for six years up to the completion of [the temple of][1] Jerusalem and another thirty years in addition to these, so that he reigned in all for thirty-six years. In this time Pythagoras the philosopher died, and Hippocrates the physician became famous. **7** Xerxes, the son of Darius, reigned for twenty years. **8** Artabanus reigned for seven months. **9** Artaxerxes, the son of Xerxes, Makrocheir (he too is called Arthasastha in Esdras), reigned for forty-one years. During his reign the events concerning Esther and Mardochaios and Amman took place; it was also during this time that Esdras acted as prophet. With the approval of Artaxerxes the high priest Esdras brought back the rest of the Jews to Jerusalem and taught them the law. And Nehemiah, Artaxerxes' chief cupbearer and a man of a family of high priests, asks the king for permission and so goes up to Judaea and Jerusalem.[2] He builds a wall around Jerusalem to protect it from attack, and he surrounds the construction workers with arms.[3] And together with Esdras he taught the people the Law of Moses, and he removed them from all elements of a Greek pagan education. And the city was built on a large scale and with a wall.

10 From Where the Seventy Weeks in Daniel Are Counted[4]

In the twentieth year of Artaxerxes' reign—from that point they say that one should count the seventy weeks mentioned in Daniel's vision, up to the coming of the Lord and the following events. For it is evident that seventy times seven make 490 years.[5] At this time Socrates was born. **11** Xerxes, the son of Artaxerxes, having succeeded to the throne, reigns

---

1 Added by me.

2 Cf. above, Chapter 45, § 13.

3 This is vaguely put and the translation uncertain.

4 This heading was no doubt originally a marginal note, adopted at some time into the text.

5 Cf. above, Chapter 44, § 13, and Chapter 45, § 12.

for two months. **12** Sogdianos reigns for seven months. **13** Darius, the son of Xerxes, nicknamed Nomios,[1] killed Sogdianos and reigned over the Persians for eighteen years. **14** Artaxerxes, the son of Darius and Parysatis, succeeded his father and reigned for forty-two years. During this time, Plato the philosopher became famous as well as Aristotle. **15** Artaxerxes, nick-named Ochos, reigned for twenty-two years. **16** Narses succeeded him and reigned for four years. **17** Darius, the son of Arsamos, reigned after Narses for six years. **18** When Alexander the Macedonian pressed upon the Persians, Bessus and his men kill Darius in Bactria, and thus the kingdom of the Persians is dissolved. It had lasted for a total of 300 years: seventy years of the Jewish exile and 230 more years. And so the reign is transferred to the Macedonians. **19** Alexander declares to Jadous, the high priest, to make an alliance with him against Darius. When he refuses, Alexander destroys the cities of Tyros and Gaza by a great effort. During the attack on[2] Tyros, he sees a satyr in his dreams, and the dream interpreter says to him: 'Tyros is yours,[3] Alexander.' Then Alexander went up to Jerusalem and subdued it and, having received a pledge of alliance from the high priest, he honoured him as a god and paid his reverence to him, and he retreated to Persia.

47 When Alexander the Macedonian had destroyed the hegemony of the Persians, the power went over to the Macedonians. It was in the seventh year of his reign that Alexander subdued the Persians and, in addition to those seven years, he rules for six years and six months also over the Persians after Darius. **2** On his death in Babylon Philip, his brother, succeeds to power in Macedonia, and Antigonos in Asia, and Ptolemy, the son of Lagos, and Arsinoe, the daughter of Meleager, in Egypt, and Seleukos Nikator in Syria. **3** Ptolemy, the son of Lagos, reigned over Egypt for forty years. At this time Epicurus, the philosopher, became famous. **4** Ptolemy Philadelphos reigned for thirty-eight years. He enslaved the Hebrews and forced them to translate the Holy Scriptures from Hebrew into Greek. This translation is made by seventy men famed among the Hebrews for their wisdom. When now the Holy Scripture had been translated and was read aloud, it is said that the king and all those in high office were astounded by the beauty of the Divine

1 Should probably be Nothos, 'the Bastard.'
2 Or: 'destruction of' (ἐν τῇ πορθήσει, etc.).
3 This is a kind of pun: sē (or: sa) Tyros (i.e. 'Tyros is yours') equals satyros (i.e. 'satyr') (Greek σὴ Τύρος). Cf. to this below, Chapter 112, § 3, and the similar pun on Thessalonica.

Word. Menedemos, the philosopher, and Demetrios from Phaleron were present at this occasion, and they shared the admiration for the power of the words. Then the king asked them: 'Considering that the Divine Word is such, how is it that no historian or poet ever has made allusion to it?' And Demetrios answered, that 'no one has ever dared to touch it, for Theopompos, who wanted to write about it, was struck by madness and saw in a dream that this happened to him because he had inquired inopportunely into divine matters. Also Theodektes, the tragic poet, who mentioned these holy books in a tragedy, was blinded, whereas others, who refrained from this daring enterprise and respected God, remained in good health.'[1] 5 Ptolemy Euergetes, the son of Philadelphos and Eurydice, who was also known as Arsinoe, reigned for twenty-six years. During this time Jesus son of Sirach, who wrote the *Book of Wisdom*, became famous among the Hebrews. 6 Ptolemy Philopator, the son of Euergetes, reigned for seventeen years. During his reign the Hebrew people, who had been brought as prisoners to Egypt, suffered the following. He ordered that his guards should give 500 of his elephants perfumed wine to drink, in order that he might use them to destroy all the Jews. But due to the prayer of the Jews, the elephants rushed in among the Macedonians' own generals and men and slew a great mass of them in the ensuing confusion. And thus the Jews were saved and could return home thanking God. 7 Ptolemy Epiphanes, the son of Philopator, reigned for twenty-four years. 8 Ptolemy Philometor, the son of Epiphanes, reigned for thirty-five years. During his reign Antiochos punished the Maccabees who did not want to eat impure food. During the reign of Ptolemy Philometor, Hyrkanos and Aristoboulos served as high priests to the Jews, and the people's party supported Hyrkanos, and the priests [supported] Aristoboulos. 9 There was a pious and righteous man by the name of Onias, who belonged to the priests and who had put an end to a drought by praying. They forced him to pray for victory, and he prayed with the words: 'Lord God, do not help the people against your priests nor the priests against your people.' The man was stoned immediately, whereupon the Divine justice at once reached them, for Pompey, the Roman general, attacked them and destroyed the city. And entering the Holiest of Holy, Pompey did out of piety not touch any of the holy objects, even if they were of great value. Rather he ordered that the temple should be cleaned and that the sacrifices should

---

1 'refrained ... health': or 'gave up this daring enterprise, were healed for placating God.'

be made. Having been entrusted with the priesthood and power over the Jews, Aristoboulos sent a vine plant of gold weighing 200 talents[1] as a gift to Pompey. **10** Ptolemy Euergetes, the brother of Philometor, reigns for twenty-nine years. Ptolemy Physkon reigned for seventeen years and six months. Ptolemy with the by-name Alexas reigned for ten years. Ptolemy II Soter, the son of Ptolemy II Euergetes and Cleopatra Euergetis, reigned for eight years. Ptolemaios with the by-name Neos Dionysios reigned for thirty years. **11** Cleopatra, the daughter of Neos Dionysios, succeeds her father at his death, and Ptolemy her brother reigns together with her. When he quarrelled with her, she had him killed and took sole control of the state. She reigns for twenty-two years.

48 That Only Four Years of Cleopatra's Reign Should be Included in the Chronological Scheme

In the fourth year of Cleopatra's reign[2] Julius Caesar, who had been made a consul by the Romans, goes down to the East accompanied by a great military force. And he conquers many of the peoples there and makes them pay tribute, and he establishes officers of his own to oversee these places. **2** Thus he made Antipater of Ascalon governor of Palestine. Antipater was the son of a certain Herodes, who belonged to the people employed at the temple and more precisely to the slaves there of Apollo. When he was a child, Antipater had been carried away by Idumaean robbers who thought that they would be able to get ransom for him. But, since his father had been reduced to the utmost poverty, Antipater remained with his kidnappers and worked for them and was raised according to their customs. **3** When Antipater, who was envied because of his great wealth, had been killed by a certain Jew called Ballichos, his children Herodes and Phasailos inherit the power. Phasailos received Idumaea and the region of Jerusalem as his part, and Herodes [received] Judaea and the Galilee. **4** When Antipater learnt that Hyrkanos, who had ruled before him, had opened the tomb of David and taken 3,000 talents[3] from it, he opened it too. He did not find any money, but he took jewellery of gold and a lot of valuable treasures. When

---

1 See Chapter 48, § 4 with n.
2 Cleopatra VII reigned from March 51 BC, and Caesar came to Egypt in late September 48.
3 The mass of one of these talents is presumably in the range 25–35 kg.

he tried to go further into the grave, to the place where the bodies of David and Solomon had been put, fire came out of the grave and killed two of his guards. **5** Having arrived in Egypt, and having suppressed the attempts of his enemies, Julius gains control of Cleopatra's kingdom. Having settled all matters of the government of the East, he then returned to Rome.

49 Gaius Julius Caesar[1]

Gaius Julius Caesar reigned for four years and seven months.[2] He was called Caesar, which means 'dissection,' since his mother died during the ninth month of her pregnancy, and they had to dissect her in order to extract him.[3] He was also called dictator, which means 'sole ruler'; dictatorship is a rule where one is not accountable to anyone. Also, the month Quintilis was renamed Julius [July] because of Caesar, for it was in this month that he acceded to sole power. **2** The same Julius subdued Germans and Gauls and Britons in very great battles, and he made 500 major cities[4] liable to pay taxes to the Romans. **3** A horse that had cloven hoofs instead of (solid) horse hoofs was born to him.[5] This horse did not accept any rider other than Caesar—just as was the case with Alexander's horse, Boukephalos. **4** When he was passing through the courtyard door of his house on his way to the Senate house, a statue[6] of him, standing in front of the door, fell down of its own accord. In addition, someone gave him a piece of writing, describing the whole plot which was being planned against him. But since he thought that it was something different, he did not look at the message but gave it to someone else for safe-keeping, and so he was killed by Brutus and Cassius in the Senate.

1 From this chapter the Chronicle of Pseudo-Julius Pollux (see Introduction) has a completely different text.

2 This could be from October 49 (the crossing of the Rubicon)–March 44.

3 This is not true but an interesting development of an original popular etymology trying to make sense of Caesar's name.

4 'major cities': πόλεις οἰκουμένας.

5 'was born to him': or 'was born and became his possession' (τούτῳ ἐτέχθη).

6 'statue': the Greek word, εἰκών, could, of course, equally well signify a picture. However, if this is meant to be outside the house, a statue is perhaps more plausible. Perhaps the author of the text was unfamiliar with the idea that statues stood outside houses, and was more used to painted surfaces.

50 Octavius Augustus

Octavius Augustus Caesar reigned for forty-six years.[1] After him the Roman emperors were called *augusti*,[2] and the month was called August, which means 'venerable'; its earlier name was Sextilis. In the night when he was born, his father dreamt that he saw the sun rise from his wife's womb. **2** Having killed Cassius and Brutus, who had murdered Julius Caesar, Anthony, imperator and consul of the Romans, came to Syria overpowered by his desire for Cleopatra. He chose not to return from there to Rome to give an account of his rule. Therefore, Augustus collected the armed forces in Italy and descended upon Anthony and, when it comes to an encounter, Anthony is defeated and, together with Cleopatra, he flees to Egypt. There Anthony made away with himself by the sword, whereas Cleopatra, who had been captured and who feared the triumph in Rome, held a snake near to herself and so dies. Her children, Helios and Selene, were captured and paraded in triumph in Rome. **3** During the time of Augustus the fourth age begins, the one Daniel calls the fourth terrible beast in the vision of the four beasts.[3] **4** Maecenas, who was a wise man, was much loved by Augustus. When the emperor was sitting as a judge once and had condemned many to death, Maecenas, who was not able to talk to him in private because of the crowd, wrote a note, saying: 'Stand up, you butcher,' and he sealed the note and threw it into the emperor's lap. On reading it the emperor rose and ordered that his rulings[4] should be annulled. **5** Further, when a soldier to whom he had taken a liking asked him to attend a meeting of a court of law,[5] he said that he himself was busy but that he would allow one of his friends to attend and to perform the duty asked of him; the soldier then said, infuriated: 'I did not send another instead of myself every time you asked for my help.' At this the emperor blushed, and he went with

---

1 'forty-six years': most probably this figure is wrong, although it could be (roughly) the time from the Battle of Actium in 31 BC until Augustus' death in AD 14 (however, this would present us with a gap in the continuous chronology after Julius Caesar, and the years between Caesar's death and Actium would not be accounted for). Approximately fifty-eight years are missing between the deaths of Julius Caesar and Augustus. Yet the most plausible correction is perhaps into fifty-six (not fifty-eight), since this is the sum given by George Synkellos (Adler/Tuffin 2002, p. 439).
2 Αὔγουστοι.
3 See the Book of Daniel (especially Chapter 7).
4 Presumably the rulings of that day.
5 'court of law': βουλευτήριον (usually of the Senate).

the soldier and helped him. **6** He had also Athenodoros the Alexandrian, a most wise man, in his following. Athenodoros checked the emperor in his least noble enterprises and corrected him. The emperor often used to praise Athenodoros in the Senate and to add that he himself had also been corrected by Athenodoros, and that he had led a bad life earlier. In his old age, Athenodoros asked for permission to return to his own country. He said that the emperor was now perfect in every kind of philosophy and practical action. However, when he was about to depart and embraced the emperor, Athenodoros bent towards his ear and asked him that, whenever he was angry, he should not order what should be done before he had counted through all the twenty-four letters of the alphabet;[1] for he knew that the emperor was quick to anger, but also easily changed his mind. On hearing this, the emperor said: 'It is good that you remind me that I am not perfect. Therefore, I will not allow you to embark on this ship.'[2] **7** This Augustus went to Delphi and asked who was going to rule after him. When the Pythian[3] priest did not answer, Augustus asked a second time, wanting to know why the oracle did not answer. At this, the Pythia said the following:[4]

'A Hebrew child, who rules among the blessed gods, tells me
To leave this house and take to the road.
Therefore, depart from our house.'

8 In the 5500th year from the Creation of the World, and in the forty-second year of his rule, there was issued a decree from Augustus that the whole world should be taxed.[5] In this year Our Lord was born, and Herod, who had been appointed by Augustus, ruled over Judaea. **9** When Augustus was about to die, a thunderbolt struck his picture[6] and wiped out the first letter

---

1 'twenty-four letters': in other words, the Greek alphabet is intended.

2 'embark on this ship' (τῆς ἐνεγκαμένης ἐπιβῆναι): or 'to travel this day,' or 'to tread the ground which brought you forth.'

3 'Pythian priest': this is in the masculine form, whereas the following, 'Pythia,' is in the feminine.

4 These verses are in a pseudo-ancient form, unsuccessfully imitating the elegiac couplet of the dactylic hexameter and the pentameter. They are known from the so-called Tübingen Theosophy, see 'La Théosophie de Tübingen,' in H. van Kasteel, *Oracles et prophétie*, Grez-Doiceau: Éditions Beya, 2011, pp. 115–125.

5 Cf. Luke 2.

6 'picture': or 'statue' (εἰκόνα). Cf. above, Chapter 49, § 4, what happened to Caesar's statue (or picture).

of his name. He then called the consuls and the senators[1] together and said, that 'I received a Rome made out of clay, but I leave it to you made of stone.' By this he was alluding to the solid strength of his power. He asked all those in office to clap their hands and to laugh at the moment of his death, as when an actor ends his performance. He did this in order to show his scorn at human life and that it is worthy of ridicule. **10** Herod[2] is not called a child-slayer only because of the children murdered in Bethlehem during his frenzy against Christ, but also because of his own children: of these, he murders three, and he then has their mother slain as well as their uncle and many other family members; he also has a great many Jews killed at the end of his life. **11** It should be noted that Herod the Great had three sons: Herod Antipas, the one who had John the Baptist beheaded; Herod Philip, to whom Herodias was first married and who became the father of Salome, who danced; and Herod Agrippa, who killed James the son of Zebedee; he was the brother of Herodias and the father of Agrippa and Ber(e)nike, and it was before them[3] that Paul was tried and defended himself.

51 Tiberius

Tiberius reigned for twenty-two years and seven months.[4] Gaius was his nephew. **2** On hearing what was said about Christ, Tiberius wanted to proclaim him a god by imperial decree.[5] But this was opposed by the Senate, and Pilate was removed from his position and sent to Rome, and he was brought into such a predicament for having had Christ crucified that he committed suicide.[6] **3** When he was ill, Tiberius was suffocated

---

1 βουλευτάς: in the Byzantine part of the text the word συγκλητικός is used (and translated by me as 'senator').

2 From this point, the material of this chapter—dealing with Palestine, Herod the Great and his family (and, in that sense, because of the interest in Christ, connected with the previous text)—is loosely added to a supposedly more original structure of the text that ends with the death of the emperor. The same phenomenon (i.e. that additional material is added and often carelessly integrated into a whole) occurs in many chapters below and will not be commented upon in each case (see e.g. Chapters 51, § 4; 52, § 4; 53, §§ 4–6, etc.).

3 'before them': or 'during their reign.'

4 Tiberius reigned AD 18 September 14–16 March 37.

5 Tiberius is portrayed in a very positive manner: with sympathy, at the very least, for the Christians, and as a righteous man.

6 Pilate was indeed recalled to Rome (see Josephus, *Jewish Antiquities* 18.89), although no mention is made of Christ. The story of his suicide is told by Eusebios, *Church History* II.7.

by Gaius who heaped many cloaks upon him. **4** It is said about Tiberius that he was reluctant to replace government officials, because he wanted to spare his subjects; and that, when he was asked why he acted in this way, he cited the proverbial expression about the flies sitting on a wound, and how, when someone wanted to scare them away, the wounded man prevented him, saying: 'Do not do that, lest others should come who are [even more] thirsty for blood.'

52 Gaius

Gaius reigned for three years and nine months.[1] He was a highly adulterous man. **2** Coming once to the Forum Gaius saw mud on the road. He then had Flavius Vespasian, who was an aedile[2] at that time, brought forward, and he ordered that the mud should be thrown on Vespasian's cloak, since he was considered not to have attended to his duties in the proper manner. The true meaning of this was that Vespasian in the future would take over public matters when they were troubled. **3** Gaius was killed by Claudius. **4** During Gaius' reign, Agrippa governs Judaea, and Simon Magus[3] is baptised by Philip, one of the Seven Deacons.[4]

53 Claudius

Claudius reigned for thirteen years and five months.[5] **2** He was a coward and had everyone who approached him searched, lest they should be carrying a dagger; at symposia he had armed guards at his side. This was taken over from him by the following emperors, too. **3** He died having eaten poisoned mushrooms. **4** During Claudius' reign, Herod Agrippa had James, the brother of John, killed by the sword,[6] and he put Peter in jail

1 Gaius, i.e. Caligula, reigned 16 March 37–24 January 41.

2 'aedile': for Greek ἀγορανόμος (officer responsible for market place).

3 For Simon see Acts 8.9–24. His story is then developed in the Church fathers and other texts, where he is portrayed as an early heretic. In this text he is referred to several times (in Chapters 53, § 5, 62, § 4, and 128, § 5, in which case patriarch John the Grammarian is referred to as a new Simon).

4 Mentioned in Acts 6.5: leaders elected by the early Christian community in Jerusalem.

5 More precisely, Claudius reigned 24 January 41–13 October 54.

6 See for this Acts 12.2.

with the intention of killing him.[1] 5 Simon Magus abandoned the Christian faith and started to converse with sorcerers, and he came down to Rome and was honoured and worshipped like a god because of his witchcraft. However, when Peter came to Rome to deal with this, Simon's power disappeared at once. 6 At the request of all, Peter encouraged Mark to use his oral teachings to the Romans and write his gospel.[2] On sending this gospel also to Egypt, Mark was made the first bishop and evangelist[3] of Alexandria. 7 Agrippa dressed in a shining golden garment and made a public speech to the Jews. When they said that he was speaking with the voice of God not of men, he greatly rejoiced—and is immediately struck down by an angel's sword[4] and dies.

54 Nero, the Son of Claudius

Nero reigned for thirteen years and eight months.[5] He was related to Aeneas, Romulus and Augustus. 2 He killed his mother and his fiancée, and he married a eunuch. 3 Because of Nero's shameful and reckless way of life, some men made an uprising against him in order to kill him. He then entreated his associates to kill him. When nobody was willing to do so, he said: 'I am the only one who has neither a friend to save him nor an enemy to kill him. The soul wants to die, but the hand is not willing to serve.'[6] His last words were: 'O Zeus, what a skilful lyre-player now dies.' He then killed himself. When he was dead, people wore the *pallium*, as if they had been released from slavery.[7] 4 When Agrippa dies, Festus is made his successor by Nero. 5 When Paul preaches the gospel during the time of Festus, he is sent to Nero to defend himself. On this occasion he does so successfully, but when he comes to Rome for a second time, he has his head

---

1 From here this chapter gives additional material of interest to the Early Church.

2 Or: 'to use his oral teachings and write a gospel for the Romans.'

3 Or, less specifically: 'herald' (κῆρυξ).

4 'angel's sword': the Greek word used (ῥομφαία) is the same as that used for the flaming sword in the Old Testament (cf. above, Chapter 20, § 3–Chapter 21, § 3).

5 Nero reigned 13 October 54–9 June 68.

6 Cf. the last words of Hadrian below, Chapter 63, § 4.

7 *pallium*: a kind of cloak (Greek ἱμάτιον). This looks like a piece of memory history: Augustus' concern with dresscodes has been reinterpreted and given symbolic meaning. At least since Tertullian (late second–early third c.), who wrote a work called *De pallio*, the word is given a Christian connotation, and the dress considered appropriate for a Christian and a philosopher.

cut off by Nero. Likewise, Nero orders that the leader of the Christians, Peter, should be crucified. **6** During Nero's reign the Jews pushed James, the brother of the Lord, from the pinnacle of the temple and killed him. Immediately afterwards, and because of the murder of James, Vespasian, general of the Romans, destroys Jerusalem.

55 Galba

Galba reigned for eight months and thirteen days.[1] He belonged to a noble family. **2** He had Otho as his co-ruler. On seeing Galba adopt Lucius as his son, Otho became jealous, and he moved the army against Galba and had him killed. **3** When Otho was asked by the soldiers for money he had promised them, he said that 'the emperor should not be forced.'

56 Otho

Otho reigned for three months and eight days.[2] He came from an undistinguished family. **2** Once, when he was performing a sacrifice in the temple, he mixed songs of Aphrodite into the holy rituals. Because of this, Vitalius rebelled against him, and Otho killed himself saying: 'Why did I have to play with long pipes?'[3] **3** Galba, Otho and Vitalius were killed by soldiers when at war. The Roman Senate proclaimed Vespasian emperor. He was besieging Jerusalem at the time; he was considered to be a sensible and courageous man.

57 Vitalius

Vitalius reigned for one year.[4] He came from a distinguished family. **2** He ordered all astrologers, astronomers and sorcerers to leave Italy by a certain date. But they circulated a document predicting that Vitalius would depart from life by a certain date—which happened. He was killed by soldiers.

---

1 Galba reigned 8 June 68–15 January 69.
2 Otho reigned 15 January–16 April 69.
3 I.e. to try to compete in a league above one's own (Greek μακροῖς αὐλοῖς).
4 Vitalius (Vitellius) reigned 16 April–22 December 69—the date is not given with the same kind of precision as in the previous cases.

58 Vespasian

Vespasian reigned for ten years and eight days.[1] He was of undistinguished parents. **2** He became emperor while he was still in Palestine besieging the cities of the Jews. He also made Josephus, the writer, his slave. He was fetched back to Rome after having been proclaimed emperor by the army, leaving Titus, his son, to continue the siege in Palestine. **3** Vespasian dies of illness. **4** Josephus tells in an admirable way the story of the capture of Jerusalem by Vespasian and Titus, his son.

59 Titus

Titus reigned for two years and three months.[2] He is the one who besieged Jerusalem. **2** He was killed by Domitian, his brother, who threw him into a wooden chest full of snow when he was ill.[3] Domitian did this on the pretence that it would cure Titus, but so he killed him. **3** Titus put fear into those in responsible positions by means of threats rather than punishments.[4] During his reign not a day passed when he did not make a gift to someone or do some good work. For it is the duty of an emperor to do noble acts and to speak the truth. He said that he who sees the emperor should not depart in sadness.

60 Domitian

Domitian reigned for fifteen years and eleven months.[5] **2** He made an enquiry into the birthday horoscopes of the noblemen of Rome and, discovering that not a few of them were destined to come to power, he had them killed on some pretext or other. For he was a man of wicked deeds and full of hatred against humanity. **3** During his reign the apostle Timothy died as a martyr, and a charge was brought against John the Evangelist,

1 Vespasian rather reigned ten years less eight days (1 July 69–23 June 79).
2 Titus reigned 24 June 79–13 September 81.
3 If we are to believe Suetonius (*Titus* X), it is true that Titus suffered from fever.
4 In this paragraph a well-known theme, the clemency of Titus, is developed.
5 If this is meant to denote the time from the death of Titus until the death of Domitian itself, it is not correct: Domitian reigned for fifteen years and four days (14 September 81–18 September 96).

who was exiled to Patmos. **4** Apollonius of Tyana, then in his prime, came to Byzantium.[1] Requested to do so by some people, he cast spells to prevent snakes and scorpions from biting, and to ward off mosquitoes, and he prevented horses from behaving haughtily or wildly, either against people or against each other. **5** Domitian ordered that †Nerva[2] should be thrown live into a fire. This he did because the astronomers had said that the man should be destroyed by dogs. But a great amount of rain fell and extinguished the pyre, and while his hands were still fettered, dogs that were running loose devoured him. **6** An astronomer, Larpus, told Domitian to his face that he would die on a certain day. Domitian ordered that Larpus should be held in fetters and be killed on the day after that day had passed. But Domitian died, and Larpus was released unharmed. **7** Domitian ordered that people of the house of David and of Christ should be killed, for he feared the coming of Christ, just as Herod had done, because the teaching had already gathered some strength. **8** Therefore, relatives of the Lord were brought into the presence of Domitian, and he asked them if they descended from David and Christ. And they confessed as much. 'And how much,' he said, 'money do you have?' 'Together,' he said,[3] 'we own nine *denarii* and some *plethra*[4] of land, from which we pay our taxes.' And they showed their hands, which were rough from work. Domitian said: 'And of what kind is the Kingdom of Christ and when will it appear?' They answered, that 'it is not of this world, nor of this earth, but heavenly and at the end of time, [when Christ will appear][5] in glory, to judge the living and the dead.' This answer made him think little of them, and he ordered that they should be released and the persecution of the Church stop.

1 Apollonius the philosopher was used in anti-Christian propaganda in Antiquity. This provoked replies from Eusebios and others, and, accordingly, he is depicted negatively in Byzantine sources. The text also mentions him as a magician in Chapter 132, § 21.

2 This story is told by Suetonius, *Domitianus* XV.3. The astrologer who is thrown into the fire was, according to Suetonius, called Ascletarion. Nerva is obvious nonsense, since he was the successor to Domitian. Of some interest, in order to explain why the name of Nerva appears like this in the text, may be that Minerva is mentioned at the beginning of the paragraph in Suetonius.

3 'he': this must refer to a spokesman of the Christians.

4 I.e. they did not possess much (a *denarius* may have been the day wage of a labourer, and a square *plethron* was 100×100 feet).

5 The words within square brackets have been supplied by me: as it stands, the text is short but logically understandable.

61 Nerva

Nerva reigned for one year and four months.[1] He was a reasonable and fair man. He recalled John[2] from exile and sent him to Ephesus, where he dies. **2** When there came tidings from Paeonia of Trajan's victories, Nerva went up the Capitol Hill and made an offering of frankincense and, standing at the altar, in the presence of the Senate and the Roman people, he proclaimed with powerful voice: 'May this bring luck! I, Marcus Nerva, adopt Trajan as my son.' **3** Nerva forbade anyone in Rome to be castrated. **4** And he dies by illness.

62 Trajan

Trajan reigned for nineteen years and six months.[3] He hated wickedness and loved justice. For on one occasion, he drew his sword in front of all the dignitaries, and he gave it to the *eparchos*[4] and said: 'Take this, and if I rule well, use it to protect me, and if not, use it against me.' Nerva selected him for office because of his ability. For he was an extremely good soldier and had achieved many successes, in Rome and everywhere. **2** Once, a friend of his was accused of treason and had his eyes put out and his beard shaved. When he, now blind, was brought to Trajan, the emperor pitied him greatly. He sent him to the city now called Traianoupolis (which he had founded in his own name) to be its ruler for the rest of his life; this he did out of compassion for the man.[5] **3** Trajan dies after having made Hadrian emperor. **4** During Trajan's reign, Ignatius Theophorus and Symeon, son of Cleopas, suffered martyrdom. Trajan ordered that the Christians should not be searched out, but if discovered, should be punished.[6] During his reign, Menander, a sorcerer and cheat of Samarian descent, who called himself Christian, succeeded Simon Magus. Cerinthus, the heresiarch, also lived at that time, as well as Nicholas, one of the Seven Deacons.

---

1 Nerva reigned 18 September 96–27 January 98.

2 I.e. the Evangelist (Apostle).

3 Trajan reigned 28 January 98–9 August 117.

4 *Eparchoi* (in the MSS frequently confused with *hyparchoi*) are sometimes mentioned in the Byzantine section of the text. In this case, the pretorian prefect is probably intended.

5 The syntax of this sentence is very loose but the meaning clear.

6 Trajan was considered a righteous pagan. This oft-repeated story goes back to Pliny the Younger, *Letters* X.96–97, and was transmitted to Byzantium via Eusebios.

63 Hadrian Aelius

Hadrian Aelius reigned for twenty years and eleven months.[1] He was fond of literature and a careful writer of prose as well as poetry. He was related to Trajan and was adopted by him as his son. **2** This Hadrian founded a city in Moesia, where he had gone to hunt, and he called it Hadrian's Hunt at his camp.[2] He also founded another city in Thrace and named it after himself. He also destroyed the city of the Jews, killing all of them through starvation or war. A sign of their complete destruction was that the monument of Solomon collapsed of its own accord. He then rebuilt the city and put a statue of himself in the temple, and he named the city Aelia after himself. He did this because he was suffering from leprosy and wanted to be cured. **3** He held a certain Similus, a man adorned with good sense and mildness and many virtues, in high esteem, and he honoured him with high office. However, having been in office only for a short time, Similus asked to be released from duty, and he lived in the countryside for seven years until he died. He ordered that the following should be written on his tombstone: 'Here lies Similus, who dwelled on earth for so-and-so many years, but who lived for seven years.' **4** Having made Antoninus emperor, Hadrian dies. He died in a violent fit of disease, crying: 'O Zeus, how horrible to wish for death but not to be given it.'[3] **5** During the reign of Hadrian there were the following heresiarchs, who were enemies of the Christian faith: Satorninus, Basileides and Carpocrates.

64 Antoninus Pius

Antoninus Pius reigned for twenty-four years.[4] He was the first of the emperors to be called pious; for he possessed every kind of virtue. **2** He died after having made Marcus Antoninus, his son-in-law, emperor.

---

1 Hadrian reigned 10 August 117–10 July 138.

2 'he called it Hadrians Hunt at his camp': this is an obscure expression, and it is unclear where 'at his camp' (ἐν τοῖς μιτάτοις) belongs. The founding story as such is known from Cassius Dio XLIX.10, etc.

3 This is somewhat reminiscent of Nero's last words (see above, Chapter 54, § 3).

4 Antoninus Pius reigned 138–161.

65 Marcus Antoninus, the Philosopher, and Verus, his Son-in-law

Marcus Antoninus reigned for nineteen years together with Verus, his son-in-law.[1] 2 This Marcus was a very wise and virtuous man, and he saved Rome from danger in many wars and was dearly loved by the citizens. He died poisoned by his own son, Commodus. In remembrance of his virtue the Senate honoured him after his death with a golden statue. 3 When Marcus fought the Germans and the Sarmatians, the army was hard pressed by thirst and therefore in danger. There is the story that members of the the legion known as the 'Legion of Melitene,' who were Christians, through their unceasing prayer to God had the enemy struck by lightning and the Romans comforted by rain. On hearing this, Marcus, it is said, was very much impressed, and he wrote that the Christians should be honoured and the legion be called 'Keraunobolos.'[2]

66 Commodus, Son of Marcus

Commodus, son of Marcus, reigned for twelve years and five months.[3] He had blond hair, similar to gold. He was fond of hunting, and they say that he killed twelve lions in one day. But he acquired gout and became very heavy. The inhabitants of Rome were struck by many disasters during his reign. 2 A certain Narcissus, who belonged to Commodus' household, throttled him in the bath (this is told by the most wise Africanus[4]). 3 During his reign Clemens Stromateus[5] became known in Alexandria; Origenes was a pupil of Clemens. Montanus, the heresiarch, also lived at that time, he who claimed to be a divine intercessor.[6]

---

1 Marcus Antoninus (Aurelius) reigned 161–180. In actual fact, Verus died in 169, i.e. some eight years into Marcus' reign.

2 I.e. the 'Thundering legion.' This anecdote is told by a great range of authors, from Tertullian (*Apologeticum*), Eusebios (*Church History* V.5) and various Church Fathers to the Byzantine chroniclers. Marcus Antoninus is a 'good' pagan emperor, a fact conveniently proven by the anecdote.

3 Commodus reigned 180–192.

4 This is (Sextus) Julius Africanus (ca. 160–240), the 'Father of Christian Chronography' mentioned in the Introduction.

5 I.e. Clement of Alexandria (ca. 150–215).

6 Intercessor (παράκλητος): or 'comforter/helper/counsellor.'

67 Pertinax

Pertinax reigned for eighty-seven days, bringing neither his wife nor his children to the palace but having them stay with their grandfather.[1] Pertinax was killed by the army. **2** During Pertinax's reign there lived Symmachus, one of the translators; he belonged to the Ebionite heresy.[2] But there was also Porphyrius, the philosopher, who wrote against the Christians, and the most wise Africanus.

68 Julianus Didius

Julianus Didius reigned for sixty-six days. He was a man of very bad character and wicked in his deeds and a lover of money, and for this reason he was killed. This was done on the vote of the Senate, while he was crying: 'What evil have I done?'[3]

69 Severus

Severus reigned for seventeen years and eight months.[4] **2** He occupied Byzantium[5] and razed its walls to the ground. The walls had seven towers, starting from the Thracian Gate and going down to the northern sea, and they were arranged in such a manner that, if someone proceeded to one tower, this was not seen at the others. But if someone shouted at the first tower, or moved a stone, the tower resounded and transmitted the sound to the next and so to all the others, one after another. Severus also had the Zeuxippos bath built for the inhabitants of Byzantium, and he gave them

---

1 Pertinax is the first emperor of the tumultuous year 193. Pescennius Niger and Clodius Albinus, also competitors for the throne, are not mentioned in this text.

2 Symmachus translated the Old Testament into Greek (in the second c. AD). His translation is referred to in this text (see Chapter 13, § 7) and there are also other fragments and testimonia, particularly through Origen's *Hexapla*. According to this text and some other sources, Symmachus was a member of the Jewish–Christian Ebionite sect.

3 Told by Cassius Dio LXX.17.5.

4 Septimius Severus reigned 193–211.

5 I.e. the City of Byzantium, the future Constantinople.

the first built-up hippodrome, and he built a hunting park[1] and a theatre for them. **3** During Severus' reign Origen was also in his prime; Origen sowed evil weeds in the earth and displayed every kind of depravity.[2] Leonides, Origen's father, also suffered martyrdom. **4** The emperor fell ill and died in battle. **5** Having won the war in Britain the emperor constructed a wall of a thousand stadia over the island, from sea to sea.[3]

70 Antoninus

Antoninus, son of Severus, reigned for six years and two months.[4] He murdered his own brother in the bosom of his mother.[5] **2** A certain mathematician[6] called Sarapion said that Antoninus would die and be succeeded by Macrinus; and he pointed out to the emperor Macrinus, who was standing with the Senate. But Antoninus was so perturbed (or rather this was the will of fate) that he did not understand who Macrinus was but ordered that a man standing close to him should be killed. But Macrinus took care to anticipate Antoninus and, when Antoninus descended from his horse in the hunting park[7] in order to relieve himself, Macrinus sent a centurion and had him killed by the sword, saying: 'You killed your brother, so I kill you.' **3** During Antoninus' reign Origenes wrote many different books which he left to posterity, among other things what is known as the *Hexapla* and the commentary on the [books of the] Hebrews.[8]

---

1 'hunting park' (κυνήγιον): or 'game preserve'/'beast-hunt' (I consider it likely that the meaning here is the same as in Chapter 70, § 2, where it must be a rather spacious place, since the emperor goes riding there). In contrast, in Chapter 117, § 2 (and 122, § 3), I take κυνήγιον (which is then preceded by the definite article) to be a proper name denoting the (ancient Roman) amphitheatre used for beast shows and, later on, for executions.

2 This is the well-known scholar and theologian (184/85–253/254) who, because of several aspects of his teachings, was condemned as an heretic, notably at the Synod of Constantinople in 543.

3 This is the Antonine Wall, constructed from 142 and only repaired during the reign of Severus.

4 I.e. Caracalla. The six years and two months mentioned correspond roughly to his period as ruler after the death of his father (February 211–April 217).

5 The brother was Geta.

6 I.e. astrologer.

7 Cf. above, Chapter 69, § 2.

8 '*Hexapla* ... Hebrews': this is obscure and the translation uncertain. *Hexapla* ('the six-fold') is the famous edition of the Bible in six versions: Hebrew, Greek transliteration of Hebrew, and four Greek translations.

71 Macrinus

Macrinus reigned for one year and two months.[1] **2** A certain Eutychianus took Avitus, who was Antoninus' son born out of wedlock, to himself, and he put a crown on his head and proclaimed him emperor. And he gave gold to the soldiers and started a war against Macrinus, and Macrinus was defeated and fled and was killed together with his son.

72 Avitus

Avitus reigned for three years and nine months.[2] He was so much like a woman that he even made Hierocles his lawful husband. **2** He was killed because of his depravities, and he died a terrible death. And so Alexander, his cousin, became emperor. Avitus begged his doctor to make him bi-sexed by means of an artificial cut in the front.[3]

73 Alexander, Son of Mamaea

Alexander, son of Mamaea,[4] reigned for thirteen years and eight months.[5] During his reign there was a famine in Rome, so that the Romans even touched human flesh. **2** Alexander went to war against Persia and was totally defeated, after which he was subjected to humiliation and was killed. And the soldiers promoted Maximinus to the throne. **3** Mamaea, Alexander's mother, who was a pious woman, sent for Origen, who lived in Antioch, to have him teach her about the mystery of Christ.

---

1 Macrinus reigned April 217–June 218.
2 This is emperor Elagabalus (218–222), born Varius Avitus Bassianus.
3 Avitus-Elagabalus' sexual orientation, and possible transgender identity, is reported by Cassius Dio LXXX.16.
4 Julia Avita Mamaea.
5 Alexander Severus reigned March 222–March 235, so this is not quite correct.

74 Maximinus

Maximinus reigned for six years.[1] He had been a shepherd and later became a soldier and was then made *strategos*[2] of Alexandria. He was promoted to the imperial throne by the people and the Senate because of his courage and good sense. **2** Later, he was treacherously killed by Maximus and Balbinus, meeting with an end worthy of his wicked mind. Maximinus started a great persecution of the Christians. This was because of his hatred against Alexander, who had many Christians with him and who paid them great respect.

75 Maximus and Balbinus

Maximus and Balbinus reigned for twenty-two days.[3] They were killed by the soldiers in the same way as the earlier caesar Gordian had been killed by Maximinus on becoming emperor;[4] for the killing happened when Philip, the *eparchos*, stopped bread from being conveyed to the army. This Philip was the father of the holy martyr Eugenia. **2** During the reign of Maximus and Gordian,[5] Africanus, the writer, became known.

76 Philip

Philip reigned for five years.[6] He was eagerly interested in Christianity and endowed with good sense and fairness. He stemmed from Bostra; there

1 Maximinus Thrax reigned 235–238, and the six years mentioned by this text would seem to be an error (see, however, below, with relevant notes).

2 In the Byzantine section of the text, a common title for a military commander.

3 Pupienus Maximus and Balbinus reigned April–July 238. The period of twenty-two days mentioned would suit better the joint reign of Gordian I and Gordian II (see following note).

4 Gordian I and Gordian II, father and son, reigned together 22 March–12 April 238 (being in open conflict with Maximinus Thrax). The Gordian mentioned here would seem to be Gordian II. See also following note.

5 Gordian II? It should be noted that Gordian III (reigned 238–244) is, if so, not referred to at all in this text, and the years of his reign are not covered. On the other hand, it should be noted (cf. above, Chapter 74, § 1) that the reign of Maximinus Thrax is said to have lasted six years (instead of the correct number of three). This error could in fact be connected to the lack of years at this point.

6 Philip the Arab reigned 244–249.

he also founded a city, which he called Philippoupolis. **2** Philip concluded a peace treaty with Shapur, the king of the Persians.[1] Philip was admired for his bodily size, for until that time no man of that size had been known. **3** Philip, together with his son, was killed by Decius when fighting for the Christians.

77 Decius

Decius reigned for two years.[2] He punished many saintly people and had them sent to their death. On the instigation of Gallus and Volusianus, he was killed by the Scythians[3] by being drowned in a swamp together with his son. Thus they met with a punishment commensurate with their brutality and, because of this, not even parts of their bodies were found afterwards.[4] **2** During Decius' reign Clemens Stromateus, Africanus and Gregory the Wonderworker lived. During Decius' reign Novatian,[5] one of the *presbyteroi*,[6] defected from the Church. For he was not willing to receive back people who had made pagan offerings and repented. During Decius' reign St Cyprian suffered martyrdom, as well as the Seven Children of Ephesus[7] and many other holy persons.

1 This is Shapur I (Σαβώρης) who reigned 240/42–270/72.
2 Decius reigned 249–251.
3 Perhaps Goths in this case (for further references to Goths and Scythians see Index of names).
4 Being known for his persecution of the Christians, Decius meets with a fitting end. This is an early example of a theme developed more systematically later: the bad death of the (un)deserving (see below, e.g. Chapter 132, § 2, on the fate of the accomplices to the murder of Michael III, or Chapter 134, § 9, on the death of emperor Alexander). A starting point for all this is provided by stories in the Old Testament, dealing with Cain and others, and the idea is also known from literature such as Lactantius' *De mortibus persecutorum*.
5 Or: 'Nauatos.'
6 Cf. above, Chapter 37, § 1, and 43, § 3, in which cases the same word is understood in a less technical sense as 'elders.'
7 I.e. the Seven Sleepers of Ephesus, a story known since Late Antiquity. These were persecuted for being Christians, or, less specifically, for refusing to indulge in the kind of idolatry demanded by the imperial cult. As related below, Chapter 97, § 4, they woke up during the reign of emperor Theodosios the Younger, i.e. when Christianity had prevailed.

78 Gallus and Volusianus

Gallus and Volusianus reigned for two years and eight months.[1] During their reign there was a great plague which started from Ethiopia and went as far as the West, and no city was spared from this menace. It lasted for fifteen years, starting in the autumn and ending at the rising of the Dog Star.[2] The disease was transmitted by clothes and by visual contact. And the Scythians crossed the Istros and ravaged and occupied the whole of the West and Italy as well as the East and Asia, with the sole exception of Ilium and Kyzikos. **2** Gallus and Volusianus were killed by the soldiers, and so Aemilian was proclaimed emperor. During the reign of Gallus and Volusianus the heresy of Sabellios began.[3]

79 Aemilian

Aemilian reigned for four months.[4] He was commander of the army in Moesia as well as of a Libyan army. With these armies, he fought the Scythians and, having achieved victory on several occasions, he was puffed up by his success and had himself proclaimed emperor. **2** Aemilian, too, is killed by soldiers.

80 Valerian and Galenus

Valerian and Galenus, his son, reigned for fifteen years.[5] **2** This Valerian went to war against Shapur, the Persian, and on being captured in the city of Caesarea, together with 400,000 men, he was flogged to death by Shapur. **3** After Valerian's death Galenus organised cavalry brigades.[6] He was the

1 Trebonianus Gallus reigned, mostly together with his son, Volusianus, June 251–August 253. It is unclear how this could be two years and eight months.

2 I.e. Sirius. This is, perhaps, odd: the heliacal rising of Sirius must have taken place somewhere in July/August. It leaves very little time in each year without the plague.

3 Sabellianism was a heresy that opposed the idea of the Trinity.

4 Aemilian reigned in 253, and the length of his reign is usually given as three months (so Eutropius, *Breviarium ab Urbe condita* 9.6).

5 I.e. Valerian and Gallienus. Valerian was captured by the Persians in 259, and the fifteen years apply to Gallienus (253–268).

6 *Tagmata*, a word with a technical meaning in the Byzantine part of the text (cf. Index of terms and concepts).

first to do so, for the Roman soldiers had to a great degree been infantry men before. Galenus, too, was killed by soldiers.

81 Claudius

Claudius reigned for one year.[1] He was the grandfather of Constantius,[2] the father of Constantine the Great. **2** During his reign the Scythians passed through and went to Athens and occupied it. And they gathered together all the books and wanted to burn them. But a sensible man among them stopped them saying that 'it is on these that the Romans spend their time so as to neglect warfare.' **3** Having promoted Aurelian to the throne this emperor dies of illness.

82 Aurelian

Aurelian reigned for six years.[3] He was killed by the army between Heraclea and Byzantium, in what is called the New Fortress.[4] And he was buried there. **2** Aurelian had a certain man[5] employed as a spy, who reported to him everything done and said. When this man was threatened once by the emperor for some reason,[6] and was frightened by this, he imitated the handwriting of the emperor and named in a document some leading men as being liable to execution. This frightened them so that they killed Aurelian. **3** Also during his reign St Chariton became a confessor for the faith. During Aurelian's reign the accursed Mani[7] was born. It is from him that the name of *Manichean* comes and has spread to so many.

---

1 Claudius II Gothicus reigned September 268–January 270.

2 I.e. Constantius Chlorus.

3 Aurelian reigned September 270–September/October 275. Quintillus is lacking between Claudius and Aurelian in the list of emperors.

4 Καινὸν Φρούριον, in Eastern Thrace.

5 'Aurelian ... man': there is a slight problem of interpretation here: perhaps the spy's name was also Aurelian.

6 'for some reason': or 'because of some accusation.'

7 The founder of Manichaeism, a gnostic, dualistic religion of considerable importance in Late Antiquity. Manichaeism proper became extinct at some later date, but followers of other, later heresies (such as that of the Paulicians) could be accused of being Manicheans. It is an interesting question whether the author of this part of our chronicle perceives something of a real threat still emanating from Mani and his teachings.

83 Tacitus

Tacitus reigned for two years.[1] He made his relative Maximinus governor of Assyria.[2] The soldiers killed this Maximinus because of the crimes which he had committed. Then they feared that Tacitus would exact vengeance on his behalf, and so they killed him, too. Thus Probus and Florianus became emperors.

84 Probus and Florianus

Probus reigned together with Florianus for two years.[3] During Probus' reign there was a great downpour of rain during which much bread[4] fell from heaven. This they collected into big heaps. **2** Having invited those involved in the killing of Tacitus and Aurelian to a banquet at Peirinthos, Probus had them all killed. He, too, was killed by his closest circle, and so Carus becomes emperor together with Carinus and Numerian.

85 Carus, Carinus and Numerian

Carus, Carinus and Numerian reigned for two years.[5] This Carus occupied Persia and Ctesiphon. This was the fourth time that these were occupied: it had happened under Trajan, under Verus, under Severus and [it happened now under] Carus. After Carus' death Carinus, who had been blinded, was killed by Apros. And so Numerian became emperor.[6] **2** During his reign St George suffered martyrdom as well as St Babylas in Antioch. He[7] was killed by Diocletian, the then *doux*[8] of Moesia.

1 Tacitus reigned September 275–June 276. Two years is therefore hardly expected as the time period for his reign.

2 I.e. Syria.

3 This is problematic, since Probus reigned 276–282 and Florianus for some three months in 276.

4 Or: 'grain.'

5 This can be understood as the two years (282–284) before Diocletian entered the stage, although Carinus went on to rule until 285.

6 This is not historically correct: Carinus outlived Numerian (cf. previous note).

7 I.e. the emperor Numerian.

8 The term *doux* is used three times in this text, always for some kind of ruler/official in the West (cf. Chapter 130, § 11, and Chapter 133, §11).

86 Diocletian

Diocletian, a Dalmatian by birth, reigned for twenty years.[1] Unable to control the situation on his own, he makes Maximianus Herculius, his son-in-law and friend, co-emperor. During their reign a great persecution of the Christians started. Diocletian and Maximianus promote Constantius and Galerius to the rank of caesars in their respective realms, and they make them their son-in-laws, persuading them to leave their spouses and take the emperors' daughters for wives: Theodora became the wife of Constantius, and Valeria that of Galerius. 2 Of these,[2] Galerius asked Diocletian for permission and was sent against the Persians to fight them. Having defeated them, he invaded the Persian palace and seized Shapur's[3] wife, and in great triumph he returned to Diocletian with bags full of precious stones and pearls. Using these, Diocletian was the first to wear a robe and shoes embellished with precious stones and gold. He also demanded that, in conflict with earlier custom, he should be hailed with *proskynesis*,[4] and he celebrated a triumph [it was called triumph because of the poetic word *thriasis*, that is, frenzy, or because the leaves of the fig are called *thria*].[5] 3 In the twentieth year of their reign Diocletian and Maximianus suddenly abdicated one day. Diocletian lived as a private citizen for twelve years. Then, when his tongue and his throat were putrified and worms came forth, he gave up his spirit.[6] But Herculius wanted to resume the rule and, when he did not succeed in this, he hanged himself. Galerius became infested with worms and gave up his soul, having first given Licinius share in the rule of the East. 4 During Diocletian's reign Adauctus the *magistros*[7]

1 Diocletian reigned November 285–May 305. Here begins Theophanes' chronicle, a major source for the Chronicle of the Logothete (see the Introduction). For a translation of Theophanes on Diocletian see Mango/Scott 1997, pp. 5–19. Cf. for Diocletian's reign also the *Chronicon Paschale* (Whitby/Whitby 1989, pp. 1–6).

2 'Of these': the Greek genitive thus translated (ὧν) is awkward.

3 This reference is problematic insofar as no Shapur reigned at the same time as Diocletian. Either there is an erroneous attribution of an episode to the wrong emperor (Narseh), or 'Shapur' is used generically for any Persian–Sasanian king (a parallel to this would be Chapter 104, § 16, where a Persian king is referred to as a 'Darius').

4 I.e. prostration.

5 The sentence within square brackets is most probably a gloss added later to the text.

6 As instigator of the Great Persecution of the Christians Diocletian had, according to early Christian and Byzantine belief, every reason to expect an unpleasant end to his life.

7 This is the first occurrence of the term in this text. Offices such as *magister equitum* and *magister officiorum* are well attested in Late Antiquity. The Byzantine *magistros* as an honorary title is known from the mid-Byzantine period. It is hard to say whether people in the later period were aware of the changes in meaning that the term had undergone.

suffered martyrdom. When his wife and two daughters were looked for, it turned out that they had fled and, in order not to lose their honour, the mother threw herself into the river together with her daughters. One should investigate whether these are counted among the martyrs.[1] **5** A certain fraudster called Theotecnus, acting upon the instigation of Maximianus, fabricated an account of the acts of Pilate during the time of Christ. These were full of every kind of blasphemy, and he sent them to every city and village together with Maximianus' order to the school-masters that they should teach these to the children, in order to make our mystery a matter of ridicule.

87 Constantius Chlorus, the Father of Constantine the Great

Constantius reigned as emperor for two years, having been caesar for thirteen years.[2] By Helena he became the father of Constantine; this happened close to the city in Dacia.[3] Maxentius and Maximinus are killed by Licinius, and from the time of Diocletian and Galerius, the Persians lived in peace with the Romans, and their royal women and children were allowed to return home. **2** Constantius was a pious man and raised his son Constantine to be so, too, and they in no way took part in the persecution of our kind. He even allowed those living under his rule to lead a Christian life without fear and without impediment. Having[4] proclaimed Constantine *augustus*[5] and emperor in Rome, Maximinus committed many atrocities against the Christians in the East, and so did Maxentius in Rome. **3** The divine Constantine proceeded towards the annihilation of the tyrants, and Maxentius is killed by him in Rome; this was when God also gave him the sign of the Cross as a token of

---

1 This could refer to several different kinds of collections containing information about who is a saint, such as a *menologion* or a *synaxarion*.

2 Constantius Chlorus was *caesar* 293–305 and *augustus*, 1 May 305–25 July 306. Cf. for his reign the *Chronicon Paschale* (Whitby/Whitby 1989, p. 6). On Theophanes see below, n. on Chapter 88, § 1.

3 'the city in Dacia': the expression is somewhat odd but should refer to Constantine's city of birth, Naissus (Niš in present-day Serbia). This was in the old Roman province of Moesia superior. Constantine made it the capital of the province of Dacia Mediterranea.

4 This chapter is structurally odd. Constantius Chlorus is phased out (his death is not mentioned), and the rest of the chapter is about Constantine.

5 σεβαστόν.

an alliance.[1] Maximinus was defeated in the East, by Licinius, who had not yet gone mad, and he fled and died of a dreadful illness. When Maxentius and Licinius had been killed, Constantine gained control of all land under Roman sovereignty, and he made many laws which favoured the Christian faith. He ordered that Friday and Sunday should be honoured, the one because of the Cross of the Lord, the other because of the Resurrection, and he ordered that no man should be condemned to crucifixion. 4 He sent his mother to the Holy Places and, having found the Holy Cross, she sent part of it and the nails to her son, and he put one[2] in a helmet to protect him,[3] and with another he embellished the bridle of his horse, and he also ordered that its[4] picture should be on his *solidi*[5] and that the sign of the Cross should be engraved on them.

88 Constantine the Great

Constantine the Great, the first true Christian among the emperors, reigned for thirty-one years and lived for sixty-five years.[6] He was baptised in Rome by Sylvester and became a Christian. 2 Fearing the Senate in Rome (this he did because of his belief in Christ), he left the city on the pretext of going to war against the Scythians. He made Licinius his brother-in-law through his sister, and then he appointed him emperor. However, when some of Constantine's men took refuge with Licinius and were demanded back by Constantine as rebels, this was not granted. Therefore, Constantine marched out against Licinius and fought him in Paeonia. There he also saw the sign of the Cross in heaven, with the

1 From this point and until Chapter 102, § 12, the *Church History* of Theodorus Lector (Anagnostes) constitutes a very important parallel to this text, with many cases of identical wording.

2 Presumably a nail went into the helmet and the bridle, respectively, although, as far as the Greek is concerned, it could refer to the Cross. See also following notes.

3 'helmet to protect him': the text is corrupt, but I take it that the sense is clear.

4 'its': this could suitably refer to either a nail or the Cross, both of which are known from Constantine's coins.

5 Greek νομίσμασι, from Constantine on the standard gold coin of ca. 4.5 g.

6 Constantine was born in (perhaps) 272 (which suits this calculation) and reigned 306–337. Cf. for his reign Theophanes (Mango/Scott 1997, pp. 19–55), and the *Chronicon Paschale* (Whitby/Whitby 1989, pp. 6–22). Constantius Chlorus' reign is not given attention by Theophanes, and the reign of Constantine is given as thirty-two years, starting in the year 304/305.

writing: 'By this sign conquer.'[1] And he made this sign in gold and put it on a spear, and so he routed the enemy. Licinius retreated and fled to Thrace. There, he was forced into battle at Philippoupolis, where he was decisively and spectacularly defeated and so pacified. **3** After this, having once again proved an enemy, Licinius was attacked at Adrianople and defeated, and he came to Byzantium and crossed over to Chrysopolis, where he was defeated once again; from there, he fled to Nicomedia. Constantine's sister comes to him [Constantine], and at her request she is given her husband's life as a gift, on condition that he should live as a private individual. But Licinius seceded and went to Thessalonica, and making a commotion there, he was killed by the army. At the time of this Licinius, St Theodore[2] also suffered martyrdom. The war between Licinius and Constantine lasted for eighteen years.[3] **4** The peace which had prevailed between the Persians and the Romans was dissolved for the following reason: there was a certain Metrodoros, of Persian descent, who pretended to be a philosopher. He went to India and the Brahmans and, by showing great continence, he earned their respect. He also built water mills and baths, which were not known [to the Indians] at that time. Since he was considered pious, he was allowed to enter the inner sanctuaries of the temples, and he took many precious stones and pearls from there. He also received stones and pearls from the king of the Indians, to be given as gifts to the emperor. But when he came back to Byzantium, he gave them to the emperor as if they were his private gifts. When the emperor marvelled at these, he said that he had sent others by the land route; these, however, had been taken by the Persians. Immediately, Constantine writes to Shapur and tells him that these should be sent to him.[4] On receiving this letter, Shapur sent no response,[5] and for this reason the peace was dissolved. From the stones that he had received, the emperor made a piece of art[6] and sent it to the peoples on the other side of the Danube. It bore the inscription: 'A gift for the greatest.' This inscription proved fatal for them.

---

1 In Theophanes, this sign appeared to Constantine at the Milvian Bridge (Mango/Scott 1997, p. 31). In Eusebios it is not stated where the emperor saw the sign.

2 This is Theodore Stratelates, high-ranking officer under Licinius and executed on his command (cf. Chapter 121, § 4).

3 'lasted for eighteen years': this is more or less a correct figure for the time from Constantine's accession in 306 until Licinius' surrender in 324.

4 This is Shapur II, ruler of Sasanian Persia 309–379.

5 'sent no response': or 'did not send anything in return.'

6 'piece of art': Greek ἔργον ('work').

5 It is said that Constantine was the first of all emperors to wear a crown, and that he was adorned with pearls and other precious stones in a rather elaborate way. He also had covers made for the Gospel in gold and with pearls and precious stones, and he offered them to the Great Church as a work worthy of admiration. He issued a law that the temples of idolatry and their incomes should be handed over to the priests of the Christians, and that only Christians should hold office or serve in the army. **6** In the twentieth year of his reign the first Council of Nicaea took place, the one against Arius.[1] **7** From there he went to Byzantium, and he took all the holy and famous fathers with him in order that they should bless the City which he had founded. He had built a palace and a hippodrome and the two delightful porticoes and the Forum, in which he erected a monolithic pillar of porphyry which he had brought from Rome, and he bound it with belts of bronze stretching around it, and he put up a statue upon it, inscribed with his own name and with the additional text: 'Because of his rays, to Constantine, who shines like the sun.'[2] This statue was the work of Phidias and had been brought from Athens. He brought the remains of the holy apostles Andrew and Luke and Timothy to Constantinople, and he placed them in the Church of the Holy Apostles. **8** He then moved against the Persians and, setting out from Nikomedeia, he arrives at Pythia Therma. There he was taken ill, and he reached Charax by way of Helenoupolis.[3] He was then overcome by violent fever and, in the ninth year[4] after the founding and inauguration of Contantinople, he died. His body was brought to the Church of the Holy Apostles and was put to rest in the *Heroon*, which he had had prepared as a burial place for the emperors.[5] He left three sons, Constantius, Constantine and Constans, having decided

1 I.e. the Council of Nicea in 325.

2 This is the famous Column of Constantine, or the Burnt Column (Çemberlitaş). The bronze belts referred to were wreaths covering the joints between the blocks of stone. Upon this there was a statue of Apollo with Constantine's features. The whole paragraph is a good example of antiquarian lore with a basis in the monuments visible in Constantinople at the time of writing.

3 All this is in Bithynia, at the Gulf of Izmit (Astacus), fairly close to Nicomedia.

4 'ninth year': this is true with some inclusive reckoning (from 11 May 330 until 22 May 337).

5 In Antiquity, a *Heroon* is the shrine (often centred upon a cenotaph or a supposed tomb) of a *hero(s)* worshipped as a founding figure of a city. In this case, the term refers to the mausoleum prepared by Constantine and his family as a burial place at the Church of the Holy Apostles. Considering Constantine's status as founding father of the City, the designation of his mausoleum as a *Heroon* is no doubt particularly fitting.

that Constantius should have the region consisting of Thrace and the East, Constantine the West towards the Ocean, and Constans, Crete, Africa and the corresponding part of Illyria.[1] **9** The[2] divine Constantine was criticised in Byzantium by the pagan philosophers for not acting justly and for deviating from the customs of the previous Roman rulers, and for having changed the faith and introduced new elements. The emperor then decided that one of the philosophers should dispute with Alexander, the bishop of Byzantium, on faith. Alexander was not versed in rhetoric, but he was a pious man and, on the day of the disputation, he said to the dialectical philosopher: 'In the name of Jesus Christ I command you to be silent and not to speak.' As soon as these words were uttered, the philosopher was silenced and remained speechless. **10** Constantine ordered Eusebios, of Pamphilos,[3] to prepare holy books[4] for the benefit of the churches of Constantinople, and he furnished him with public means for this. And, apart from the other holy books, he wrote[5] sixty books with beautiful decoration[6] on deer skin. The divine Constantine builds the Church of St Irene and the Church of the Holy Apostles and the Church of St Mokios and that of Agathonikos the martyr, as well as that of the Archangel Michael in Anaplous, and in Sosthenion, a place where he also heard and saw divine omens in a wondrous way. **11** St Metrophanes was the bishop of Byzantium before Alexander. **12** The emperor first started to build a city to bear his name in the plain[7] in front of Ilium, on the site of the grave of Ajax.[8] However, God ordered the emperor in a dream to found his city, which now is called Constantinople, at Byzantium instead. But when he saw that the inhabitants of the City were few, he chose people from noted families in Rome and other places, and he built large houses which he bestowed on them, and he made them live in the City. **13** During

1 'corresponding part of Illyria': there is a problem in the Greek text, and the translation is hypothetical.
2 From here at the latest, the text consists of material that seems loosely added to the main structure of the chapter, running from the accession of the emperor until his death. There is also some overlap between the narrative before and after this point.
3 This is Eusebius of Caesarea (Eusebius Pamphili), the chronicler etc. (cf. above, Chapter 35, § 5).
4 Or: 'Bibles.' Cf. on this the book covers mentioned in § 5 above.
5 Or: 'had written'; probably, Eusebios is the intended subject.
6 'with beautiful decoration' (γράψας ἐφιλοκάλησε): or 'in beautiful calligraphy.'
7 'plain': the text is corrupt here, but the meaning seems clear.
8 Or: 'Aias.' There were two Greek heroes of this name fighting at Troy. Presumably, this is Ajax the Great, the Telamonian.

Constantine's reign many pagan peoples welcomed Christianity, from the Celts and the Galatians in the West, but also[1] the innermost[2] Indians, and bishops were sent to them by Constantine with the twofold purpose of investigating their regions and of proclaiming the faith. Likewise, the Iberians[3] as well as the Armenians become Christians; this started with Tiridates, who was of Parthian descent. Persians likewise became Christians during the time of Symeon, bishop of Ctesiphon; together with him, also Ustaxades, the eunuch, who was the teacher of Shapur,[4] suffered martyrdom.

89 Constantius

Constantius reigned for twenty-four years and Constans for seventeen years, whereas Constantine died after a very short time.[5] He died in the following way. Accompanied by a great military force, he went towards his brother Constantius.[6] This he did in order to share some matter with him, but it caused consternation in Constantius' mind, and he feared that his brother was coming against him with rebellion in mind. Constantius had engaged bad counsellors who were inciting him to conflict and fear, and thus to war, rather than diverting him from such thoughts; therefore, he went out against Constantine. When battle is joined, Constantine is found at the rear amongst the last of those fleeing, and is killed. Thus Constans gained control of the whole of the West. 2 In the seventeenth year of Constans' reign, Magnentius, a rebel who had appeared in Gaul, killed Constans in his sleep after a hunt.[7] On learning this, Constantius, who was in Antioch, makes Gallus, his brother-in-law through his sister, caesar, with the duty of managing the Western parts of the empire. He himself

---

1 The text is slightly anacoluthic, and the 'from' (in 'from the Celts etc.') is not followed up.

2 'innermost': Greek οἱ ἐνδότεροι, i.e. the people furthest into India.

3 I.e. the Georgians.

4 In this instance, the Greek form is Σαβώριος (otherwise Σαβώρης).

5 Constantius II reigned 337–361, Constans 337–350, and Constantine II 337–340. Cf. Theophanes (Mango/Scott 1997, pp. 55–76), and the *Chronicon Paschale* (Whitby/Whitby 1989, pp. 22–36).

6 This should probably be Constans, see Theophanes (Mango/Scott 1997, p. 58) and others.

7 This was in 350.

continued to fight the Persians; this was already his third campaign against them. Gallus defeated Magnentius. Then he turns against Constantius, but Constantius has him pacified with flattery and favours, and then has him killed. **3** At first Constantius did not confer Gallus' position on anyone, but, when there was a great movement of the Persian army, he gave it to Gallus' brother Julian, whom he brought from Athens and made caesar. In this, Constantius made no less of a mistake than in his championship of Arius, which made him do a great deal of evil to Athanasios, bishop of Alexandria, and Paul of Constantinople. **4** Having marched against the Persians and learning that Julian was rebelling against him, Constantius, who because of his constant worries had become ill from black bile, died at Mopsou krene (this is situated on the slopes of the Tauros[1]). Jovian, who was a *protiktor*[2] at the time and who later became emperor, arranged the transportation of his body and laid it to rest close to Constantius' father's body in the *Heroon*.[3] **5** Weak-minded as he was, Constantius was persuaded by Eusebios of Nicomedia to become an Arian and to remove the word *homoousios*,[4] on the grounds that it was not attested. **6** On the death of the patriarch Alexander, Paul the Confessor is elected. Paul having been deposed, Eusebios, bishop of Nicomedia, places himself on the patriarchal throne with the help of bribery. After him there was Paul again, and after him Makedonios, the opponent of the Spirit,[5] who started no less a persecution of the Christians than the idolaters. **7** Close to the Church of Irene, Constantius founds the Church of God's Wisdom, a most beautiful church, but not of the same design or of the same beauty or size as the one to be seen there now.[6] And he conducted the inauguration ceremony of this church; this was when Eudoxios, the pupil of Eunomios, was patriarch. **8** During Constantius' reign St Ephraim the Syrian was prominent in deed and word. He has left many useful writings to posterity.

1 I.e. in south-eastern Anatolia.

2 This was a Latin title, originally for members of an imperial bodyguard, later for courtiers. Later in Byzantium *protiktores* are officers under the *domestikos* of the *scholai*. Whether the author of this text is aware of the changing meanings of the term remains unclear.

3 This is the mausoleum at the Church of the Holy Apostles in Constantinople (cf. above, Chapter 88, § 8).

4 The Arian creed claimed that the Son is subordinate to and not consubstantial with the Father.

5 Greek πνευματομάχος: i.e. he supported a kind of Arianism.

6 I.e. the St Sophia (= (Church of the) Holy Wisdom), erected new during Justinian in the sixth c.

9 When the army killed the young(er) Dalmatius,[1] Gallus was saved because he was ill and Julian because of his tender age. They were allowed by Constantius to reside and be educated in a village close to Caesarea, where Julian went about with his hair cropped short and pretended to adopt monastic practices. Having both become readers in the Church the brothers wanted to found a church dedicated to the martyr Mamas. But the place that was allotted to Julian for building did not accept this.

90 Julian the Apostate

Julian reigned as emperor for two years; he had been a caesar for four years and six months.[2] He was the cousin of Constantius.[3] He had been brought up by Eusebios, the bishop of Nicomedia. He was short in stature and to the highest degree able to control his need for sleep, food and sex. But otherwise and with regard to religion he was of an evil disposition. For, having been initiated to the Christian mysteries, he later disregarded these and preferred the Hellenic belief, and he exchanged the true belief for the bad, and virtue for wickedness and deviousness of the mind. **2** Julian opened the coffin of the Forerunner[4] and committed his bodily remains to the fire and scattered the ashes.[5] The wicked sinner also ordered the statue of Christ at Paneas,[6] the one put up by the woman with the haemorrhage, to be torn down and taken away, and he put an image of Zeus in the place of the image of Christ.[7] He also burnt the bodies of many saints, not, however, with impunity. **3** For, when he went to war against the Persians, he was tricked by the deserters to set fire to his boats. Having

1 This is Flavius Dalmatius Caesar, killed by soldiers in 337. He was the nephew of Constantine I and the son of Flavius Dalmatius Censor.

2 This is, however computed, imprecise: Julian was caesar November 355–February 360, joint *augustus* until 3 November 361, and sole ruler until 26 June 363. Cf. for Julian's reign Theophanes (Mango/Scott 1997, pp. 76–83), and the *Chronicon Paschale* (Whitby/Whitby 1989, pp. 36–42).

3 They had a common paternal grandfather in Constantius Chlorus but different grandmothers: Helena (in the case of Constantius) and Theodora (in the case of Julian) respectively.

4 I.e. John the Baptist.

5 Several of the anecdotes in the following are known from Church historians, including Eusebios and Theodorus Lector.

6 Greek εἰκόνα. Paneas is Caesarea Philippi, in the Golan Heights.

7 The story about this woman is first told in Eusebios, *Church History* VII.18.

then marched for quite some time through deserted and hilly regions, his army ran out of all necessary provisions, and all those who accompanied him suffered much. When the time came for battle, Julian turns in flight and is wounded by a spear and, with blood streaming through his nostrils, he took the spear in his hands and brandished it in the air and said: 'Be satisfied, Nazarene!' And thus his devious soul departed, and his body was carried away to Tarsos. 4 At[1] the death of Constantius, Julian became sole ruler, and he shamelessly adopted Hellenism and washed off holy baptism with the blood of sacrifices. He had Eusebios, the foremost of the imperial eunuchs,[2] killed for wrongdoing, striving (indeed!) for a reputation of righteousness. He even expelled all eunuchs from the palace and, out of hatred of Constantius, he rejected his wife, who was Constantius' sister.[3] He also expelled all cooks and barbers, and he prohibited the use of camels, oxen, donkeys and mules for the public post;[4] he allowed only horses to be used for this. 5 The same emperor issued a law that no Christians should be allowed to be engaged in the teaching of Hellenic learning. But Apollinarios, using the Holy Scriptures as his material and imitating the style of all poets, wrote works by which the Christians could be educated.[5] 6 Having fortified himself with divination, sacrifices and the fraud of demons, Julian marched against the Persians. It is at this time that he is said to have received a prophecy worded as follows:[6]

'Now we, all the gods, have set out to gain trophies at the Wild Beast River.[7]
I, furious Ares, will lead them on, raising the din of war.'

1 The following additional material aims at characterising Julian further.

2 Cf. the title of *proteunouchos* in Chapter 114, § 4.

3 'and, out ... sister': the Greek text is unclear and may be corrupt, and the translation partly hypothetical. Cf. Mango/Scott 1997, p. 77; also Theodorus Lector 57.3–9.

4 δημόσιος δρόμος, cf. Latin *cursus publicus*.

5 As reported by Sozomenus (*Church History* V.xviii; VI.xxv), father and son (both called Apollinarios and here, probably, conflated into one person) were engaged in the rewriting of the Bible so as to give it a more classical form and make it palatable for an educated audience.

6 This oracle is also known from Theophanes (and older texts, such as Theodorus Lector, see Mango/Scott 1997, pp. 82–83).

7 παρὰ Θῆρι ποταμῷ: Julian was mortally wounded in the battle of Samarra on the river Tigris (with other words: An Appointment in Samarra).

91 Jovian

Jovian reigned for eight months.[1] He confessed in front of the army that he was a Christian. Julian knew about him. Once, when he walked behind him, Jovian stepped on Julian's cloak, and Julian turned to him and, seeing no one but him, said: 'If only it had been a human!' This Jovian was chosen emperor by all the army, on the grounds that he was pious beyond any doubt and mild and fair. 2 Having concluded a peace treaty with the Persians, Jovian ate a poisonous[2] mushroom on the way home from Persia, and he died. 3 Wishing to save the people left behind, Jovian was forced to cede Nisibis, a very great and populous city, to the Persians.[3] The same emperor said to the army, that 'I am not able to command an army which has been accustomed to the Hellenic religion during the reign of Julian.' On hearing this, the army confessed to him that they were all Christians.

92 Valentinian

Valentinian reigned for thirteen years.[4] Because of his righteousness, he was praised and admired even when he made a display of severity. For they knew that his severity was the result of thought, and he always gave priority to justice, and he was not deflected from his course or dissuaded by anyone when he had made up his mind about a matter. 2 Valentinian was proclaimed emperor by the army after Jovian and, on being asked to name an associate ruler, he said: 'I will take the associate I want.' On his arrival at Nicomedia, he was asked by the magistrates about his choice of a co-ruler. And Daglaiphus, a senator, replied: 'If you love your kin, greatest emperor, you have a brother; but if you love the empire, consider whom you clothe in the purple.' But Valentinian trusted nature most, and he appointed

---

1 Jovian reigned 27 June 363–17 February 364. Cf. for his reign Theophanes (Mango/Scott 1997, pp. 83–85), and the *Chronicon Paschale* (Whitby/Whitby 1989, pp. 42–44).

2 Or: 'poisoned' (πεφαρμαγμένον).

3 This is an additional anecdote, intended to further underline the piety of Jovian.

4 The total of Valentinian's reign lasted from 26 February 364 to 17 November 375 (it should perhaps be noted that, for most of that time (from 26 March 364), he reigned over only the Western part of the empire). Therefore, thirteen years can be accepted as the correct number with inclusive reckoning (26.2–1.9.364 = year 1; 1.9–17.11.375 = year 13). Cf. for Valentinian's reign Theophanes (Mango/Scott 1997, pp. 85–97), and the *Chronicon Paschale* (Whitby/Whitby 1989, pp. 44–48).

his brother Valens, and he gave the West to himself, having learnt about an insurrection of some tribes there, and he gave the East to Valens. **3** As far as ruling the empire was concerned, Valentinian had learnt from a certain Sallustius that he would gain possession of it, and he promised that if he should attain such power, Sallustius would have whatever he wanted. However, when he had become emperor and was asked by Sallustius for the office of *eparchos* according to his promise, he said that it was not right for him to keep true to his commitment if this should bring harm to the state. **4** During Valentinian's reign, a certain woman had her property taken from her by Rodanos, the *praipositos*.[1] The emperor gave judgement on the matter, and he ordered the *praipositos* to give her back her belongings. However, the *praipositos* did not obey. On learning this, the emperor asked that the woman should come before him. She kneeled in supplication before the emperor during races at the hippodrome and, when she had asked about the matter and spoken of the *praipositos*' disobedience, the emperor ordered that a great fire should be kindled in the Sphendone[2] and that the *praipositos*, who was standing at his side, should be burnt there in his dress of office,[3] and that all his belongings should be given to the woman. **5** This emperor also razed the city of Chalcedon to the ground, and he built the great aqueduct from its stones and brought water into the City. **6** Having defeated the Sarmatians as well, and seeing their ambassadors coming, he asked if these people were Sarmatians. And on learning that the best of them had come to him, he was deeply distressed[4] and said: 'It bodes ill for the Romans, if such people deem it fit to become ambassadors.' It is said that his excessive reaction caused a vein to dilate and an artery to burst, and that the resulting haemorrhage led to the emperor Valentinian's death.[5] **7** Valentinian, who was most orthodox, appointed Ambrose bishop in Milan, and it is said that Ambrose censured the unjust magistrates during the time of this emperor. **8** The Goths treated Valens badly, and he asked the most divine Valentinian to send an army to assist him. Not only did Valentinian not give him this, but

1 This anecdote, illustrating the righteousness of the emperor, bears a certain resemblance to other stories about how emperors intervene against the magistrates on behalf of humble individuals. See, e.g., below, Chapter 130, § 31, on a story about emperor Theophilos and how he dealt with the theft of a horse.

2 Or: 'Sphendon,' a curved tribune at the hippodrome's U-turn, where executions were carried out.

3 μετὰ τῶν ἀμφίων τῆς ἀξίας.

4 Or: 'filled with anger' (πλησθεὶς θυμοῦ).

5 This story is told in Ammianus Marcellinus XXX.6.

he even reproached him, saying that one should not defend a man who fights against God. **9** During Valentinian's reign, Basil and Gregory,[1] who had been educated by Himerios and Prohairesios, famous sophists, flourished. Basil and Gregory were also taught by Libanios, the sophist in Antioch.

93 Valens

Valens reigned for three years.[2] **2** During his reign the Goths crossed Lake Maiotis in pursuit of a deer and arrived in Thrace. There, they split into two factions that fought each other. One of the factions asked for an alliance with Valens. This was given to them, on condition that they became Christians. This is why they became Arians on being baptised, for this is what Valens was. When Valens after this was resident in Syria, the Scythians[3] crossed over and penetrated to the City, showing no regard for the peace treaty. Valens arrived and fought them but, being defeated, he fled to Achyron, a village close to[4] Adrianople, and he was burnt to death there. **3** Valens committed many atrocities against the orthodox: people were burnt together with their ships at sea, or drowned, and exposed to many kinds of torture. He plundered the whole Church and, having done against Basil what the Theologian wrote about in the *Epitaphios*, he came to Caesarea.[5] At this time also Galates, the son of Valens, and his wife Domnika were grievously afflicted by illness. **4** And Demosthenes, who was one of Valens' cooks, on talking to Valens criticised Basil and committed a linguistic error at which the teacher said: 'See, we have even seen an illiterate Demosthenes!' **5** Valens had many people killed who were suspected of aspirations to rule because their name began with the letter theta.[6]

1 Basil the Great and Gregory the Theologian, of Nazianzus.

2 Valens reigned as emperor of the East from 28 March 364, at first with Valentinian as colleague in the West. From 17 November 365 to 9 August 378 he reigned (always in the East) with Gratian as his colleague. Cf. for Valens' reign Theophanes (Mango/Scott 1997, pp. 97–101), and the *Chronicon Paschale* (Whitby/Whitby 1989, pp. 46–48).

3 I.e. still the Goths.

4 In fact, Achyron was the villa at which Constantine the Great died.

5 Valens was a champion of Arianism and therefore an enemy of Basil. The 'Theologian' is (cf. above) Gregory of Nazianzus, who wrote a funeral oration on Basil.

6 This superstition was alive in later times and was shared by emperor Maurice (see below, Chapter 107, § 6).

94 Gratian

Gratian, son of Valentinian, reigned for three years alone and for another three years together with Theodosios.[1] For, having brought Theodosios the Great from Spain in order to fight the Scythians who were plundering Thrace, he appointed him emperor in Byzantium. He himself dwelled in Rome. **2** A certain Briton called Maximus was greatly vexed at the fact that Theodosios had been honoured with the imperial title by Gratian, while he himself had not received any sign of honour. He therefore stirred up the inhabitants of Britain to rise against Gratian, and he sends Andragathios against him. Andragathios entered the City in a covered litter after having spread a rumour that it was Gratian's wife who was coming. Overwhelmed by his love for his wife, Gratian went to the litter and uncovered it. There, Gratian sees Andragathios, who immediately had him killed by the soldiers. Gratian was transported to the imperial mausoleum by Theodosios. **3** Gratian was able to shoot so accurately and so far, that some people said that Gratian's arrows had their own mind. **4** During Gratian's reign Meletios, patriarch of Antioch, was in Constantinople and, on finding that Demophilos controlled the churches, he brought Gregory the Theologian from Nazianzus in order to destroy the Arian error.

95 Theodosios the Great

Theodosios the Great reigned for sixteen years.[2] He was Spanish by birth, and he had a wife named Placilla, by whom he had Arkadios and Honorios. When Placilla died, he married Galla, Gratian's sister. **2** And he marched against the Scythians and killed all of them. And he had all the rebels in Rome who had killed Gratian's family executed, as well as Andragathios, who had killed Gratian himself. **3** During Theodosios' reign, the second

1 Gratian reigned (as senior emperor of the West, then of the whole empire) with his brother Valentinian II, 17 November 375–19 January 379, then, together with Valentinian II, as senior emperor of the West (having ceded the East to Theodosios) until 25 August 383. Cf. for Gratian's reign Theophanes (Mango/Scott 1997, pp. 100–101), and the *Chronicon Paschale* (Whitby/Whitby 1989, pp. 48–51).

2 Theodosios reigned 19 January 379–17 January 395. Cf. for his reign Theophanes (Mango/Scott 1997, pp. 101–113), and the *Chronicon Paschale* (Whitby/Whitby 1989, pp. 49–55).

synod in Constantinople took place,[1] at which Gregory the Theologian was expelled from the Church.[2] **4** During Theodosios' reign the head of John the Baptist and the bodily remains of the holy martyrs Terence and Africanus were brought to Constantinople, and they were deposited in the Church of St Euphemia in Petra. The same Theodosios brought the great Arsenios from Rome, having heard about his wisdom and his knowledge of divine matters. And he committed his children, Arkadios and Honorios, into his care to be taught the Holy Scripture by him. He also made Arsenios *basileopator*.[3] When this Arsenios was praying to God one night he heard a voice saying: 'Arsenios, flee humankind and be saved.' **5** This Theodosios razed to the ground those Hellenic temples that Constantine the Great had not destroyed but only ordered to be closed. **6** On his deathbed Theodosios makes Arkadios emperor in Constantinople and of the whole East, and he has Honorios elected emperor of the West to reign together with Placidia. Honorios had his palace in Ravenna, whereas Placidia, the daughter of Gratian, resided in Rome. During their reign Genseric[4] took Rome and made the empresses prisoners. **7** During the time of Theodosios the Great, Gregory the Theologian taught the orthodox in the church which is now dedicated to Anastasia, the martyr; it was only a small chapel at that time. The historian[5] says that the large complex was called Anastasia either because of the resurrection of the true faith, or because of a pregnant woman who fell down there and died, yet was resurrected by the prayer of the orthodox.[6] **8** Theodosios ordered Demophilos either to renounce his Arian error or to leave ecclesiastical office. Thus he left the Church, which the Arians had dominated for forty years. The synod and the emperor put Gregory by force and against his

---

1 This is the Second Ecumenical Council, of 381, also known as First Council of Constantinople.

2 This is not quite correct: he resigned as bishop of Constantinople, but returned to Nazianzus and resumed office as bishop there.

3 *Basileopator* ('father of the emperor') is an interesting title, vaguely suggesting the role of protector of a young emperor. It is used in this text for Arsenios, Stylianos Zaoutzes and Romanos Lekapenos (see Index of terms and concepts). It may be that the title was invented no earlier than the ninth c., and that the present occurrence should be considered an anachronism.

4 This is the Vandal king (Greek Γιζέριχος), who reigned 428–477.

5 This remark possibly hints at an influential chronographer used as a source. Cf. also below, Chapter 107, § 3.

6 The name Anastasia being an adjectival form of the word 'resurrection' (Greek ἀνάστασις).

will on the throne; for he had suffered much, and he had delivered the City from the outrage of the heresies. However, on learning that the Egyptians were envious on his account, the holy Gregory gave a valedictory speech and withdrew from the episcopal see of his own free will, and Nektarios was made patriarch by the emperor in his stead. **9** Theodosios brought the body of Paul the Confessor[1] to the City and laid it to rest in the church called St Paul's, which Makedonios, who was Paul [the Confessor]'s opponent, had built. During Theodosios' reign Heliodoros, who wrote what are known as the *Aithiopika*, was bishop of Trinke.[2] He also writes the *Poem of Gold*, in iambic metre, to the same Theodosios.[3] **10** Because of the murders that had been committed in Thessalonica,[4] Theodosios went to Milan together with a great many people, and with the *hyparchos*[5] and his son. There he is excluded from church for a long time by Ambrose. However, after much prayer and demonstrations of repentance, he was reluctantly received and, having offered the customary gifts, Ambrose ordered him away from the altar area and instructed him in the duties of priests and emperors. When Theodosios came to Constantinople he issued an edict about this; the emperors who preceded him had stood within the sanctuary. In Antioch, the statue of his wife Placilla was torn down in protest against the extreme taxation. The emperor was infuriated on her behalf and, although he threatened the city with complete ruin, he was held back by the law on anger that Ambrose had made him write.[6] **11** It was also at this time that John Chrysostom, a *presbyteros* in Alexandria, wrote the *Andriantes*.[7] **12** When Theodosios dies in Milan, his body is brought to the City by Arkadios and put to rest there.

1 This is the bishop of Constantinople already mentioned above (see Chapter 89, § 3).

2 The Byzantines were convinced that Heliodoros was a Christian and identified him with a bishop of Trikkala in Thessaly (so Socrates, *Church History* V.22), although, according to what is said in the romance itself, its author was from Emesa in Syria.

3 Or: *On the Manufacture of Gold*. This is probably an anachronistic reference to a later author, together with what is a misunderstood reference to Theodosios III (715–717).

4 A massacre perpetrated in 390 by Gothic soldiers at least formally under Theodosios' command.

5 This title (more often than not confused with *eparchos*) can denote the governor of a province. In this case, perhaps the *magister officiorum* (supervisor of imperial administration) Rufinus is intended (so Theophanes, see Mango/Scott 1997, p. 111).

6 I.e. that death sentences should be carried out only after a delay of thirty days: see Codex Theodosianus 9.40.13.

7 These were homilies referring to the tearing-down of statues of the imperial family in Antioch in 387.

96 Arkadios

Arkadios came from Rome and reigned for twenty-two years;[1] he had left Honorios in Rome. He set up his own military unit, which he called the 'Arcadic.'[2] He also raised the pillar at the Xerolophos,[3] placing his own statue on top. He also founded a city in Thrace which he called Arkadioupolis. 2 During his reign, as a result of an intrigue by the *augusta*[4] Eudoxia and the patriarch of Alexandria, Theophilos, John Chrysostom was exiled and sent to Koukousos.[5] Having bid farewell to Olympias, daughter of Seleukos the former *eparchos*, and to other pious[6] ladies, John left the church. And immediately fire burst forth from the sanctuary and burnt everything. In the same year, the Isaurians marched against the empire and pillaged the land as far as Cappadocia. During the time of the same Arkadios the bodily remains of the holy Samuel, the prophet, were also brought to the City, and they were deposited in his church near Hebdomon.[7] 3 Having fallen ill, the same emperor dies. 4 At[8] the death of Nektarios, Arkadios brings John from Antioch and makes him patriarch. John belonged to the nobility and was held in high esteem, as even Libanios attested: for, when his pupils asked him whom he would put at the head of his school in his place, Libanios said: 'John, if he had not been stolen by the Galilaeans.'[9] Between John and Epiphanios of Cyprus there was some bad feeling because of Eudoxia. John told Epiphanios that he would die on a ship. Likewise, Epiphanios predicted John's death in exile. To his friends, who escorted him when he set out, Epiphanios said: 'I make haste, I make haste, leaving to you the palace, the City and the show.' 5 At the death of John, Arsakios is appointed patriarch. 6 Gainas revolted against Arkadios and inflicted much evil upon

---

1 Arkadios reigned as junior emperor (caesar) to his father 383–395 and as senior emperor (*augustus*) of the East until 408. It is difficult to see how twenty-two could be correct here as number of years of his reign. Cf. for Arkadios' reign Theophanes (Mango/Scott 1997, pp. 113–124), and the *Chronicon Paschale* (Whitby/Whitby 1989, pp. 55–61).

2 For this interpretation see Mango/Scott 1997, p. 115 (Mango/Scott: 'the Arcadiaci').

3 An area (hill) of Constantinople.

4 I.e. senior empress.

5 Present-day Göksun, Kahramanmaraş Province, south-central Turkey.

6 σεμνάς.

7 A suburb of Constantinople (seven miles from the Milion in the City centre and therefore called Hebdomon, 'the seventh'); present-day Bakırköy.

8 From this point, the chapter provides additional material, chiefly well-known anecdotes about John Chrysostom.

9 I.e. the Christians. The story is told by Sozomenus, *Church History* VIII.2.

the City.¹ However, when open war broke out on land and sea, he and his followers perished.

97 Theodosios the Younger

Theodosios the Younger, son of Arkadios, reigned for thirty-three years.² On the advice of his own sister Pulcheria, and of Paulinos, who was a friend of his, he married Eudokia from Athens, a most beautiful woman. **2** The emperor went to the Great Church, where a beggar offered him a remarkably large apple. On seeing this, the emperor together with the Senate marvelled, and the emperor gave the beggar one hundred *solidi*³ and sent the apple to the empress. She sent it to Paulinos, the man who had arranged her marriage, who was ill. In his turn, Paulinos sent it innocently to the emperor when he came back to the palace. The emperor recognised the apple and hid it and, entering the palace, he asked the empress about it. She said that she had eaten it. He asked her under oath of his own salvation whether she had sent it to anyone. But she repeated that she had eaten it. Then the apple was brought out, and there was great sorrow, and they were estranged from each other. The emperor also had Paulinos sent for and killed. On hearing this, the empress set out for the Holy Land, because she had been insulted, and she dies there, in Jerusalem. When she was about to die, she swore solemnly that she did not understand the accusation made against her with regard to Paulinos. **3** The emperor Theodosios sent for the bodily remains of John Chrysostom and brought them into the City and had them deposited in the sanctuary of the Church of the Holy Apostles. During his reign, the bodily remains of the saints Stephen and Lawrence were also interred.⁴ **4** The

---

1 Gainas was a Goth who served as *magister militum* in the East Roman/Byzantine army. The revolt took place in 400 and led to the death of a great many Goths.

2 Theodosios II reigned 1 May 408–28 July 450—that is, well over forty-two years. Forty-two is the number of years indicated by Theophanes and the *Chronicon Paschale*, whereas Malalas (see Jeffreys et al. 1986, p. 91) has fifty years, seven months. However, perhaps we should detract the period of rule of his sister Pulcheria (408–416), in which case the computation of thirty-three years is more or less correct. Cf. for Theodosios II's reign Theophanes (Mango/Scott 1997, pp. 124–160), and the *Chronicon Paschale* (Whitby/Whitby 1989, pp. 61–80).

3 Greek νομίσματα, the standard gold coin of ca. 4.5 g.

4 I.e. they were reburied in Constantinople. St Stephen is the Protomartyr, and St Lawrence another early martyr (third c.).

third synod in Ephesus[1] also took place during his reign, when the seven children awoke who had fallen asleep in the time of Decius.[2] **5** The king of the Persians also went out against the Romans. The emperor sent Procopius the *stratelates*[3] against them. The king of the Persians tells Procopius: 'I am willing to conclude a peace treaty for fifty years with the Romans, if a Persian of my choice is defeated in single combat. However, if the man of your choice is defeated in single combat by him, I shall receive fifty *kentenaria*[4] and all the customary gifts.' When this had been agreed upon, the Persian fighter came forward. The *stratelates* chose Areovindos, *komes* of the *foideratoi*.[5] And they went out armed, on horseback, Areovindos holding a javelin.[6] First, the Persian charged at him, but Areovindos escaped by twisting sideways, and he struck the Persian with the javelin and then, throwing him from his horse, killed him. Then the king of the Persians accepted the peace treaty. On returning to the City, Areovindos was received with great honours by the emperor, and he was promoted to *hypatos*.[7] **6** The same emperor razed the land walls of the City to the ground and, adding two other spaces in-between, he built a new wall within sixty days. **7** After some time the emperor went out riding, but his horse fell, and he was hurt and had to return to the City on a stretcher. He then sent for his sister Pulcheria and told her about Marcian, who was to reign after him: 'For this,' he said, 'John the Theologian disclosed to me when I was in Ephesus.' And sending for Marcian he said to him in the presence of Aspar and the Senate: 'It has been revealed to me that you will become emperor after me.'[8] And two days later he died. **8** The[9] empress

1 This was in 431.

2 This is the well-known story of the Seven Sleepers (cf. above, Chapter 77, § 2).

3 *Stratelates* is a title with changing meaning in Byzantine sources. It can be synonymous with *strategos* (military commander), or a Greek equivalent of *magister militum*, or, as may be the case several times in this text, a modest honorary title.

4 I.e. 50×100 Byzantine *litrai* ('pounds of calculation,' cf. below, Chapter 127, § 1) of gold, ca. 1,600 kg, or 360,000 gold *solidi*.

5 A *komes* is a (military) leader, in this case of the allies of the empire (or of a specific military unit from the theme of Anatolikon).

6 σόκιστρον.

7 This (i.e. ὕπατος) is translated as 'consul' above (cf. Index of terms and concepts). Having once denoted the highest office in the Roman empire, this develops into an increasingly insignificant title.

8 This is a short statement: an elaborate speech would have been appropriate.

9 From this point, additional material is given. Although Pulcheria ruled on her own, she is not recognised as a ruler by being given a chapter of her own (cf. the similar case of Irene, mother of Constantine VI, also denied a chapter of her own (see Chapter 124, especially § 21)).

Pulcheria managed the empire in a most excellent way although she was young.[1] She also taught her brother to live chastely, and she dedicated her virginity to God and persuaded her sisters, Arkadia and Marina, to do the same. **9** On the death of Arsakios, St Attikos is appointed patriarch. During Theodosios' reign Aspar and Ardabourios are made *domestikoi*[2] of the East and the West respectively. On the death of Attikos, Sisinios is made patriarch. On his death Nestorios became patriarch. When he had been ousted, Proklos is appointed patriarch instead of him. It was at this time that the body of Chrysostom was translated to the City.[3] **10** During Theodosios' reign, during the service in the Kampos,[4] a child was lifted into the air for several hours. This child also heard a divine voice saying that one should not add the words 'the one crucified for our sake' to the *trishagion*;[5] however, these words are sung to the present day. **11** The emperor Theodosios was extremely easy to influence, and he was prone to listen to suggestions from people close to him. He even signed documents without reading them. Realising this, his sister Pulcheria cunningly smuggled a document into his hands by which his spouse Eudokia was sold as a slave. This document he signed, but he was heavily criticised by Pulcheria. **12** When Proklos died Flavian, a most holy man, was made head of the Church. There[6] were four tribes of Goths: the Goths, the Hypogoths, the Gepids and the Vandals. From these,[7] the Avars began to cross into Roman territory. After the emperor Theodosios' death Pulcheria had Chrysaphios executed; he was a eunuch who had great influence over Theodosios and was also a devoted follower of Nestorios.[8] **13** The *eparchos* of the City Kyros, a most learned and able man, built the City walls[9]

---

1 This is an interesting statement: it is not said that she was competent 'although she was a woman,' but rather 'although she was young.'

2 A *domestikos* is mostly (and also in this case) a high-ranking military officer. See further qualifications of the term in Index of terms and concepts.

3 Cf. above, § 3.

4 The Kampos tou tribounaliou or Field of Mars, a space outside the City used for military rallies.

5 A prayer to the Trinity. See also Chapter 102, § 3, and Mango/Scott 1997, p. 207, n. 6 (with further references in index).

6 'There ... territory': this is quite clearly a marginal note, which has crept into the text at a secondary stage.

7 'From these' (ἐξ ὧν): this is a little odd; perhaps 'From these (regions),' or 'Of these.'

8 The patriarch mentioned above, § 9.

9 Cf. above, § 6, where the same building project is referred to. That the same story is told twice seems indicative of the bad integration of additional material into the text.

and, when the emperor was sitting in the hippodrome, the people[1] shouted: 'Founded by Constantine, restored by Kyros.' Kyros thus becomes an object of envy, and he is falsely accused of being a Hellenizer. He is therefore arrested and tonsured, and he is appointed bishop of Smyrna.[2]

98 Marcian

Marcian reigned for six years and five months.[3] He was crowned by the patriarch Anatolios. The same most divine Marcian married Pulcheria, the sister of the emperor Theodosios. She was fifty-four years of age and still a virgin. 2 During Marcian's reign the fourth synod took place at Chalcedon.[4] 3 The bodily remains of the holy prophet Isaiah were also brought from Paneas and came to the City, and they were deposited in the Church of St Lawrence. In the third year of his reign Pulcheria died. She founds the Churches of the Most Holy Mother of God, in Chalkoprateia[5] and in Blachernai.[6] 4 Having been hurt in his feet Marcian fell ill and died after five months. 5 When[7] on a military expedition, Marcian was taken ill and was left behind in the city of Sydima. When he regained his strength, he made friends with two well-to-do brothers. Going out hunting together with them, at noon he lay down to rest and went to sleep. When the brothers wake up, they see Marcian sleeping in the sun while an eagle hovers over him.[8] They are struck by this, and they say to him when he wakes up: 'If you become emperor, what will you give us?' He did not believe what they told him, but said nevertheless: 'I will consider you as I would my father.' Then they gave him 200 *solidi* and sent him to the City, telling him to remember them. 6 On entering the City, Marcian attached himself to

---

1 'people' (δῆμος): or '(circus) party factions' (in which case, however, a plural form would suit better). Cf. Chapter 108, § 5.

2 This is strange punishment for someone suspected of paganism. However, the passage is a garbled version of its source (see Theophanes in Mango/Scott 1997, pp. 151–152).

3 Marcian reigned 25 August 450–27 January 457. Cf. for his reign Theophanes (Mango/Scott 1997, pp. 160–169), and the *Chronicon Paschale* (Whitby/Whitby 1989, pp. 81–84).

4 This is the Council of Chalcedon (Fourth Ecumenical Council), of 451.

5 At the area of the Copper Market, close to St Sophia.

6 In north-western Constantinople, later important for its palace complex.

7 From here on the chapter contains additional information.

8 Or: 'he is covered by an eagle.' This is one of several episodes where a glorious future is predicted to somebody in a similar way. A closely parallel passage involving an eagle is Chapter 116, § 2.

Aspar and Ardabourios. Then he went to Africa together with Aspar and was captured. When Marcian was sleeping in the courtyard of Genseric, an eagle once again came down and covered him. On seeing this, Genseric first thought of having Marcian killed, since otherwise he would become ruler. However, after considering the matter he came to the conclusion that it is impossible to hinder God's design, and he therefore made a peaceful settlement with him and sent him away. 7 Flavian died during Marcian's reign, and Anatolios is made patriarch.

99 Leo the Great

Leo the Great, the Butcher, reigned for eighteen years.[1] He had been promoted to the throne by Aspar and Ardabourios because of his competence[2] and for being orthodox. For these two wanted to rule the empire, but the Senate would not allow it since they were Arians. Then, when he saw that they were not totally loyal to him but wanted everything to be managed by themselves, the emperor Leo had them killed. Further, Leo wrote a letter to Anthemios, the emperor in Rome, to the effect that 'I have killed Aspar and Ardabourios, lest anyone should oppose my orders.' *Makel* is the Latin word for butcher.[3] 2 During Leo's reign, the robe[4] of the Most Holy Mother of God was brought from Jerusalem. It had been found by a most pious Jewish woman, a virgin, and it was brought together with the bodily remains of St Anastasia, and it was[5] deposited in her sanctuary.[6] During Leo's reign there was also the great fire at the Neorion,[7] which went down all the way to the Church of St Thomas. During his reign, a layer of dust, one span thick, also fell from heaven and was deposited on the roof-tiles. 3 In the days of Leo there was also the holy Daniel, the Stylite,

1 Leo I reigned 7 February 457–18 January 474, i.e. eighteen years with inclusive reckoning (counting a new year from 1 September each year). Cf. for his reign Theophanes (Mango/Scott 1997, pp. 169–187), and the *Chronicon Paschale* (Whitby/Whitby 1989, pp. 84–91).

2 Or: 'virtue' (ἀρετή).

3 Or: 'slayer/murderer.' This sentence may be a gloss.

4 Greek ἐσθής, her robe otherwise being referred to as ὀμοφόριον (see Chapter 131, § 30, and Chapter 136, § 32).

5 Or: 'they were' (if the remains of St Anastasia are included).

6 The robe was deposited in the Church of St Mary (St Soros) at Blachernai. The remains of St Anastasia were deposited in a church built for the occasion.

7 This is a harbour area at the Golden Horn.

in Anaplous. The emperor had great confidence in him. **4** Leo dies from an illness. **5** During Leo's reign Anatolios dies, and Gennadios is chosen as patriarch. **6** Leo made Markianos *oikonomos*.[1] He belonged to the sect of the Katharoi[2] originally, but had come over to the Church. During the fire[3] he mounted the roof-tiles of St Anastasia with the Gospel in his hand and thus protected the building from harm. **7** During Gennadios' patriarchate the hand of the painter who depicted the Saviour as Zeus withered; this man was healed by Gennadios through prayer. It is said that the other way of depicting the Saviour, with short curly hair, is nearer to the truth.[4] **8** During Leo's reign Stoudios founded the Church of St John and placed monks there from the monastery of the Akoimetoi.[5] **9** During Leo's reign the body of the prophet Elisha[6] was translated to Alexandria, into the monastery of Paul the Leper. For he cured a leper, made himself a leper and was put to rest in the monastery of the Leper. **10** During Leo's reign Isokasios, the *quaestor*,[7] was accused of Hellenism and was brought before the *eparchos* of the city with his hands tied to his back. Poseos, the *eparchos*, said to him: 'Look at yourself, Isokasios, to what condition you have been reduced.' Isokasios said: 'I see that, and I am not surprised. I am a human and I have been struck by human misfortunes. May you judge me as you judged together with me.' On hearing this, the emperor felt pity and released him. **11** During Leo's reign, 1,300 years after the reign of that Romulus who founded Rome, Romulus becomes emperor, and so the empire, which started with a Romulus, ended with a Romulus; this was when Odoacer, king of the Goths, seized power.[8]

---

1 Person engaged in the management of an organisation (often a cleric in charge of church or religious institution).

2 This may be a reference to Novatianism or, possibly, an anachronistic reference to the Paulicians.

3 See for the same fire above, § 2.

4 This story is taken from Theophanes. It goes back to Theodorus Lector 107.21–24.

5 This is the famous Stoudios monastery, founded by Flavius Studius in 462. The Akoimetoi ('Monastery of the sleepless ones,' so called because of the monks' constant recitation of the divine liturgy) was an already existing institution in the City.

6 Or: 'Elissaios,' mentioned several times above (see Index of names).

7 A high-ranking jurist.

8 Romulus Augustulus was made emperor 31 October 475, i.e. after the death of Leo I. He was ousted from the throne in 476, this marking the fall of the Western Empire.

100 Leo the Younger

Leo the Younger, his grandson, born from Zeno and Areadne,[1] reigned for ·
one year.[2]

101 Zeno

Zeno reigned for seven years.[3] He was ousted from the throne by Basiliskos.
For, when Zeno was dwelling in Thrace, a coup was staged against him; this
coup was carried out by Verina in cooperation with Basiliskos, her brother,
and Armatos,[4] her nephew. Out of fear of them Zeno left Thrace together
with Ariadne and, bringing a sufficient amount of money with him, he flees
to a stronghold in Isauria. However, some years later Zeno, accompanied
by Ariadne, regained the capital, and he was welcomed back by the Senate,
and he put Basiliskos and Armatios to death. **2** During Zeno's reign there
was a terrible earthquake in Constantinople, and many churches, secular
buildings and porticoes were razed to the ground. The catastrophe also
hit the city[5] of Nicomedia. **3** A certain Marianos predicted to him that 'a
former *selentiarios*[6] is going to take over your throne as well as your wife.'
He therefore had a certain Pelagios, a *patrikios*[7] and former *selentarios*, a
most wise man, held in jail. On Zeno's command this man was killed during
the night by the men set to guard him. **4** A short time after this, Zeno went
down with dysentery and died. Zeno belonged to the Acephalite heresy.[8]

---

1 Or: 'Ariadne,' see below, Chapter 101, § 1.
2 Leo II reigned 18 January–17 November 474. Cf. for his reign Theophanes (Mango/
Scott 1997, pp. 186–187), and the *Chronicon Paschale* (Whitby/Whitby 1989, pp. 91–92).
3 This is not correct: it may be said that Zeno reigned for seventeen years (so some MSS
and also Theophanes and the *Chronicon Paschale*), 9 February 474–9 January 475 and August
476–9 April 491 (if we ignore the period from January 475 until August 476). Cf. for his reign
Theophanes (Mango/Scott 1997, pp. 187–210), and the *Chronicon Paschale* (Whitby/Whitby
1989, pp. 92–98).
4 Or: 'Armatios,' see below.
5 μητρόπολις.
6 Courtier with responsibility for order in the palace.
7 Honorary title well attested since Constantine I.
8 This was a monophysite heresy originating in Alexandria in the late fifth c. Its name
derives from the fact that it was left without its original leader at an early date. That Zeno
died of dysentery was, perhaps, not considered a coincidence: he was a heretic and he
'devoted himself to unnatural pleasures and unrighteous acts' (see § 5).

5 Zeno[1] devoted himself to unnatural pleasures and unrighteous acts. **6** During his reign the bodily remains of the apostle Barnabas were found in Cyprus under a carob-tree. On his breast the corpse had the Gospel of Matthew in Barnabas' own handwriting. With this as a pretext, Cyprus was made a metropolitan see independent of Antioch. Zeno deposited this gospel in the palace, in the Church of St Stephen. **7** During Zeno's reign Perozes the Persian was defeated in battle by the Huns.[2] He took from his right ear the extremely lustrous and excessively great pearl, which he wore, and threw it away, lest anyone should wear it after him. **8** During the earthquake[3] the ball on the statue in the Forum[4] fell down, as well as the statue of Theodosios the Great on the pillar at the Forum Tauri. **9** On the suggestion of Illos, the *magistros*, the same Zeno exiled Verina. Areadne exhorted Urvicius to kill Illos and, when Illos came up to the hippodrome armed with his sword, Urvicius grabbed him and had his right ear cut off.[5] Because of this he[6] tried to organise a rebellion against Zeno.

102 Anastasios Dikoros

Anastasios Dikoros, the former *selentiarios*, also of the Acephalite heresy, reigned for twenty-seven years.[7] **2** During his reign Vitalian from Thrace rebelled. Together with Thracians and Scythians he came pillaging as far as Anaplous. Marinos, the *hyparchos*, fought a sea-battle against him using Median fire and native sulphur (this had been prepared

---

1 From here (or from the previous sentence) additional information about the emperor's reign is given.

2 This is Sasanian king Peroz I, killed by the Hephthalites (or White Huns) at the battle of Herat in 484.

3 Cf. above, § 2.

4 The statue of Constantine the Great, cf. above, Chapter 88, § 7, and below, Chapter 104, § 8.

5 'grabbed ... off': the Greek is ambiguous and could mean that Urvicius had his own right ear cut off. See, however, Theophanes (Mango/Scott 1997, p. 196), from which it is clear how the passage should be understood.

6 Illos.

7 Anastasios reigned 491–518. Cf. for his reign Theophanes (Mango/Scott 1997, pp. 210–249), and the *Chronicon Paschale* (Whitby/Whitby 1989, pp. 98–103).

by Proklos, the philosopher), and he burned the barbarians' ships.[1] But Vitalian managed to escape and saved himself together with some few others. **3** When the emperor, persuaded by Severos the Acephalite, wanted to add to the *trishagion* the words 'holy He who was crucified for our sake, may He have mercy upon us,' and the logothete[2] and the *hyparchos* had mounted the ambo[3] in the Church to announce this, there was a public uprising, and people shouted: 'Another emperor for the City!' Burning many houses, creating much confusion and insulting the emperor, they came to the cistern close to St Mokios, which this very emperor had built. And killing the *hegoumenos* of the monastery of St Philip, a man loved by the emperor, they mounted his head on a spear and shouted: 'This is the friend of the enemy of the Holy Trinity.' They killed a woman, too, who lived in seclusion and whom the emperor trusted, and they dragged the two bodies to the Stoudios monastery and had them burnt there. This frightened the emperor in such a way that he temporarily abandoned the heresy. **4** During Anastasios' reign Moundaros,[4] the leader[5] of the Saracens, was baptised by the orthodox. However, Severos sent two bishops to him wishing to make him part of his own heresy. Realising the absurdity of their dogma Moundaros, feigning seriousness, said to them: 'I have received a letter today that the archangel Michael is dead.' When they said that this is impossible, he said: 'So how, according to you, could God be crucified naked, if Christ did not have two natures—if, as you say, not even an angel can die?' On hearing this, they were much astonished at the natural wit revealed by his suggestion, and they retired in shame. **5** Anastasios, in his dreams, saw a terrible apparition who held a book in his hand with writing[6] and who said to him: 'Behold, because of your lack of faith, I

---

1 For other examples of the use of liquid, or, as it is more often referred to, Greek fire (an incendiary weapon employed in naval battles), see Index of terms and concepts. In the present instance, the invention is credited to Proklos, whereas below, Chapter 113, § 4, it is (taking that the same weapon is meant) credited to Kallinikos.

2 The title refers to different kinds of senior public servants, usually (at least at this time) active at the court and heads of imperial departments. See also Index of terms and concepts.

3 This is an elevated platform, or projection, in front of the iconostasis in a church, from which texts of the liturgy etc. were read out or political manifestations were made (for the latter see, e.g., below, Chapter 133, § 3); i.e. a functional equivalent to the pulpit.

4 Or: 'Alamundaros.'

5 φύλαρχος.

6 κώδικα γεγραμμένον.

wipe out fourteen years of your life.' And[1] while thunder and lightning surrounded the palace, and the emperor was left totally alone and fled from one place to another, the Fury overtook him in the small chamber called the *Oaton*,[2] and there he was found dead shortly afterwards.[3] **6** It is said that he cried out some days after his burial: 'Have mercy upon me and open [the tomb]!' But the guardians of the mausoleum said: 'There is another emperor now'; at which he answered: 'I do not care. Send me to a monastery.' But they left him. It is said that the tomb was opened a short time afterwards and that he was found to have eaten his arms[4] and the boots he was wearing. **7** Since Anastasios was a heretic, Euphemios, the patriarch, supported people who rebelled against him. On learning this, and having overpowered the insurgents, the emperor Anastasios said to the holy Euphemios: 'Your prayers, Great One, have covered your friends with soot.' He then made Makedonios patriarch instead of him; on this patriarch he inflicted much harm, since he did not yield to the emperor's heresy. For it is said that something terrible happened upon Makedonios' death in exile: he is supposed to have made the sign of the cross although he was dead. **8** Shortly before an earthquake in Neocaesarea[5] a soldier, who was travelling on the road, saw two persons walking towards the city and behind them another one who cried: 'Take care of the house where Gregory's tomb is.'[6] When the earthquake came, the greatest part of the city was razed to the ground except for the part where St Gregory was. **9** Anastasios melted down many bronze statues[7] and made a statue of himself that he put on the pillar in the Forum Tauri. For the earlier statue, representing Theodosios the Great, had fallen down and been

---

1 More consistent versions of this story are found in Theophanes (Mango/Scott 1997, pp. 248–249), Malalas (Jeffreys et al. 1986, p. 229), and the *Chronicon Paschale* (Whitby/Whitby 1989, pp. 102–103). This text has the interesting addition (as far as I know, unique) about the emperor's flight through the palace. However, there is a logical lacuna at the point indicated here and, in contrast to the chronicles mentioned above, we are not told how anyone could know about his dream.

2 The 'Egg-chamber.' This is somewhat problematic: it could be an (anachronistic) reference to the domed hall, probably built by Justinian II, in which the Council in Trullo was held (in 692). However, why this hall should be referred to as a 'small chamber' (κοιτωνίσκος) remains unclear.

3 αἰφνίδιον.

4 Or, perhaps, 'the sleeves of his tunic.'

5 Present-day Niksar in Northern Anatolia.

6 I.e. Gregory the Theologian, of Nazianzus. On the house cf., perhaps, Chapter 95, § 7.

7 'statues (of living creatures)' (ζῷδα).

shattered by the earthquake. **10** During Anastasios' reign a certain man from the guild of goldsmiths, a clever man, indicated to money-dealers and others hands and feet of statues and other items which were of pure gold, and he told them that he had discovered a treasure. By this he fooled many and reduced them to poverty. When his fame spread, he was arrested and brought to Anastasios. He brought as a gift to the emperor a horse's bridle made of gold and covered with pearls. The emperor accepted this, but said: 'Truth is, you do not fool me.' And he exiled the man to a certain fortress where he also died. **11** During his reign Deuterios, the bishop of Byzantium, who was an Arian, dared to say while he was baptising a barbarian: 'So-and-so is baptised in the name of the Father, through the Son, and in the Holy Ghost.' Upon which the baptismal font dried up, and the barbarian, terrified, fled naked from the place—which made the miracle known to everyone. **12** During the reign of Anastasios two bishops, one orthodox and one Arian (the Arian was a dialectic philosopher, whereas the orthodox was pious and a faithful Christian), were holding a discussion. The orthodox one suggested that they should abandon the discussion and step into a fire, and thus it would be shown who was the truest Christian. When the Arian refused to do so, the orthodox one entered the fire alone and continued the discussion from there without being hurt.[1]

103 Justin the Thracian

Justin the Thracian, the Great, reigned for nine years.[2] He was a superb military man and a warm supporter of the orthodox faith. **2** He also made the afore-mentioned Vitalian his friend and honoured him with the title of *stratelates* and allowed him the right to speak his mind in front of the emperor. However, Vitalian was killed by the inhabitants of Byzantium; they were enraged with him because of the rebellion mentioned earlier.[3] **3** Amantios the *praipositos*,[4] who built and had decorated the Church of

---

1 Cf. to this (the Book of) Daniel, Chapter 3, where Shadrach, Meshach and Abednego are sent into the fiery furnace but remain unscathed.

2 Justin I reigned 518–527. Cf. for his reign Theophanes (Mango/Scott 1997, pp. 249–265), and the *Chronicon Paschale* (Whitby/Whitby 1989, pp. 103–108).

3 See above, Chapter 102, § 2.

4 Here perhaps the head chamberlain (the functions of which were later fulfilled by the *parakoimomenos*).

St Thomas the apostle, is said to have given money to the same Justin who was a *komes* of the *exkoubitoi*[1] under Anastasios, in order to have Justin proclaim his cousin Theokritos emperor. Justin had Amantios killed together with those who had planned the rebellion with him, and he seized the throne himself. **4** To Justin's reign belong the occurrences concerning St Arethas and the people in the city of Negra, as well as the actions undertaken by Elesbaas, king of the Ethiopians, against the Himyarites.[2] **5** During Justin's reign an edict was issued that we should also celebrate the feast of the *Hypapante*.[3] **6** During his reign a star appeared in heaven, above the Chalke Gate of the palace,[4] shining for twenty-six days and nights. And there was a terrible earthquake, and Constantinople suffered damage at various places. But the great city of Antioch suffered indescribable damage, and almost all of the city collapsed and became the grave of its inhabitants. For such was the wrath of God upon them, that fire even came out of the earth and painfully consumed the survivors. The earth also opened in the middle of Pompeiopolis in Moesia, and the city, together with its inhabitants, was swallowed up, and the people who were under the earth cried from below: 'Have mercy upon us!' **7** During Justin's reign, a gigantic woman from Cilicia also appeared. She was taller by one cubit than any tall person and very broad—so much so that people paid her an obol[5] per person to watch her in workshops and public buildings. **8** The same emperor showed great concern for the city of Antioch, helping with its reconstruction and supporting its survivors. So grieved was the emperor for the city that he even set aside his diadem and the *porphyra*,[6] and dressed in sackcloth and ashes and mourned for several days. **9** Justin died and left his nephew Justinian as emperor. **10** Justin recalled all priests and pious orthodox men who had been unjustly exiled by Anastasios. **11** During his reign the city of Edessa was flooded by the river Skirtos which flows through the middle of the city and provides riches and enjoyment to it. The flood drowned the city and its houses. When the flood receded, a stone slab was found on the river bank. It was inscribed with

---

1 Leader of an imperial elite guard unit.
2 Ella Atsheba, or Kaleb of Axum, was an Ethiopian king (reigned ca. 520–540) who invaded the Himyarite kingdom of Jemen in defence of the Christians living there. Arethas was the leader of the Himyarites, and Negra a city.
3 Celebrating Jesus' presentation at the Temple and Mary's purification.
4 Copper Gate: the main entrance of the Great Palace.
5 Generically for a small coin: the ancient *obolos* was not in use at this time.
6 An imperial dress.

hieroglyphics, reading as follows: 'The Skirtos river will leap with evil leapings for the citizens.'[1] **12** A certain Eulalios had been a rich man but had died poor. He had made Justin his heir in his will and had entreated him to take care of the upbringing of his three young daughters who had been left behind, and give them a dowry. Eulalios had also begged the emperor to pay all his debts to his benefactors and to save his personal papers. Justin fulfilled all this in a way befitting an emperor and, in doing so, amazed everyone who heard about the matter.

104 Justinian

Justinian reigned for thirty-nine years.[2] He made a procession in the middle of the City[3] and distributed a great amount of largesse. **2** He made the *Novels*, and he also published an edict about bishops, managers of hospices, *oikonomoi* and managers of orphanages, namely that they should not be able to bequeath anything other than what they had before they started in their profession.[4] **3** He also completed the public bath at Diegesteus,[5] begun by the emperor Anastasios. **4** Antioch did not stop shaking until it was revealed to a pious man that one should write on the lintels: 'Christ [is][6] with us, stop!' This done, God's wrath stopped, and from then the city was called God's city.[7] **5** During Justinian's reign there was a public uprising, and the people burnt down St Sophia and the colonnades leading to the Forum.[8] They insulted the emperor Justinian and hailed Hypatios and crowned him at the *kathisma*[9] in the hippodrome. This uprising was checked by Belisarios, Moundos and Narses, who killed 35,000 people as well as Hypatios himself in the hippodrome. **6** Justinian rebuilt the Great

---

1 This is a kind of wordplay in Greek. Skirtos means the 'leaping/jumping (river).'

2 Justinian I reigned 527–565. Cf. for Justinian I's reign Theophanes (Mango/Scott 1997, pp. 265–354), and the *Chronicon Paschale* (Whitby/Whitby 1989, pp. 108–137).

3 I.e. on becoming emperor.

4 Similarly Malalas (Jeffreys et al. 1986, p. 249) and Theophanes (Mango/Scott 1997, p. 267 and p. 269, n. 22).

5 Or: 'Dagistheus,' an area of Constantinople named after a certain Dagistheus, probably an Ostrogothic hostage of the late fifth c.

6 'is': or, possibly, 'be.'

7 Θεούπολις.

8 These were the so-called Nika riots in 532, which almost cost Justinian his throne and neck.

9 The imperial box.

Church of God[1] so as to be more beautiful and bigger than before, and he provided a *troparion*[2] to be sung in it: 'The only begotten Son and Word of God.' The feast of the *Hypapante*[3] also started to be celebrated, which had not before been counted as one of the dominical feasts.[4] **7** During his reign there was also the fifth synod, the one against Severos.[5] In his tenth year the first inauguration of the Great Church took place and, after the death of Theodora, his wife, there was the inauguration of the Church of the Holy Apostles.[6] **8** During his reign there was also a plague in Constantinople, so that people who died remained unburied, for there were not enough stretchers in the churches and the houses[7] to carry them away. The emperor had a thousand stretchers made. When these proved insufficient, he ordered that as many waggons as possible should be prepared together with horses, in order to carry away the dead on these.[8] This deadly disease continued for two months, July and August.[9] There were also much loud and terrifying thunder and lightning, and many people were burnt to death, and there was a great earthquake, too, which affected the whole world. And in Constantinople many houses and churches collapsed, and many people were killed. The walls at the Golden Gate[10] also fell down, as well as the lance carried by the statue in the Forum.[11] And the earth continued to shake for a long time. Because of his grief, the emperor walked uncrowned in the processions of the birthday of Christ and of Holy Epiphany,[12] and he did not give the customary banquets during the twelve-day period in between, but distributed everything to the poor. It is said that the sea receded two miles because of the earthquake and that many ships were destroyed by the back-flow of the water. Also, the dome of the Great Church collapsed.

---

1 I.e. St Sophia; on the first church at the same site and with the same name, see above, Chapter 89, § 7.

2 An early form of Byzantine hymn.

3 Cf. above, Chapter 103, § 5.

4 I.e. a feast in honour of Christ.

5 This looks like a conflation of two events: the 536 condemnation of Severos (cf. Mango/Scott 1997, p. 315) and the fifth synod, taking place in 553 (cf. Mango/Scott 1997, p. 334).

6 The original Church of the Holy Apostles was erected by Constantine I and inaugurated around 330.

7 Or: 'institutions' (οἶκοι).

8 'carry ... these': i.e. to the cemeteries outside the City walls.

9 The plague is generally dated to 541–542.

10 A gate towards the southern end of the City land walls.

11 The statue of Constantine the Great, cf. above, Chapter 88, § 7, and Chapter 101, § 8.

12 Or: 'Theophany' (ἅγια Θεοφάνια).

The emperor had this rebuilt higher and stronger, and he held a second, more splendid and brilliant, inauguration ceremony of the same church.[1] 9 When Justinian heard about men engaged in homosexual practices, he investigated the matter and, having found the people, in some cases he had their genital organs cut off, in some cases he ordered that sharp reeds should be introduced into the openings of their genitalia and that they should be paraded naked in the Forum. Among these, there was a great number of public figures, senators and not a few members of the higher clergy. Having had their property confiscated and been led naked round the Forum in this way, these people died a pitiable death. This caused great fear, and the rest was chastened. For, as they say, 'may the pine-tree cry when the cedar falls.'[2] 10 Justinian also set up the column called Augusteus;[3] on top, he put an equestrian statue of himself. In its left hand the statue was holding a spherical apple, as if he had conquered the whole world. Its right hand the statue held upright as if pointing at the Persians and calling: 'Stand still and do not tread on Roman soil.' 11 Justinian also sent Belisarios, the *strategos*, with an immeasurable number of men and with ships and much gold to wage war on the Vandals and to lay Africa waste. When Belisarios, through shrewdness and sense, had ravaged everything, he laid hands on Gelimer and brought him back to the City together with great wealth, and he held a triumph in the hippodrome, and he distributed largesse in the City. On this occasion, Justinian had *solidi* struck with his own picture on the one side and that of Belisarios, armed, on the other, and with the legend: 'Belisarios, the Glory of the Romans.' However, what envy has been wont to engender in cases of great luck, it brought forth against Belisarios, too. For he was slandered, and he was removed from the power and the glory, and Solomon was sent out as *strategos* instead of him. However, when Solomon was unable to hold on to what Belisarios had acquired, he ceded everything to the Vandals. 12 There was a certain coppersmith called Andreas who had a tawny, blind dog that performed tricks. Without showing this to the dog, Andreas took rings (these were made of gold and silver and iron) from people in the crowd standing around him, and he put the rings on the ground and covered them with earth. And he gave a command to the dog, and the dog

---

1 This refers to St Sophia. Several earthquakes in the 550s damaged the structure, especially the dome. The rededication of the church took place 23 December 562.
2 Zechariah 11.2.
3 This was between the Great Palace and St Sophia.

dug out the rings and gave each back to its owner. Likewise, the dog was able to sort different emperors' *solidi* by name when they had been mixed up. But he was also able to indicate, from the men and women standing there, who were pregnant or prostitutes or adulterers, and who were pitiful people and who were miserly. All this he did correctly and, therefore, it was said that he had a spirit of divination.[1] **13** The same emperor had very many remarkable building projects carried out, of churches as well as cities; he also had the five-span bridge over the Sagaros river[2] built. Prokopios, the historian, wrote about these building projects in eight books.[3] **14** Towards the end of his life, Justinian inspired the dogma about the corruptible and the incorruptible, a dogma alien to the true belief in God.[4] Justinian died having made his nephew Justin, who was then *kouropalates*,[5] emperor. **15** Gelimer escaped from Belisarios and fled to a mountain stronghold of the people of the Marousioi. Among these, neither bread nor wine nor olives are produced, but, like unreasoning animals, they eat barleycorns and rice-wheat boiled. Therefore, Gelimer writes to Faras, whom Belisarios had left as his guard, and asks him to send him bread, a sponge, and a cithara. Faras was at a loss about this, until the man who carried the letter told him, that 'he asks for bread because he wants to taste it and see it again, a sponge because of his tears and because he is unwashed, so as to soothe his eyes, and a cithara to sing about his misfortune.' On hearing this, Faras was deeply upset, and he bewailed human fate, and sent Gelimer everything he was asking for. **16** When Chosroes the Persian was ravaging the whole of the East, Justinian brought Belisarios from the West and made him *strategos* of the East and sent him against the Persians. When he had taken up arms and marched against the Persians, Belisarios impressed the ambassadors of Darius[6] so much by the weaponry employed and by his army (he showed himself to them when he had gone on what was allegedly a hunting expedition), that they went to

---

1 'spirit of divination': πνεῦμα Πύθωνος (cf. Acts 16.6).

2 The Sangarius river (present-day Sakarya) in north-western Anatolia.

3 These are the *Peri ktismaton*, or *Buildings of Justinian*.

4 This is the so-called aphtartodocetist heresy, a kind of monophysitism maintaining the incorruptibility of Christ's body. For further reference see Mango/Scott 1997, p. 321 with n.

5 Originally designating an official responsible for the construction and maintaining of palaces, it may have been a purely honorary title at this time.

6 At this time Chosroes I ruled (see above). Perhaps the name of Darius is here used generically for 'the Great King.' Cf. Chapter 86, § 2, where it may be that the name of Shapur is used in a similar way, i.e. generically for a (Sasanian) ruler.

Chosroes and made him accept a truce with the Romans. So much did the Persians as well as the Romans admire Belisarios, and he reached a fame that could only be matched by what he achieved when he brought Gelimer as a prisoner and Vittiges, the two kings, to Byzantium.[1] After this, he was accused of plotting against Justinian, the emperor, and he dies from grief and has all his property confiscated.

105 Justin

Justin reigned for thirteen years.[2] He was generous and fond of building. He had a wife named Sophia. Being pious and orthodox he embellished the churches built by Justinian, that is, the Great Church and that of the Holy Apostles, with treasures and vestments, and he gave them all kinds of income. **2** When the factions were rioting, the same Justin went up to the hippodrome, and he told the blue party, 'for you, emperor Justinian is dead,' and the green party, that 'for you, emperor Justinian lives on.' On hearing this the factions became quiet. **3** The same Justin also builds the palace of Sophianai, an extraordinary and glorious and most admirable building, and he named it after his wife.[3] He also had works carried out on the island of Prinkipos, which was his suburban property, and had a palace built there too. The same Justin also built the Church of the Holy Apostles Peter and Paul in the Orphanage.[4] It was also he who added the two apses to the Church of the Blachernai, so as to make it cruciform. **4** Narses, the *koubikoularios*,[5] was loved by the emperor, and for this reason he was slandered in front of the emperor by those accustomed to see something suspicious in everything.[6] The emperor sent Narses to Alexandria against

1 The text is corrupt here, and the translation uncertain. Cf. Theophanes: 'The Romans praised Belisarius for having gained greater glory from this achievement than when he had brought the two emperors Gelimer and Vittigis as prisoners of war to Byzantium' (Mango/Scott 1997, pp. 320–321).

2 Justin II reigned 565–578. Cf. for his reign Theophanes (Mango/Scott 1997, pp. 354–369), and the *Chronicon Paschale* (Whitby/Whitby 1989, pp. 137–138).

3 This was on the Asiatic side of the Bosphorus (probably present-day Çengelköy) and not the same palace as that mentioned below, § 6.

4 Close to the Acropolis point in Constantinople (see Mango/Scott 1997, p. 362, n. 1).

5 A eunuch appointed to the emperor's bedchamber (or a lady appointed to an empress's bedchamber, see Chapter 124, § 18 (*koubikoularia*)). It may be that there is no distinction from *koitonites* (see Chapter 131, § 7).

6 'by … everything' (Greek ὑπὸ τῶν εἰωθότων ἴσως πάντα ὑπονοεῖν): this is vague.

enemy forces, and he acquitted himself in a most excellent way. This Narses had the Church of the Most Holy Mother of God built, in which the bodily remains of the holy martyrs Probos, Tarachos and Andronikos were also deposited. **5** The emperor sent Tiberios, the *komes* of the *exkoubitoi*, against the Huns, who were on the move and were pillaging the Thracian part of the empire. After this, Justin was taken ill and, having adopted Tiberios as his son, he proclaimed him caesar. **6** He also builds the palace in the Harbour of Julian and names it after his wife, Sophia.[1] He cleaned the harbour and erected two statues of himself and his wife in the middle of it, and he renamed the harbour after Sophia [as well]. **7** Being weighed down by illness the emperor summoned the patriarch[2] and the whole of the Senate, and brought Tiberios forward and declared him emperor in the presence of everybody. And he said as follows: 'It is God Himself, not I, Who made you a good man and Who gives you the position of emperor. Honour Him, so that you may be honoured by Him. Do not delight in bloodshed. Take no part in murder. Do not requite evil with evil. Do not lose your temper with anyone, like I have done. I did this, and I suffered defeat and was then repaid according to my crimes. I beg you to judge me in God together with those who suggested these crimes to me.[3] Do not be elated by the honour of your imperial title. Treat everyone as yourself. Realise who you were and who you are now. Do not be arrogant against your kin; thus you will avoid sinning. You know who I was. And what am I now, being face to face with death? All these people around us are your slaves and your children. Pay attention to the army. Do not appoint anyone who is cowardly and without good sense. Do not let them persuade you, that "your predecessors did it this way." I recommend this to you and I exhort you out of my own experience. Those who have riches should be allowed to enjoy them and profit by them. To those who do not have you should, if they are good people, be generous. You know that I preferred you to my own kin. Honour and respect your mother, who was once your empress. For earlier you were her slave, now you should be like a son to her.' When the emperor had said this, and the caesar had fallen to his feet, the emperor added: 'If you wish, I am; if you do not wish, I do not live. God,

1 This is close to the area of the Great Palace of Constantinople, on the Marmara Sea.
2 Eutychios.
3 'I beg … to me': this is hardly correct. Better (but less lenient towards other parties) is Theophanes: 'But I shall bring to justice before Christ's tribunal those who have done that to me' (Mango/Scott 1997, p. 368).

Who made heaven and earth, has put other things into your heart which I have forgotten to tell you.' So Justin died, and Tiberios succeeded to the throne. **8** During Justin's reign Narses founds the so-called Monastery of the Katharoi, and he builds a most beautiful church. Justin also renovates Valens' great aqueduct. He also builds another aqueduct, the so-called Adranes, and he furnishes the City with an abundance of water. **9** During Justin's reign John Nesteutes is appointed patriarch.[1]

106 Tiberios

Tiberios reigned for four years.[2] **2** When he went up to the hippodrome, the factions[3] cried: 'Let us see, let us see the *augusta* of the Romans.' And he declared: 'The church opposite to the communal bath of Diegesteus bears the same name as the *augusta*.' Then the factions chanted: 'Long live the *augusta* Anastasia!' But Sophia, Justin's wife, was hurt in her feelings. For she did not know that he already had a wife, and she had made friends with Tiberios under Justin, and persuaded Justin to make him emperor because she wanted to marry him and remain *augusta*. However, Tiberios had Sophia removed to the palace in Julian's harbour, and he ordered that *koubikoularioi* and others should wait upon her and keep her under surveillance. But he honoured her like a mother and ensured her every comfort. **3** Tiberios also built the public bath in the Blachernai, and he renovated many churches and hospices. **4** Tiberios sent Maurice and Narses against the Persians. Maurice returned after a major victory, and the emperor received him with great honours and made him his son-in-law. He married his other daughter to Germanos, and he made Maurice as well as Germanos caesars. **5** Having eaten early sycamore-figs, remarkable to look at but poisonous,[4] Tiberios, when on the point of death, had Maurice proclaimed emperor.

1 This is not correct: John IV was appointed in 582, long after Justin's death.

2 After having been appointed caesar 7 December 574, Tiberios became *augustus* 26 September 578, and died 14 August 582. Cf. for Tiberios' reign Theophanes (Mango/Scott 1997, pp. 369–374), and the *Chronicon Paschale* (Whitby/Whitby 1989, pp. 138–139).

3 μέρη.

4 Or: 'poisoned' (πεφαρμαγμένα).

107 Maurice

Maurice reigned for twenty years.[1] He had a brother-in-law called Philippikos who founded a monastery in Chrysopolis in his own name. He had been appointed *stratelates* by Maurice and, together with the armed forces, he marched against the Persians and, with Herakleios, the *strategos*, he performed many brave acts against them. **2** Maurice builds in the Karianos district,[2] and he erects the portico in it, and he has his achievements depicted there. He also issued an edict for the performance of the liturgy[3] to the Most Holy Mother of God in Blachernai and for the procession, and he had the public bath in Blachernai completed. He is also the founder of the Church of the Forty Holy Martyrs close to the Staurion.[4] **3** During Maurice's reign the Chagan, the leader of the Avars, broke the peace treaty and marched into Thrace and destroyed many Roman military units. The emperor went out against him and when he came to Daonion,[5] in that same night a woman was giving birth there, and she uttered piteous cries. The emperor sent someone forth to find out what had happened, and he saw a child born without eyes and eyelids, who had neither hands nor arms, and who had a fishtail growing from the hip-joint. In the outskirts of Byzantium too, one child was born with four feet, and another with two heads. People who write history[6] say that it signifies no good for the cities in which such children are born. On the same day the emperor's horse collapsed and died. **4** The emperor considered these incidents as forebodings and he returned to the City sending Priskos, his own son-in-law, against the Scythians[7] with the whole army. These forces defeated the Scythians but then turned against the emperor. Maurice, the emperor, became angry with them and, since war was imminent between

1 Maurice reigned 582–602. Cf. for his reign Theophanes (Mango/Scott 1997, pp. 374–418), and the *Chronicon Paschale* (Whitby/Whitby 1989, pp. 139–143). An outstanding source for Maurice's reign is Theophylact Simocatta (Whitby/Whitby 1986).

2 Ta Karianou: this was in the region of Blachernai, and there was also a palace there.

3 Or, perhaps, 'litany' (Greek λιτήν).

4 As stated in the text, this Staurion is situated close to the church of the Forty Holy Martyrs. It may be one of two locations in the City with this name, and it may be a courtyard off the Mese, deriving its name from the column of Phokas (so A. Berger, *Untersuchungen zu den Patria Konstantinupoleos*, Bonn: Habelt Verlag, 1988, pp. 316–317).

5 Close to Heraclea in Thrace.

6 'People who write history' (οἱ δὲ τὰς ἱστορίας γράφοντες): obviously a category that does not include the author of this text. Cf. above, Chapter 95, § 7.

7 In this case, the Avars.

the Romans and the barbarians, the emperor suggested to the *strategos* to whom the army had been entrusted that he should betray the soldiers to the enemy because of the insurrection they had contemplated against him. This indeed happened. A large number of men were captured, and the Scythians brought them to be ransomed by the Romans. But the emperor told the Chagan to release them without ransom paid. The Chagan declared on his part: 'I give everyone back to you if I get one *solidus* for each.' When the emperor did not accept this, the barbarian demanded a half *solidus* for each. When the emperor did not accept even this, the barbarian was infuriated and had 12,000 men executed in the Kampos tou tribounaliou. 5 For this reason, and from this moment on, everyone began to hate Maurice. But he repented and, considering the judgement that is to come, he preferred to suffer the consequences of his sin in this world and not in front of the dread tribunal.[1] And he sent supplicatory letters together with great gifts to the patriarchal thrones, to hermitages and monasteries that they should pray for him that he should suffer punishment in this world. 6 He had also committed a sin earlier against his brother-in-law Philippikos because of the letter phi. For it was said that such a person[2] would succeed Maurice as emperor. However, Philippikos had sworn solemnly to Maurice that he was not guilty of what was implied by the suspicion. 7 While Maurice was praying to God to be freed from his sin, he saw the following in a dream, namely that a great crowd was standing in front of the icon of Christ at the Chalke Gate of the palace and that a voice came from the icon, saying: 'Bring Maurice unto me.' And they brought him there and placed him there, and the divine voice says: 'Maurice, where do you want me to give you what you deserve, here or in the time to come?' Trembling, Maurice answered: 'Kind Lord, here and not there.' And at once, the voice ordered that he and his wife and children and all his relatives should be turned over to Phokas, the *stratelates*. 8 Waking up, Maurice sent his *parakoimomenos*[3] at once to bring Philippikos to him. On seeing the *parakoimomenos* coming at such an hour, Philippikos despaired of his life and asked for Holy Communion.

---

1 The way in which, in the following, the story of Maurice's sins and fall is told seems rather convoluted, and it may be that the text mirrors several sources that have not been worked into a consistent whole.

2 I.e. a person whose name began with the letter phi. Cf. to this superstition above, Chapter 93, § 5.

3 The highest-ranking official guarding the emperor's bedchamber, usually a eunuch (an exception to this rule is Basil I). It has been suggested that the mention of a *parakoimomenos* for Maurice may be an anachronism (cf. Theophanes 285.7 (= Mango/Scott 1997, p. 410)).

He then went to the emperor, leaving his wife wailing in sackcloth and ashes. Coming to the emperor, Philippikos fell at his feet. The emperor asked the *parakoimomenos* to leave, and he himself fell at Philippikos' feet, saying: 'Forgive me, brother, for I have sinned gravely against you. For I suspected that you were plotting against my life. But now I have realised that you are innocent. Hence, I beg you to tell me if you know of a *stratelates* called Phokas in the *tagmata*.'[1] Philippikos said: 'I know of one, who some time ago was sent away from the army and who spoke against you.' And the emperor said: 'What is he like?' And Philippikos said: 'Cowardly and insolent.' And the emperor said: 'If he is cowardly, he can be a murderer too.' And so the emperor told Philippikos about his dream. And Philippikos said: 'See, My Lord, how God is not stopped by a letter if He wants to give the throne to someone!' **9** Then the *magistrianos*,[2] who had been sent away, arrived, and he carried an answer from the holy men: 'God saves your soul, and He accepts your repentance, but you will leave this earthly life in great pain and anguish.' On hearing this, Maurice thanked God from the bottom of his heart. **10** Sophia, the wife of Justin, and Constantina, the wife of Maurice, had a crown[3] made for the emperor, extraordinary and very valuable. Having seen this and admired it, Maurice took it to the church on the day of Holy Easter and offered it to God.[4] **11** When autumn came, the emperor wrote to Peter, the *strategos*, and ordered him to winter in Sclavonia.[5] But the people opposed this and, as a consequence, the leading officers gather the crowds at one place and promote Phokas, the *stratelates*, to emperor. When Peter and the other leading officers came to the City and told the emperor this, Maurice, who was aware of the people's hatred against him, stripped himself of his imperial robes (this was in the middle of the night) and embarked on a *dromon*[6] together with his wife and children, and tried to evade the insurrection of the people. However,

---

1 The *tagmata* were, at least later (eighth or early ninth c.), elite guards stationed around Constantinople. It could be that the term is used here anachronistically or in a less technical sense.

2 Member of the staff of the *magister officiorum*, often used for carrying messages (see Mango/Scott 1997, p. 363, n. 7, and p. 415, n. 23).

3 στέμμα.

4 I.e. it was deposited in St Sophia (cf. Theophanes (Mango/Scott 1997, p. 406f.). It is related that emperor Leo IV took the crown and decided to wear it, with disastrous results (see Chapter 123, § 9).

5 This is probably in Macedonia/Greece (cf. Mango/Scott 1997, p. 669, n. 2).

6 A fast warship ('runner').

although he with difficulty reached St Autonomos,[1] he was not able, as had been intended, to take refuge in a fortress. For suddenly he is attacked by violent fits of arthritis that immobilise him. **12** Phokas was greeted by the people and entered the City and the palace. He sent his son Theodosios to Chosroes, the king of the Persians, to remind the king of the services he had rendered him, and that Chosroes had control over the Persian kingdom thanks to him.[2] Chosroes gathered the Persian forces and marched against the Romans under Phokas, and he destroyed many Roman cities and villages.

108 Phokas the Usurper

Phokas the Usurper reigned for eight years.[3] He crowned Leonto, his wife, *augusta*. **2** When Phokas went to the chariot races and there was some dispute as to the seating of different groups, the factions cried: 'Maurice is not dead! He lives! Ask him!' Then the accursed man moves towards murdering Maurice. And Maurice was brought in chains to the harbour of Eutropios.[4] As a preliminary punishment the bloodthirsty man orders that Maurice's five sons should be slaughtered in full view of their father. Maurice bore this misfortune with equanimity and kept repeating: 'Thou art righteous, O Lord, and righteous is Thy judgement.' And when the family's nurse stole away one of the five children and put her own in its place to be killed, Maurice protested and called for his own child to be fetched and killed. Then Maurice himself was executed, and the wretched Phokas ordered that their heads should be set up in the Kampos tou tribounaliou. And the inhabitants of the City went out and looked at them, until they started to smell; then Phokas allowed them to be handed over to Maurice's friends. **3** Shortly after, Maurice's wife and her three daughters were falsely accused of plotting against Phokas, so he had them executed at the mole of the Eutropios harbour. Indeed, the lawless man had everyone related to Maurice executed. **4** Following this, Philippikos was tonsured and took up service in Chrysopolis and lived there quietly until he died.

---

1 Close to Nicomedia.

2 This is a little unclear, or downright confused: Theodosios was the son of Maurice, and the acting subject should be Maurice (who had helped Chosroes).

3 Phokas reigned 602–610. Cf. for his reign Theophanes (Mango/Scott 1997, pp. 418–427), and the *Chronicon Paschale* (Whitby/Whitby 1989, pp. 143–152).

4 At Chalcedon.

And from that time a constant sequence of all kinds of disasters befell the state. Chosroes the Persian broke the peace; and the Avars pillaged Thrace and destroyed both the Roman army camps there; and a most severe winter came which made the sea freeze and the fish die. **5** Phokas put on chariot races, but in the evening he had drunk a lot of wine and was slow to appear, and the people[1] cried: 'Wake up, Phokas! Once again you have drunk from the cup; once again you have lost your mind.' At this he went mad, and he had many people maimed and many people's heads cut off. But the mob set fire to the *praitorion*,[2] and all the prisoners there got out and escaped. **6** The same Phokas builds an *armamenton*[3] close to the Magnaura palace,[4] and he placed there a column he had built with his statue on top. **7** His son-in-law Krispos, the *patrikios*, who could not bear any longer to see the unrighteous murders and the horrible acts committed under Phokas, wrote to Herakleios, who was *strategos* of Africa[5] and who had a fleet at his disposal, to move against the usurper Phokas.[6] This Herakleios equipped many ships and an army, and he arrived from Africa at Constantinople. He also brought with him the Acheiropoietos icon of Our Lord and God.[7] And when fighting broke out in Sophia's harbour between [the forces of] Phokas and Herakleios, the accursed man was defeated and fled to the palace. **8** A certain Photinos, whose wife had been seduced by Phokas, entered the palace together with soldiers. He ejected Phokas dishonourably from the throne, and he stripped the wretched man of the imperial dress and dressed him in a black tunic and put a collar around his neck[8] and brought him in disgrace to Herakleios who, on seeing Phokas, said: 'This, you wretched man, is how you ruled the state.' Phokas said, despairingly:

---

1 'people': or '(circus) party factions' (Greek δῆμος). Cf. Chapter 97, § 13.

2 The city *eparchos*' residence that also contained a prison.

3 This was probably an arsenal for the building of ships for the imperial navy. Cf., however, Chapter 122, § 14, in which case the term denotes a stable.

4 The Magnaura (or Manaura), i.e. 'Magna Aula,' was (perhaps) originally the Senate House. It was a large building close to the Chalke Gate and St Sophia, and it was used for receptions and ceremonies. Later, it also came to accommodate a school (see Chapter 130, § 35).

5 This is Herakleios the Elder, exarch of Carthage, who then sent his son, also named Herakleios, with a fleet to Constantinople.

6 From here and until Chapter 122, § 15, the *Short History* of the patriarch Nikephoros constitutes a parallel text of some importance (cf. Introduction).

7 I.e. an icon not made by human hand. Later on, the same icon is taken out by Herakleios (see Chapter 109, § 6).

8 As one did with prisoners.

'May you rule better and more justly.' Then Herakleios ordered that first Phokas' arms and legs should be cut off and that then his shoulders should also be amputated, and his genitalia should be cut off and put on a stake, because of the countless wanton acts which he had committed; and then his head should be cut off and what was left of the infamous man's body should be dragged to the so-called Forum Boarium and consigned to the flames. **9** It is reported that in the days of Phokas a holy monk used to dispute with God and to say repeatedly: 'My Lord, why did You give the Christians such a lawless emperor?' An unseen voice came to him saying: 'Since I could not find a worse one to match the wickedness of the inhabitants of the City.'

109 Herakleios

Herakleios reigned for thirty years.[1] The patriarch Sergios crowned him in the chapel of St Stephen in the palace. His fiancée Eudokia was crowned *augusta* also together with him and, with the marriage crown added, he was made a bridegroom as well as emperor. He was proclaimed emperor in the Great Church by all the Senate and the people. Krispos, Phokas' son-in-law, helped him and advised him in this. **2** Shortly after, the emperor made Krispos *strategos* of Cappadocia, and sent him out, showing him many signs of favour. However, on arriving there Krispos started to slander Herakleios and to plan an uprising against him. When Krispos came back to Constantinople,[2] the emperor had the accusations against him written down on paper[3] and, in the presence of the Senate, he hit him on the head [with them][4] and said: 'You miserable man, you did not make a [proper] son-in-law; how then will you make a true friend?' He then made Krispos a cleric and exiled him to the Chora monastery, in which he also died. **3** The Persians occupied Cappadocia, Damascus, and Palestine and the Holy City, and they killed many tens of thousands of Christians with the help of the Jews. They also imprisoned Zacharias, the patriarch of Jerusalem, and they took the Holy Cross and carried it off to Persia. Likewise, they occupied Egypt, Libya and all land as far as Ethiopia. They came to Chalcedon and occupied it. The

---

1 Herakleios reigned 5 October 610–11 February 641. Cf. for his reign Theophanes (Mango/Scott 1997, pp. 427–475), and the *Chronicon Paschale* (Whitby/Whitby 1989, pp. 152–189).

2 The Greek here is a little problematic but the meaning seems clear.

3 'paper': Greek χάρτου, i.e. papyrus.

4 The meaning is here a little uncertain.

emperor Herakleios sent ambassadors to Chosroes and asked for peace. Chosroes, however, sent them away, saying: 'If your emperor renounces the crucified one and worships the sun, then I will make peace.' **4** The Avars also made an expedition against the City and, when Herakleios sent ambassadors to them asking for peace, they agreed to this. The emperor then went out to the Long Wall[1] with a large baggage train to meet the Chagan and, having received pledges from him and having concluded a truce, he rejoiced with him. However, the Chagan rescinded the treaty and the oaths, and marched suddenly against the emperor treacherously. The emperor barely managed to return to the City, whereas the barbarian took the whole of the imperial baggage and retinue and then turned back, pillaging the whole of Thrace in the hope of achieving peace.[2] Once again the emperor sent ambassadors to the Chagan, reprimanding him and exhorting him to peace. And the Chagan was embarrassed by the benevolence shown by the emperor and made peace with him. **5** Having celebrated Easter emperor Herakleios wanted to march out against Persia. For this he had taken money[3] from the holy institutions[4] and vessels from the churches, and he had struck *solidi* and *miliaresia*.[5] Chosroes sent a great force with Saitos as commander against the Romans, and so he laid the whole East to waste. Saitos came to Chalcedon and besieged it for a long time. And he called Herakleios to him and, feigning friendliness, he talked to him about peace. Trusting his treacherous words, Herakleios sends seventy noblemen with him to Chosroes as ambassadors. Chosroes received these dishonourably, and he brought them in chains to Persia. Chosroes ordered that Saitos should be flogged, on the ground that he had seen Herakleios and not apprehended him, and he condemned the ambassadors to imprisonment and hardships. As a result the emperor was struck by great dejection and sorrow. Then Chosroes sent another leader on a new expedition against the Romans, a man called Sarbaros, and he came to Asia [Minor] with a very great force and ravaged Roman territory. **6** When the emperor Herakleios, as has been mentioned, intended to march against Persia, he said the following to the patriarch: 'I entrust this City and my son

---

1 The so-called Anastasian Wall in Thrace, some sixty-five kilometres from the City, stretching from the Marmara Sea to the Black Sea.

2 Or rather: a more favourable peace (however, it is likely that the form of the text is due to a less than careful treatment of a source).

3 Or: 'valuables' (χρήματα).

4 εὐαγῶν οἴκων: for the passage cf. Theophanes (Mango/Scott 1997, p. 435).

5 I.e. gold and silver coins respectively (cf. on their relative value Chapter 121, § 18, with n.).

into the hands of God and the Mother of God, and to you.' And he entered
the Great Church and put on black shoes[1] and said his prayers. On seeing
him humbling himself so much, George the Pisidian[2] said: 'Emperor, having
dressed in black shoes, you will dye your foot red with Persian blood.' The
emperor took the Acheiropoietos icon of God-man[3] in his hands. He then
started on his campaign against the Persians, going by boat through the
Black Sea. He took many Turks and many men from other peoples with him
as allies, and he set out against the Persians with a very great force. **7** The
Avars dissolve the truce and approach the wall of Byzantium, setting
everything outside the City on fire.[4] And as if they had made a division
between themselves, the Persians ravaged the East, and the Avars destroyed
everything in Thrace. Although the citizens were worn out and in despair,
when they joined battle with the Avars, with the help of Bonos, the *patrikios*,
and Sergios, the patriarch, they slaughtered many thousands of them, set fire
to their ships, and drove them back to their own country. **8** On learning of
Herakleios' approach Chosroes joined battle with him often, but because of
God's assistance the Persians were always totally defeated. When the
emperor was approaching his city,[5] Chosroes sent one satrap with 30,000
hoplites against him. When battle was joined, all these were killed. But the
Persians who were left and had escaped raged against Chosroes, and they
shut him into one of the royal palaces, and they put gold and silver and pearls
and precious stones before him, saying: 'Eat these, and enjoy the things for
which you brought the Romans against us.' And thus they punished him with
famine and thirst and let him die. **9** But Herakleios destroyed the cities of
Persia, and he tore down the fire temples[6] on which the abominable
representation of Chosroes was found, placed on the house ceiling as if in
heaven. Chosroes had the stars and the sun and the moon painted there, and
himself surrounded by angels, and he had arranged for artificial thunder and
for it to rain when he wished. The emperor razed all of this to the ground and
made it into dust. On hearing this, Sarbaros, who happened to be on Roman
territory, writes an apology to Herakleios, saying that 'it was against my

---

1 Instead of the red ones otherwise worn by the emperor.
2 Poet and contemporary of Herakleios who wrote about the emperor's expedition
against the Persians in 622.
3 I.e. Christ.
4 This is the Avar attack of 626.
5 Ctesiphon.
6 πυρεῖα. This passage is closely paralleled in Nikephoros' *Short History* (see Mango
1990, p. 57).

wish, but on the decision of Chosroes, that I acted as I did against the Romans.' The emperor then wrote a friendly letter to him and summoned him. Thus Sarbaros came to the emperor who was in Persia. But when the emperor asked for his ambassadors and learnt that they had been killed in a terrible way by Chosroes, he was filled with anger and he showed no mercy but killed and burnt and destroyed the whole of Persia for six years. In the seventh year he brought the Holy Cross from Persia to Jerusalem and raised it there. He then returned in joy and peace to Constantinople. 10 During Herakleios' reign Muhammad, the leader of the Saracens, appeared. He came from Yathrib[1] and he, together with many of his people, met with the emperor and asked for a place to live, which was given to him. I consider it necessary[2] to say something about Muhammad's background. 11 Muhammad stemmed from Ishmael, the son of Abraham. For, Nizaros, the descendant of Ishmael, has two sons, Moundaros and Arabias. These had many children, and they settled in the Madianitis desert. They also traded with their camels. Being poor and an orphan, the already mentioned Muhammad entered the service of a rich woman named Chadiga, who was his relative; he was to take care of her camels and to engage in trade. But after a short time he felt greater freedom, and he became intimate with the woman and married her. In that way, he received her camels and her wealth as his own. 12 Coming to Palestine, Muhammad associated with Jews and Christians, and he sought out their writings.[3] The ailment called epilepsy befell him and, on realising this, his wife was very distressed. She grieved over the fact that she had been joined to a man who was not only poor, but also an epileptic. But he tries to comfort her by saying, that 'I see a vision of an angel called Gabriel, and it is because I cannot support that sight that I fall down.' But she had a friend, a monk, who was exiled there because of false beliefs, and she told him everything, including the name of the angel. At this, he reassured her and said: 'He is telling the truth, for this is the angel who is sent to all prophets.' Thus the woman was persuaded by the false father, who belonged to the Kallistratos monastery. He had been thrown out of the City because of his heretical beliefs, and he preached to women of the same tribe [as Muhammed belonged to] that Muhammad was a prophet. Thus this heresy was generally

---

1 I.e. Medina.

2 'I consider it necessary' (or: 'I have come to the conclusion that it is necessary,' Greek ἀναγκαῖον ἡγησάμην): this is reminiscent of the way in which the story of the rise of Basil I (Chapter 131, § 8) or the death of evildoers (Chapter 132, § 2) is introduced.

3 'writings' (Greek τινὰ γραφικά): or 'matter that he could write about,' or 'scriptures,' referring to the Bible.

accepted in the region of Yathrib. **13** Muhammad dogmatically decreed to his subjects that whoever kills an enemy or is killed by an enemy will enter paradise. He said that paradise was a place of carnal food and of intercourse with women, and that the intercourse was continuous and the pleasure lasted for a long time, together with other reckless and foolish statements. **14** Muhammad left Abu-Bakr as his successor. And, after having been forced into skirmishes by the Romans very often, the Arabs won a decisive victory,[1] and from that time on they had the better of the Romans. **15** Let us now go back to the main story. Having accomplished this, Herakleios returned to Constantinople. Hearing of his approach, the inhabitants of the City, because of their unrestrained love for him, all went out to the palace of Hieria[2] together with the patriarch and Constantine, the emperor who was his son. They carried olive branches and torches to welcome him, and they hailed him. And his son stepped forward and fell at his father's feet, and Herakleios embraced him, and they kissed each other, with tears in their eyes. And having thus received their emperor, they hailed him and entered the City rejoicing. **16** This Herakleios was deceived by Athanasios, the patriarch of the Jacobites, and by Sergios the Syrian, the patriarch of Constantinople, and he fell into the heresy of the monotheletes.[3] Later he was struck by hydropsy, too, from which he died. He was punished in a terrible way. For the ailment had gone so far that, when he wanted to urinate, he had to press a board against the abdomen; for his genital organ turned upwards and sent the urine towards his face. This was punishment for his lawlessness, because of his most lawless marriage with his own niece.[4]

110 Constantine, Son of Herakleios

Constantine, son of Herakleios, reigned for one year.[5] He is killed with poison by his own stepmother.

---

1 Or: 'started to achieve victories.' If a specific victory of the Arabs is on the author's mind, it could be the battle of Yarmouk in 636.

2 Or: 'Heria,' at the Asiatic shore opposite of the City.

3 Monotheletism is the doctrine of the one will of Christ's human and divine natures. This is a monophysite development, condemned as heretical in 681.

4 This is the Martina mentioned below (see Chapter 111, § 1, etc.).

5 In actual fact, Constantine III reigned just over two months as senior emperor (11 February–20 April or 24/26 May 641). Cf. for his reign Theophanes (Mango/Scott 1997, p. 474).

111 Heraklonas

Heraklonas reigned together with his mother Martina for four months.[1] But the Senate rejected Heraklonas, and they had his nose slit and Martina's tongue cut out, and they sent them into exile. **2** They promoted Constans, the son of Constantine, grandson of Herakleios, to the throne.

112 Constans

Constans reigned for twenty-seven years.[2] During a *selention*[3] he said to the Senate: 'My father Constantine reigned for some time with his father, my grandfather Herakleios, during his father's lifetime, but only for a very short time after his father's death. For, the envy of Martina, his stepmother, removed him from life to benefit Heraklonas, who was born illegally from her. Now, thanks to your and God's decision she has been removed with her child, so that the empire of the Romans should not be ruled by people of illegitimate and illegal descent.[4] I beg you to be my counsellors and friends and the examiners of my rule.' Then, honouring them with gifts, he dismissed them. **2** During Constans' reign there was a violent storm that tore up many trees and threw down pillars and crushed ships. **3** Also Mauias, the leader of the Arabs, reached Rhodes. Having got control of[5] the Colossus of Rhodes he had it pulled down, 1,360 years after its construction. The Colossus was bought by a Jewish merchant who loaded its bronze onto 700 camels. Mauias came with his ships to Phoinike,[6] where the emperor Constans lay in waiting with the Roman fleet, intending to fight a sea-battle with Mauias.[7] In the night the emperor dreamt that he was in the city of Thessalonica. When he woke up, he recounted his dream to his dream interpreter, who said: 'My emperor, I would that you had not slept during this night and that

---

1 Heraklonas reigned together with Constantine III from February 641. The four months may refer to his period as sole ruler (20 April–September of the same year). Cf. for his reign Theophanes (Mango/Scott 1997, pp. 474–475).

2 Constans II reigned 641–668. Cf. for his reign Theophanes (Mango/Scott 1997, pp. 475–491).

3 A solemn meeting of emperor, his advisers and the Senate.

4 The text is here a little problematic, but the meaning suggested seems plausible.

5 'got control of' (παραλαβών): or 'come to.'

6 Phoinix in Lycia (see Mango/Scott 1997, p. 482).

7 'intending ... Mauias': or, possibly, vice versa, i.e. that it was Mauias' plan to fight the emperor.

you had not dreamt! For that you were in Thessalonica is to be interpreted as "give someone else the victory."[1] The victory goes to your enemy.' And so it happened. When they clash, the Romans are defeated. The emperor saves himself with difficulty and returns in shame to Constantinople. 4 Unable to change the saintly Maximos[2] to his own heretical belief, this Constans had his tongue and his hand cut off. He also sent St Martin, the pope of Rome, into exile. 5 After this, Mauias, the leader of the Arabs, sent ambassadors to Constans proposing a peace treaty. Mauias did this because the Arabs had rebelled against him, and he suggested that the Arabs, to achieve the peace, should pay a daily tribute to the Romans of 1,000 *solidi*, one horse, and one slave. But Constans did not accept this. 6 Constans left Constantinople and moved to Syracuse in Sicily. He wanted to move the seat of government to Rome since he was hated by the inhabitants of Byzantium for being a monothelete and a heretic. Although this was against his will, he left his three sons and his wife in the City. 7 Constans was murdered in Syracuse in Sicily washing himself in the bath-house. He was hit on the head with a jar by Andreas, and he died. The Syracusans proclaim Nizizios the Armenian emperor, a dignified and most beautiful man.

113 Constantine, Son of Constans

Constantine, son of Constans, reigned for sixteen years.[3] When he learnt about the murder of his father, he went to Sicily with a very great fleet and captured Nizizios and all of his father's murderers and had them decapitated. He did the same with Justinian, the *patrikios*, the father of Germanos who became patriarch. But Germanos, who was a rather violent man, he made a eunuch. This emperor was called Pogonatos, for he had departed beardless to exact revenge for his father, but returned with a beard. 2 Having returned to Constantinople he reigned together with his brothers. However, when they tried to plot against him, he prevailed, and he had the noses of Herakleios and Tiberios slit, and he sent them into exile. 3 During his reign a great

---

1 In Greek: θὲς ἄλλῳ τὴν νίκην, i.e. a combination of syllables very much reminiscent of the name of the city. A similar interpretation, involving the name of the city of Tyros, is recorded above, Chapter 46, § 19.

2 This is Maximos the Confessor.

3 Constantine IV reigned 15 September 668–September 685. Cf. for his reign Theophanes (Mango/Scott 1997, pp. 491–506).

Arab fleet, with very many units,[1] went out and reached Kyzikos and came as far as the Golden Gate and the Kyklobion.[2] With regular skirmishes taking place, they wintered in the bay of Kyzikos for seven years, as they made war upon Constantinople. But by the grace of God they were defeated by the inhabitants of Byzantium, and their wretched[3] fleet returned home. During their retreat, when they were once more forced to join battle by the *strategos* of the Kibyrrhaiotai,[4] they were defeated, and their ships were burnt by liquid fire. For Kallinikos, an architect from Helioupolis in Syria who was a refugee with the Romans, had invented liquid fire, and he burnt the Arab ships and destroyed them, men and all. Thus the Romans, thanks to the invention of the liquid fire at that time, returned in great triumph.[5] 4 The Mardaites[6] came to Lebanon in Syria and gained control of it. This greatly terrifies Mauias, and he sends ambassadors to the emperor suing for peace and promising a yearly tribute. The emperor receives the ambassadors and then sends them back together with John Pittigaudes, the *patrikios*, to talk to the Arabs. For John was adorned with great experience and good sense. The Arabs came to admire his good sense and his astuteness, and they agreed to furnish the Romans a yearly tribute of 3,000 [...][7] of gold, 8,000 prisoners,[8] and fifty thoroughbred horses. It was agreed that this tribute should be paid for thirty years, and so a general peace prevailed between the Arabs and the Romans. 5 Likewise, the Scythians who lived in the West, the Chagan and the kings from more distant regions and the *kastaldai*,[9] sent gifts to the emperor and sued for peace. The emperor accepted this and confirmed the peace. And so, great tranquillity ensued in the East as well as the West. 6 Under this emperor

---

1 κεφαλαί.

2 A suburb on the European shore of the Marmara Sea, present-day Zeytinburnu.

3 θεοβύθιστος στόλος: '(to be) sunk by God.'

4 Kibyrrhaiotai was a *thema*, i.e. a division of the Byzantine empire and/or the military forces therein. Kibyrrhaiotai was primarily a naval organisation, and it was stationed at the southern coast of Asia Minor.

5 The invention of Greek, or liquid, fire is credited to Proklos above, Chapter 102, § 2.

6 An obscure group of Christians (sometimes identified with Maronites) in the border area between Byzantium and the Caliphate. Below, § 8, a Mardaite *tagma* (military unit), in the service of the Byzantines, is mentioned.

7 Theophanes has the same text, and Mango/Scott 1997 (p. 496, with n. 3) suggest *solidi* or pounds. Cf. the following note.

8 I.e. slaves. Theophanes (cf. previous note with reference to Mango/Scott 1997) gives the number of prisoners as fifty, whereas *De administrando imperio* 21.15–16 mentions 800.

9 Or *gastalds*: Lombard local governors (cf. Mango-Scott 1997, p. 497, n. 6).

the Bulgarian people crossed over[1] and, splitting from their kinsmen, they settled at Varna in a region of forests and mountains. On hearing this, the emperor went out against them with ships and an army. Seeing this massive attack coming, and despairing for their lives, the Bulgarians take refuge in a stronghold and make themselves secure. Now, since the Romans were unable to join battle with them because of the marshes and the location's impregnability, the abominable[2] people became more audacious. It also happened that the emperor suffered a violent attack of gout and had to return to Mesembria,[3] leaving it to the *strategoi* to make an ambush and drive the Bulgarians out. But when the cavalrymen spread the rumour that the emperor was fleeing, the *strategoi* fled, although they were not being pursued. On seeing this, the Bulgarians went after them and killed many by the sword. And then they crossed over and audaciously gained control over Roman territory, over-running it and taking prisoners. This forced the emperor to sue for peace with them and, to the shame of the Romans and because of our many sins, he agreed to pay them a yearly tribute. For he who had subdued everyone was defeated by the abominable people. 7 Having achieved peace everywhere, the emperor united the holy churches and gathered an ecumenical synod of 289 fathers in Constantinople, and he confirmed the dogmas of the previous five holy synods.[4] He crowned Justinian, his son, as co-emperor. 8 When Mauias the Arab died, Abimelech came to power. Sending ambassadors to the emperor, he asked for peace and offered a yearly tribute of 365,000 gold *solidi*, 365 slaves, and 365 thoroughbred horses. This he did so that the Mardaite *tagma*[5] should be withdrawn from Lebanon. 9 Having reigned for seventeen years, this pious Constantine departed from life.

---

1 I.e. over the Danube and into Byzantine territory.

2 τὸ μιαρὸν ἔθνος: a common way to describe the Bulgarians.

3 Present-day Nesebar in Bulgaria.

4 This is the Sixth Ecumenical Council, or Third Council of Constantinople, taking place in 680/681 and, among other matters, being concerned with putting an end to monotheletism (cf. above, Chapter 109, § 16).

5 Cf. above, § 4.

114 Justinian, his Son

Justinian, his son, reigned for sixteen years.[1] He sent a message to Abimelech to confirm in writing[2] what had been agreed during his father's reign, and he sent orders and removed 12,000 Mardaites—what foolishness! Thus he curtailed the Roman realm. For from then on and until the present day, Romania has suffered terrible evil from the Arabs because of the removal of the Mardaites. **2** Justinian also dissolved the peace with the Bulgarians, and he went on an expedition to the Western parts of the empire where, in some cases by war, in some by persuasion, he won many groups of Slavs over to his side. He then returned. From these Slavs he selected 30,000 men and made them into an army, calling them the *chosen people*.[3] He armed them and made them his own special force and, trusting to their help, he dissolves out of folly the peace between the Romans and the Arabs. And taking the selected, or, rather, this unholy people, as well as the other army units, he set off towards Sebastopolis.[4] To this city also the Hagarenes came, and they protested saying that he should not pervert what had been agreed upon under oath, for God will judge and take vengeance. However, the emperor did not listen to this talk of peace, and he marshalled the troops for battle. At this, the Hagarenes unfolded the written peace document and put it on a spear and rushed against the Romans. And when they clashed, 20,000 of the Slavs deserted to the Hagarenes, and so the Romans were routed terribly, and an immeasurable number of them were slaughtered. The righteous judgement and the victory went to the enemy, teaching that, even if you are dealing with an enemy and with non-believers, you should never break an oath sworn in the name of God. **3** When the emperor had fled and, in great shame and defeat, had arrived at the coast of Leukaton,[5] he had the remaining 10,000 Slavs killed. And after this the Hagarenes behaved even more audaciously, and they ravaged Romania more vehemently, having also the Slav refugees to help them. When the emperor entered the City, there was a solar eclipse that made even the stars appear. **4** Justinian

---

1 Justinian II reigned 685–695 and 705–711. Cf. for his first period of reign Theophanes (Mango/Scott 1997, pp. 506–515).

2 Or: 'to confirm what had been agreed upon in writing.'

3 Or: 'most treasured among peoples' (λαὸν περιούσιον): this is an echo of Exodus 19.5.

4 Some 200 kilometres south of Samsun, present-day Sulusaray.

5 Leukate in Theophanes, present-day Yelkenkaya Burnu, across the gulf from Yalova (see Mango/Scott 1997, p. 511 and 512, n. 3).

took an interest in building activity relating to the palace. He built the so-called *Triklinos* of Justinian and arranged the area round the palace. He had his *sakellarios*[1] and *proteunouchos*[2] Stephen to do this. This was a bloodthirsty and cruel man who maltreated the workers and showed them no compassion; he even went as far as to beat the emperor's mother. He also treated the inhabitants of the City badly, and he made unjustifiable demands of a fiscal kind upon the citizens.[3] Through this, he made the emperor hated in the City. **5** Wanting to build a platform for the people and a place for them to stand the emperor asked Kallinikos, the patriarch, to make a prayer for the deconsecration of the Church of the Most Holy Mother of God, the one close to the palace, for he wanted to prepare an open courtyard with a fountain[4] and a platform[5] for the people, so that the so-called *saximodeximon*[6] could be performed there. The patriarch said: 'We have a prayer to say when a church is founded, but no prayer has come down to us for a church's deconsecration.' However, being put under pressure and requested to perform the prayer, he said: 'Glory to God, Who endures everything, now and always and to the end of time.' And immediately they destroyed[7] the church. **6** Leontios the *patrikios* had been suspected of coveting the throne and had been held in detention for this reason for two years. He was then sent by Justinian as *strategos* to Hellas. There he met Paul, a friend of his, who was a monk and an astronomer,[8] and this Paul predicted that Leontios would become emperor. To him and to his other friends Leontios said in private: 'Look, the emperor will send people after me, and he will cut off my head. Anyway, it is not true what you promise me about the rule.' But they said: 'If you do not hesitate, it will soon come to pass.' **7** And he took them along and broke into the public prisons, collecting a large mob around him. When he came out to the Forum, his men shouted to all the people: 'All Christians to St Sophia.'

1 A fiscal official, serving the imperial treasury.
2 'First of the eunuchs' (at the imperial court).
3 This sentence is difficult and the translation hypothetical.
4 φιάλη (cf. Chapter 130, § 36).
5 βάθρα. The text seems somewhat repetitive here. Perhaps this is done with rhetorical calculation, the second mention of the platform being part of the actual words spoken to the patriarch.
6 This was a ceremony at which the emperor inspected racehorses (cf. the description below, Chapter 130, § 36).
7 Or: 'deconsecrated' (Greek καταλύω, as above).
8 I.e. astrologer.

And when the crowd had gathered, they cried: 'Let the bones of Justinian be exhumed.' Then, coming to the hippodrome, Leontios is proclaimed emperor. And, when dawn broke, he brought Justinian to the hippodrome and had his nose slit in the Sphendone and exiled him to Cherson.[1] The crowd seized the *sakellarios* Stephen, who was also a eunuch, and Theodotos, the *genikos*,[2] and they tied ropes round their feet and dragged them through the Mese[3] and had them burnt in the Forum Boarium.

115 Leontios

Leontios reigned for three years.[4] **2** During his reign the Arabs went on an expedition and occupied Africa.[5] On learning this, Leontios sends the *patrikios* John, who was an able man, with the Roman fleet. John routed the enemy and liberated Africa. He then sent a report back to the emperor, and he spent the winter there. On learning this, the *protosymboulos*[6] sent a great Hagarene force against John and chased him away. John then returned to Romania intending to gather a greater force. **3** When, on his journey back to the emperor, John had come as far as Crete, the expeditionary force was led astray by their own commanders and made a bad decision. They killed John the *patrikios* and, cursing the emperor, they proclaimed Apsimaros, who was *droungarios*[7] of the Kibyrrhaiotai, emperor and renamed him Tiberios. **4** When Leontios was cleansing the Neorion harbour,[8] bubonic plague hit the City and killed a great host of people. **5** Apsimaros arrived with the fleet and anchored at Sykai.[9] Even though the City did not wish to betray Leontios, treason took place, and

1 Chersonesus Taurica, in the Crimean Peninsula.
2 I.e. he worked for the *genikon*, an office responsible for the collecting of general taxes (according to Mango/Scott 1997, p. 513, he was 'head of the state treasury,' i.e. *logothetes tou genikou*).
3 The main street of Constantinople, running from the area of the Great Palace until the City Wall.
4 Leontios reigned 695–698. Cf. for his reign Theophanes (Mango/Scott 1997, pp. 515–518).
5 For this expedition see Mango/Scott 1997, pp. 516–517.
6 Literally: 'first counsellor,' either denoting the caliph, or the (Arab) commander-in-chief (see Mango/Scott 1997, p. 497 and p. 500, n. 1).
7 This is a military rank, encountered here for the first time in this text.
8 Cf. above, Chapter 99, § 2.
9 At Galata across the Golden Horn.

the gate at the Blachernai was opened. Apsimaros was able to apprehend Leontios, and he had his nose slit and exiled him to the Dalmatos monastery.[1] Also, after beating all Leontios' friends and confiscating their belongings he sent them into exile.

116 Apsimaros, Also Known as Tiberios

Apsimaros reigned for seven years.[2] During his reign there was a great plague, and the Romans raided Syria and slaughtered as many as 200,000 people. **2** Apsimaros exiled Philippikos, son of the *patrikios* Nikephoros, to Cephalonia, since he was thought to be dreaming of becoming emperor. For he said that in a dream he had seen his head being covered by an eagle.[3] And having heard this, the emperor sent him into exile. **3** Justinian, who was in Cherson, made it known that he intended to regain the throne. This alarmed the inhabitants of Cherson, who discussed whether they should put him to death or send him to the emperor. On learning this, Justinian flees to Chazaria,[4] and the Chazar gave him his own sister, Theodora, for wife. Being informed of this, Apsimaros sends an embassy to the Chagan,[5] promising him many gifts if he turns over Justinian to him alive or, otherwise, lets him have his head. On learning this, Justinian secretly went down to Cherson and, gathering some men, sailed to the Istros estuary. There was a storm, and because of this storm everyone lost hope of survival. One of Justinian's intimates said to him: 'My Lord, if you are saved and God gives you the throne, give your word that you will not exact vengeance from any of your enemies.' But Justinian said with great fury: 'May the Lord let me drown on the spot rather than that I should spare any of them.' **4** Having been saved from the storm, Justinian sent a message to Terbelis, the Bulgarian, with a promise of an alliance and a guarantee that Terbelis should be able to retain his inherited kingdom and also should receive many gifts from Justinian. Terbelis did not only agree to an alliance but offered his services as well. For together with Justinian

1 This is in the City.

2 Apsimaros (Tiberios II/III) reigned 698–705. Cf. for his reign Theophanes (Mango/ Scott 1997, pp. 517–522).

3 Cf. Marcian (see above, Chapter 98, § 6).

4 I.e. the Chazar (Khazar) empire, north of the Black Sea.

5 This would seem to refer to the Chazar ruler, not, as otherwise, to the ruler of the Avars.

he arrived at the capital with a very great force. **5** Justinian entered the City together with a small number of his kinsmen. He went through the aqueduct,[1] aided by the treason of some people in the City, and he emerged at St Anna, into the building called Deuteron (Second) thereafter because of him.[2] He took up temporary residence in the Blachernai palace and so regained his throne. On learning this, Apsimaros fled to Apollonias.[3]

117 Justinian

Justinian took over the throne for a second time.[4] After he had given many gifts[5] to Terbelis he cut off part of Romania and gave him what is now called Zagoria. **2** He sent people to apprehend Apsimaros, and impaled Herakles, Apsimaros' brother, and all the magistrates who had been his comrades-in-arms[6] on stakes on the City wall. He bound Apsimaros and Leontios with chains and brought them to the *kathisma* in the hippodrome, where he placed his foot on their necks until the end of the first race, while the people shouted: 'You have walked on a snake and a basilisk, and you have trampled on a lion and a dragon.'[7] He then sent them to the Kynegion[8] and had them decapitated. He also had Kallinikos, the patriarch, blinded and exiled, and he destroyed many people in the City, causing great fear. **3** He sent for Theodora, who was from Chazaria, and Tiberios, her son, and they ruled together with him. **4** He dissolved the peace treaty with the Bulgarians and marched against them. Then,

1 I.e. he presumably went through the Valens aqueduct (cf. Theophanes: Mango/Scott 1997, p. 522).

2 'called ... him' (τὸ λεγόμενον δι' αὐτὸν ἔκτοτε δεύτερον): i.e. referring to the fact that it was the second time that an intruder entered the city through the aqueduct.

3 Perhaps Apollonia ad Rhyndacum in north-western Anatolia (see Mango/Scott 1997, p. 524, n. 5).

4 Justinian II reigned for the second time 705–711. Cf. Theophanes (Mango/Scott 1997, pp. 522–533).

5 Or: 'to achieve this, he gave many gifts etc.,' i.e. stressing that the bond with Terbelis was the reason why Justinian managed to regain the throne (cf. 116, § 4).

6 There is probably a minor textual problem at this point, but the meaning seems clear.

7 A paraphrase of Psalms 90(91).13.

8 The Kynegion mentioned here is probably the (ancient Roman) amphitheatre used for beast shows and, later on, for executions (cf. R. Janin, *Constantinople Byzantin*, Paris 1964, 2nd ed., p. 14). However, in other instances in this text the term *kynegion* may refer to a hunting park (see Chapter 69, § 2, with note).

having been defeated, he took refuge in a fort and, having hamstrung his horses, boarded a ship and returned to Constantinople ignominiously. Feeling a grudge against the inhabitants of Cherson, where he had been in exile, he sent the *patrikios* Mauros and had them all slaughtered and their 'infants dashed against the earth.'[1] **5** Philippikos, also known as Bardanes, who lived there as an exile, had managed to bring some soldiers over to his side and to make them loyal to himself as a result of Justinian's rudeness and brutality. They hailed him as emperor and sent him with a fleet towards the City. On hearing this, Justinian was even more fearful and angry, and he went up to Sinope[2] to get more exact information about the matter. When Philippikos arrived at the City with the fleet, Justinian, who had been abandoned by everyone, escaped to Damatrys.[3] However, he was apprehended at once by Philippikos, who had his head cut off and sent to the Scythians.[4]

118 Philippikos, Also Known as Bardanes

Philippikos, also known as Bardanes, reigned for two years.[5] To those who met him and talked to him, he seemed to be a learned and sensible man. Yet his actions proved him to be a man whose conduct was in every way improper, incompetent and shameful. He was no real orthodox Christian,[6] and was not ashamed to move against the Holy Synod, trying to overthrow it.[7] **2** During his reign also the Bulgarians took prisoners from as far as the Golden Gate and returned home. **3** When chariot races had been held and the green party had won, Philippikos decided to go to the Zeuxippos bath together with his retinue and with instruments, to bathe and to have a banquet with humble citizens. When he was resting (that is, having a siesta), the *patrikios* George, also called Boraphos, and the *patrikios* Theodore Myakes suddenly burst in, together with soldiers

---

1 'babies ... earth': cf. Psalms 137.9.

2 On the Black Sea.

3 This may be Samandra at the mountain of St Auxentios close to Constantinople (for this see Mango/Scott 1997, p. 531, n. 11).

4 I.e. back to Cherson where he had been an exile.

5 Philippikos reigned 711–713. Cf. for his reign Theophanes (Mango/Scott 1997, pp. 531–534).

6 κακόδοξος.

7 He was a monothelete.

from Thrace. They seized Philippikos and took him to the *ornatourion*[1] of the green party[2] and had him blinded. On the following day, they brought the people into the Great Church and crowned Artemios the *protasekretis*[3] as emperor.

119 Artemios, Also Known as Anastasios

Artemios, also known as Anastasios, reigned for two years.[4] He was a most learned man, and he appointed most learned and able men to be *strategoi* in command of the cavalry units of the *themata* and to hold civil office. Therefore, the political situation remained stable. He had the *patrikioi* Theodore and George blinded and exiled to Thessalonica. 2 The Arabs took arms against Romania on land and at sea, and it was reported to the emperor that they were coming towards the City. The emperor began to build *dromones* and biremes and to renew the sea walls. He also strengthened the land walls with catapults for darts, and he fortified the City with other armaments, and he filled the granaries with crops. 3 It was also during his reign that Germanos was translated from the metropolitan see of Kyzikos to Constantinople. And Artemios published a decree of translation,[5] which was approved by the vote and scrutiny of the most God-loving *presbyteroi* and deacons and the Holy Synod.[6] It read as follows: 'In the reign of emperor Artemios, Divine Grace, which always takes care of what is weak and supplies what is lacking, transfers Germanos, the most holy president of the metropolitan church of the people of Kyzikos, and makes him bishop of this God-protected, imperial City.' 4 On learning that a Hagarene fleet had sailed to Phoinix,[7] to cut timber there, the emperor sent a fleet under

---

1 This was probably an assembly hall or room in which the *urna* used for drawing lots (in order to allocate starting positions in chariot races) was placed (see Mango/Scott 1997, p. 534, n. 6, with further references). There is great variation as to the correct form of this word (*armatourion*, etc.). Anastasius Bibliothecarius, Theophanes' Latin translator, has *oratorium*.

2 I.e. faction in the hippodrome.

3 The joint chief of the offices *asekretis*.

4 Artemios, i.e. emperor Anastasios II, reigned 713–715. Cf. Theophanes (Mango/Scott 1997, pp. 534–536).

5 κιττατώριν μεταθεσίμου (cf. Mango/Scott 1997, p. 537, n. 3).

6 ἱερὰ σύγκλητος ('Sacred Senate').

7 Perhaps (so Mango/Scott 1997, p. 537, n. 5) modern Fenaket, on the coast by Rhodes, rather than Phoinike (or Phoinix) in Lycia, probably referred to above, Chapter 112, § 3.

the command of a cleric by the name of John, whom they also called Joannakes, to burn down the woods at Phoinix and destroy the Hagarene naval force. But the fleet rebelled and turned against the emperor, and they killed Joannakes with swords. Having done this, they sailed back towards the imperial City in open rebellion. Arriving at Adramyttion,[1] they found Theodosios there, who was a tax-collector and a pious man and who did not pursue any selfish interests, and they proclaimed him emperor, for they did not consider that they had any real leader of their own. However, Theodosios fled into the mountains and went into hiding. But when they found him, they acclaimed him and forced him to become emperor. 5 On learning this, Artemios fortified the City and fled to Nicaea. 6 The Constantinopolitan fleet and that of Theodosios continued to fight each other for six months. Having passed over to the Thracian part of the empire Theodosios reached the City with a great force, and he entered the City through the single wall at the Blachernai gate and, taking much booty and sparing no-one, the marine soldiers plundered the City and robbed its leading men. They took hold of the patriarch Germanos and the officials loyal to Artemios and brought them to Nicaea. On seeing the soldiers coming, Artemios asked for and received a pledge of personal security, and put on a monk's habit, whereupon Theodosios had him exiled to Thessalonica. 7 Leo the Isaurian, who was *strategos* of the Anatolikon, fought on behalf of Artemios and did not subordinate himself to Theodosios. He had Artavasdos the Armenian, *strategos* of the Armeniakon, as a supporter, and had agreed to give him his daughter in marriage.

120 Theodosios of Adramyttion

Theodosios reigned for two years.[2] 2 During his reign Masalmas, the leader of the Saracens,[3] campaigned against the Romans. On arriving in the region of Amorion he writes to Leo, *strategos* of the Anatolikon: 'The empire of the Romans is yours. So come and let us talk about peace, and I will do anything you want.' 3 Leo sent *hypatoi* to him to conduct peace talks and, when he had been acclaimed emperor, he goes to Nicomedia with a very

---

1 Or: 'Adramytion,' in north-western Asia Minor, present-day Edremit.

2 Theodosios III, of Adramyttion, was acclaimed emperor in May 715 and abdicated in March 717. Cf. for his reign Theophanes (Mango/Scott 1997, pp. 538–541).

3 I.e. the Umayyad prince Maslamah ibn Abd al-Malik.

great army. There he happens to meet Theodosios' son, and he apprehends him as well as his imperial retinue and the palace officials, and he arrives at Chrysopolis. But Theodosios received a pledge of security from Leo and ceded the throne to him, becoming a cleric together with his son.

121 Leo the Isaurian

Leo the Isaurian reigned for twenty-four years.[1] **2** His story is more or less as follows. The leader of the Arabs was Yezid.[2] Two young Jewish men, enemies to God and claiming to be pursuing the astrological science, come to the royal court of the Arabs and make statements to Yezid: they predict a long life for him if he can make the icons of Our Lord Jesus Christ and of the Mother of God disappear from all churches under his rule. And he, who loved life, followed the advice of the cheats, and he upset all the churches in his territory. Yet the wretched man was deceived, and divine justice struck him before a year had passed. **3** His son, who succeeded him to the throne, wanted to kill the two Jews for being false prophets. On learning this, the two Jews went away to Isauria. When they were refreshing themselves at a well, behold! There was Leo, still a youth, with good looks and well grown. He was a simple craftsman and earning his living from this, and he now unloaded his pack-animal and also sat down at the well to eat his lunch. **4** Then these men, who were devotees of sorcery, reveal to him that he will control the sceptres of the Roman empire. Now, considering his own simple state, Leo is doubtful about this, but the godless men assure him with oaths that this is what is going to happen. And they ask him to swear that, if this should come to pass and they should ask him for something, he would give it to them without hesitation. Close by was the Church of St Theodore. At once the simple craftsman Leo went inside and, touching the sanctuary's holy railings, gave as guarantor Christ's great martyr.[3] All the while the Jews were

---

1 Leo III the Isaurian reigned 717–741. Cf. for his reign Theophanes (Mango/Scott 1997, pp. 541–574).

2 This story is confused. This should be the Umayyad caliph Yazid b. Abd al-Malik (cf. Theophanes, Mango/Scott 1997, pp. 555–556). However, the chronology does not make sense, since he reigned 720–724, and Leo the Isaurian is said to come into prominence during Yezid's son's reign.

3 I.e. St Theodore (Theodoros Stratelates), executed under Licinius (cf. above, Chapter 88, § 3).

standing at the door of the church, and they received his oath. And so each of them returned immediately to his place of origin. **5** At that time the *patrikios* Sisinios was *strategos* of the Anatolikon. During his time in office Leo served as a soldier there and was quickly promoted to a very high rank. For he was appointed *spatharios*[1] by Justinian Rhinotmetos,[2] and he was sent to the West, and on returning in great triumph Theodosios made him *strategos* of the East. **6** Having gained the throne in the way just described, the seers, who had made the prophecy about him, came to Leo and took his hand and asked him to fulfil his promise. When he declared himself ready to grant it to them, these enemies of God said: 'The following we demand of you, emperor: that you erase any depiction of the Nazarean Christ and of his mother and of all the saints from every account of ecclesiastical history. If you do this, you will reign through your kin for a hundred years.' The wretch, who was not firm in his faith, very readily promised to do what was asked and proceeded at once to act. **7** A son named Constantine was born to the impious emperor Leo.[3] During his baptism, it is said that he discharged terrible, foul-smelling excrement into the baptismal font. This was a bad sign.[4] **8** For, shortly afterwards the emperor sent for the patriarch Germanos and started a discussion with him, which had a hidden purpose. He censured all the emperors before him and all the priests as having been idolaters in their reverence for the holy icons. But the great Germanos said: 'Listen, emperor! When our Lord Jesus Christ appeared in flesh and walked among men, every kind of idolatry ceased, and every idol disappeared and was banned. For the prophet Zechariah says: "The Lord Sabaoth says: I will cut off the names of the idols from the land, so that they shall be remembered no more."[5] However, we have been told that the icons will be torn down, but not during your reign!' The emperor interrupted: 'During whose reign, then?' 'During Konon's,' answered the patriarch. And the emperor retorted: 'Truly that is I, and I have been called by that name since my childhood.' And the great Germanos said on his part: 'My Lord, let it not come to pass, that this abominable evil be perpetrated during your reign!' On hearing this the upstart, the enemy of God, roars

---

1 Early on denoting an imperial bodyguard, but at this date probably an honorary title.

2 I.e. emperor Justinian II.

3 This is Constantine V, born 718.

4 From this came the nickname of the future emperor, Kopronymos ('Named from dung').

5 Zechariah 13.2.

like a wild beast[1] and becomes exceedingly displeased and calls the patriarch an idolater, and he strikes him with his own hands and drives him out of the palace. And in this brutal and impious way, he starts the heresy and, having torn down the icon of Our Lord Jesus Christ at the Chalke gate,[2] he holds a *selention* against the icons. He also summons the venerable Germanos unto his presence for a second time, in the belief that he will be able to convince him to sign a document against the holy icons. But Germanos in no way yielded either to flattery or to threats from the upstart. Instead he placed his *omophorion*[3] on the holy altar of the Great Church and renounced his priesthood and went into exile. 9 The enemy of God appoints Anastasios, the *presbyteros*, as patriarch instead of Germanos, since Anastasios supported the emperor's impious decision. The emperor had every icon of Our Saviour and of the Mother of God and of the saints torn down and burnt, and he started a great persecution, subjecting many priests and monks and laymen to various kinds of punishment as well as death. Close to Chalkoprateia there was a modest palace in which, in accordance with an ancient decree, there lived an *oikoumenikos didaskalos*[4] together with twelve men from the aristocracy who were his assistants. These men pursued every kind of science and they preserved the dogmas of the Church, and they also received imperial funding, and likewise books. Emperors did not make any public judgement or decision without consulting them. The beast of ill-omened name[5] summoned these men, and tried to persuade them. When they did not accept his view but criticised him, he ordered that a great amount of wood should be collected and set on fire, and that the men should be burnt with their buildings and books and all other belongings. Because of this the *proedros* of Rome[6] also rebelled and made a peace treaty with the Frank, and he stopped sending tribute, and he condemned Anastasios and his

---

1 'roars ... beast' (ὡς ἀνήμερος θὴρ βρύξας): this expression is of a common type (cf. below, Chapter 128, § 7). It should be remembered that the man's name was Leo, 'Lion.'

2 'Copper Gate' (Χάλκη): of the Great Palace. That the emperor inaugurated iconoclasm by tearing down an icon at the Chalke is highly doubtful.

3 A kind of scarf worn (in this case) by bishops.

4 'universal teacher': a title used in different epochs, sometimes referring specifically to a teacher at the Patriarchal School at St Sophia.

5 I.e Leo = 'Lion' (cf. above, § 8).

6 The pope. The actual historical meaning of this is uncertain: perhaps the increasing problems in the relationship with the pope were economically motivated rather than due to iconoclasm.

men. **10** Masalmas was waiting for Leo to honour his promises. However, when he did not receive anything from Leo and realised that he had been cheated, he moved against the imperial City. And he reached Abydos and, having transferred a very large force to the other side,[1] he writes to Souleiman,[2] the *protosymboulos*, to come with his fleet at once. And in the month of August Masalmas laid siege to the City, building a palisade to encompass the land wall, and he inflicted severe damage on Thrace. On the first day of September[3] Souleiman arrived with ships of great size, triremes and *dromones*, to the number of 1,800. **11** The emperor sent the navy against them with its fast ships, and with liquid fire[4] he made their numerically superior, fearful ships catch fire, so that some of them ran into the sea walls in flames, whereas others sank with all hands, in the deep sea, and yet others were driven as far as Oxeia and the other islands, still burning.[5] From this the inhabitants of the City gained confidence, for the enemy had been struck by a major catastrophe. **12** The enemy spent the winter close by the City. When spring came, plague struck, combined with famine, and destroyed an immeasurable number of them. The survivors joined battle with the Bulgarians in Thrace and were for the most part killed. On the fifteenth of August[6] as they set out from the City with a violent gale blowing, some were killed at Proikonnesos[7] and at other beaches, while others were lost at sea when a violent hail-storm combined with powerful wind hit them and made them all go down. A mere five ships out of the 1,800 were, against all expectation, saved, and this remnant made the Roman victory and their own utter destruction known in their country. **13** On hearing that the Hagarenes were trying to destroy the City, Sergios, the *strategos* of Sicily, crowned one of his own men as emperor (this man was called Basil, and his nick-name was Onomagoulos), and he also appointed officials. On hearing this, the emperor sent Paul there carrying his orders and accompanied by a fleet.

---

1 I.e. to the European side of the Hellespont. Abydos is located on the Asian shore of the Hellespont.

2 Sulayman b. Muad (see Mango/Scott 1997, p. 541, n. 1).

3 This was 1 September 717.

4 I.e. Greek fire.

5 I.e. to the Princes Islands in the Marmara Sea (Oxeia is present-day Sivriada).

6 This was 15 August 718. Since this is the day of the feast in celebration of the Assumption of the Virgin, the text may suggest that the Virgin once more protected the City from its enemies.

7 Or: 'Prokonesos,' i.e. Marmara Island.

Now, on learning that the Saracens had been routed and that Leo reigned, the Sicilians betrayed Basil and the other officials to Paul, who had all of them decapitated on the spot as rebels. **14** Together with other *patrikioi*, the *patrikios* Niketas Xylinites made friends with Terbelis; this was achieved through letters, much money and gifts, and they urged him to go to war against Leo. However, some Bulgarians betrayed them and revealed their names to the emperor, who had them all killed by the sword. **15** The same Leo crowned Constantine, his son, on the tribune of the Hall of the Nineteen Couches.[1] **16** Leo also baptised Jews by force, with the result that henceforth Jews were called Montanists.[2] He also sent John of Damascus,[3] also known as Chrysorroas[4] (this was because of his wisdom), into exile, and he called him Mansour, that is, 'blasphemous.'[5] **17** He betrothed the daughter of the Chagan, the chief of the Scythians,[6] to his son Constantine, and had her converted to Christianity and renamed her Irene. Having been instructed in the Holy Scripture this girl came to excel in piety, and she became a critic of the impiety of others. **18** Because of the pope, Leo often committed unfriendly acts against Rome, and he ordered that the churches should pay a yearly tax. The Hagarenes also went to war against all Romania, and they took many prisoners and returned home. And there was a great earthquake that caused churches and houses[7] to collapse, and it also brought down the statue of Arkadios at the Xerolophos,[8] as well as the land walls of the City and of Nicomedia and Nicaea, and it made the sea recede from its boundaries in certain places. On learning that the walls had fallen, the emperor made a speech in which he said:

1 Δεκαεννέα Ἀκούβιτα: a reception hall (in the Great Palace) also used for formal dinners.

2 Montanism is a Christian heresy known since the second c. Theophanes has: 'In this year the emperor forced the Jews and the Montanists to accept baptism' (Mango/Scott 1997, p. 554).

3 Ca. 676–749, prominent defender of icons.

4 'golden flowing,' or 'of the Golden Stream' (so Mango/Scott 1997, p. 565).

5 'that is, blasphemous': or 'which is blasphemy.' As it stands, the passage is obscure. Much clearer is the corresponding passage in Theophanes: '... John, whom the impious emperor Constantine subjected to an annual anathema because of his pre-eminent orthodoxy and, instead of his paternal name, Mansour (which means 'redeemed'), he, in his Jewish manner, renamed the new teacher of the Church Manzeros' (Mango/Scott 1997, p. 578; for Μάνζηρος (Aramaic 'bastard') see Mango/Scott 1997, p. 579, n. 7).

6 I.e. the Chazar Chagan.

7 Greek οἴκους (large houses, palaces, institutions).

8 Cf. Chapter 96, § 1.

'You who live in the City are not able to rebuild the walls yourselves. So we have ordered the City governors to demand one *miliaresion* for each *solidus*; this money the state will collect and rebuild the wall.' From this the custom has prevailed to give the *dikerata*[1] to the City governors. **19** In the middle of all this the most abominable Leo gives up his soul, dying of dysentery.[2]

122 Constantine Kopronymos

Constantine, his son, called Kopronymos,[3] reigned for thirty-four years,[4] and he turned out to be a 'devious leopard, born of a most terrible lion; from the seed of a snake, a cobra and a flying serpent.'[5] **2** This emperor inherited both his father's throne and his impiety, and he distanced himself even more from God and the Mother of God and from all His saints. And starting with this, he devoted himself to magic and recklessness and the invocation of demons and the cutting up of intestines and other evil practices as well as to hunts and chariot races; thus he became a suitable instrument of the Antichrist. For he drifted into such extreme senselessness that he even published a general decree that no one at all should be called holy and that, whenever they were found, one should spit upon the bodily remains of holy men and not ask for their intercession ('for they have no power,' the impious man added). 'Nor [he added] should one invoke Mary's intercession (for she has no power), nor call her Mother of God.' To illustrate this, he took a pouch full of gold in his hand, and he showed it to everyone and asked: 'What is it worth?' And they said: '[So and so] much,' at which he emptied it of the gold and asked again: 'What is it worth?,' to which they answer: 'Nothing.' 'So,' he said, 'it is with Mary, too' (for the godless man did not deign to call her Mother of God). 'She deserved honour as long as she had Christ within her. But when she had given birth to Him, she was no

---

1 The nominal worth of the *miliaresion* would be 1/12 *solidus*. The *dikerata* mentioned should be understood as two carats per *solidus* (one carat = 1/24 *solidus*). In other words, the latter is another way of expressing the same ratio as that intended by the first. Cf. Mango/Scott 1997, p. 572 and 574, n. 6.

2 This is the typical death of an evil emperor.

3 See above, Chapter 121, § 7.

4 Constantine V reigned 741–775. Cf. for his reign Theophanes (Mango/Scott 1997, pp. 574–620).

5 This is partly reminiscent of Isaiah 14.29.

different from any other woman.' What blasphemy! Save us, Lord![1] **3** These attitudes caused no little despondency amongst the Christians, with the result that everyone came to hate the emperor, and they attached themselves to Artavasdos, who was a *kouropalates* and the emperor's brother-in-law. For it happened that Constantine went out against the Arabs in the region of Opsikion,[2] and Artavasdos was with him, and they watched each other suspiciously. At some point they clashed with each other, and Biser,[3] who was also the confidant of Constantine, was killed by Artavasdos, and Constantine fled in fear to Amorion. After this, terrible battles ensued between them. Artavasdos wrote to the *magistros* Theophanes, who was his friend and who took care of his interests in the City, and asked him to receive him. And, having been received by the *themata*, he was proclaimed emperor. [Artavasdos] having entered the City together with Anastasios, the false patriarch, all the people cursed Constantine and proclaimed Artavasdos as orthodox emperor. So Constantine arrived at Chrysopolis with his people, but, not achieving anything, he returned to Amorion. Artavasdos had the holy icons put up again everywhere, and the Church regained its earlier order. Holding the venerable Cross and standing in the ambo, Anastasios, the patriarch, swore: 'By Him who was nailed to this, Constantine the emperor said to me, that "you should not consider Christ, who was born from Mary, as the son of God, but as an ordinary man, [born] just as I was born from my mother [also called] Mary."' On hearing this, the people cursed Constantine. Artavasdos went out and started to levy an army. On learning this, Constantine moved against him and, joining battle with him, routs him. And Artavasdos reaches Kyzikos and takes refuge in the City. When Constantine reached Chalcedon he crossed to the Thracian side and, establishing himself at the land-wall, went as far as the Golden Gate and showed himself to the masses. Thereupon, Artavasdos opened the gates and joined battle again, but was decisively defeated. Since Constantine had taken control of the fleet, the City was struck by severe famine, with the result that a bushel[4] of barley was sold for twelve *solidi*, and other commodities at similar prices. Since people were dying and wasting away, Artavasdos was forced to release them so that they could leave the City.

---

1 In this passage, Constantine and the iconoclasts are probably accused of more than they ever stood for.

2 A *thema* in north-western Asia Minor.

3 This man (Biser or Bishr) is mentioned several times in Theophanes (for this passage see Mango/Scott 1997, p. 575; see also p. 556, n. 2, etc.).

4 μόδιος (equalling approx. seventeen litres).

Niketas, the son of Artavasdos, gathered a sufficient force and went as far as Chrysopolis, where the emperor crossed over and pursued him and, when he caught up with him, had Niketas arrested and put into fetters. Arriving at the City, Constantine showed Niketas to his father through the wall. Then suddenly, having arranged his men in battle-order he entered the City through the land-wall and apprehended Artavasdos and the *patrikios* Vaktangios. He had Artavasdos blinded, together with his two sons; but as for Vaktangios, he had his hands and feet cut off and beheaded him in the Kynegion, and he had many others of the leading men killed and their belongings confiscated. Having organised chariot races, the emperor brought in Artavasdos together with his sons as well as the patriarch Anastasios and his friends. The patriarch was led in the procession, sitting on a donkey and facing backwards. For, once, when he was a *synkellos*,[1] he had been walking behind Germanos the patriarch, and he had stepped on his *omophorion*. And Germanos had turned around and said to him: 'Don't hurry, the Diippion[2] is waiting for you.' After having thus terrified him, Constantine restored Anastasios to the patriarchal throne, for the patriarch sympathised with him in matters of the creed.

4 During Constantine's reign a great many signs began to appear out of nowhere on people's clothes, and on the churches' holy vestments there appeared very many crosses dripping with olive oil, and so the Divine wrath in the form of bubonic plague struck, not only the inhabitants of the City, but also those in the surrounding areas, causing terrible devastation. And in addition many people were subject to hallucinations and terrible portents, and on seeing these they died. Thus entire households were wiped out, and there were not enough people to bury the dead. When every house was thus destroyed because of the impiety of the tyrant, the emperor took all the wealth belonging to the City's householders and brought it to the palace and stored it there. The wrath even reached the impious Anastasios, and he ends his life by the most pitiable ailment, the so-called *chordapsos*.[3] **5** When the upstart[4] hears that the Saracens are fighting each other, he marches out to Syria, and he occupied Germanikeia, Theodosioupolis and Melitene and made everyone there a prisoner.[5] And using the fore-mentioned plague as a

---

1 Belonging to the patriarch's staff as an adviser.
2 The gates of the hippodrome in Constantinople.
3 A bowel disease. This is of course a symbolic punishment.
4 I.e. the emperor (Greek τύραννος).
5 The cities in question are present-day Kahramanmaraş (Germanicia Caesarea), Erzurum, and Malatya, all in East Anatolia (Turkey). They had been lost by the Byzantines in the seventh c.

pretext, he took his relatives, who were Armenians and Syrians and heretics, and resettled them in Byzantium and in Thrace. These people keep the heresy of the upstart alive to the present day.[1] **6** At this time a son was born to the emperor Constantine from the Chagan's daughter, the Chazar woman; he was named Leo.[2] **7** Being elated in his mind because of the victory he had achieved, the godless man gathers a synod against the holy icons in the Blachernai and, in defiance of the prescriptions, he ascended the ambo.[3] Holding Constantine, bishop of Sylaion, by the hand, he pronounced the following: 'Long live Constantine, the ecumenical patriarch!' During this synod the shameless priests talked a lot of nonsense about the Lord, and they stretched their abominable hands into the air and shouted the following miserable words: 'Today salvation comes to the world, for you, emperor, have delivered us from the idols.' Such did the unholy traffickers of Christ do. **8** Shortly afterwards the emperor committed deeds worthy of himself against the patriarch. For, when the avenging spirit[4] learnt that the patriarch had told many people that the emperor had said to him, 'Christ is not God; therefore I do not consider Mary to have given birth to God,' he [the emperor] became mad with rage against him [the patriarch] for having disclosed his secret, and inflicted many blows on him and paraded him in front of the people during the chariot races, and had him spat at and dragged away.[5] Then, having detained him, he sends *patrikioi* to him and says: 'What do you say now about our belief and about the synod which we convened?' Now the patriarch, who was totally confused in his mind and who thought that he would be able to placate the emperor again, answered: 'You believe rightly and rightly did you convene the synod.' But they laughed at this and said to him, that 'this is precisely the thing we wanted to hear from your foul mouth.' And at once they took him away and had him beheaded and dumped his body in the Pelagios,[6] where formerly there had been a church of the holy martyr Pelagios. This church the God-hated emperor had had torn down, and he had made a

---

1 This was probably written down in the ninth c. Cf. below, § 13, with another example of the tendency to refer back from the viewpoint of 'today.'

2 This is emperor Leo IV, born 750.

3 This is the 754 iconoclast synod of Hieria, the concluding session of which took place in the Blachernai.

4 ἀλάστωρ, i.e. the emperor.

5 The Greek is slightly incoherent.

6 Ta Pelagiou, i.e. (perhaps) the 'district/quarter (or 'ditch': so Mango/Scott 1997, p. 610) of Pelagios (Pelagion).'

burial place for criminals there and called it Pelagios. And in the place of Constantine he has Niketas, who was a eunuch and a Slav, appointed patriarch. **9** Likewise, he had the holy man Peter and the pious Stephen, who came from Mt Auxentios Theophoros,[1] killed, and he ordered that they should be dragged to the Pelagios and dumped there. And many other leaders and monks he delivered to a terrible death on account of the holy icons. **10** The emperor went to war against the Bulgarians by land and by sea and, having routed them, he entered the City in arms, carrying the enemies' weapons, and he paraded the Bulgarians in fetters in a triumphal procession. **11** At this time a winter storm came, and there was such a great, bitter cold that the northern sea of the Pontos[2] became hard as stone for a distance of a hundred miles, and the open sea froze to ice to a depth of thirty cubits. When it snowed upon this, the surface towered up for another twenty cubits, so that the sea assumed the shape of dry land and wild and tame animals could walk over the cold. In the month of February, through the Providence of God, this sea-water was split into very many mountain-like pieces and, by the force of the winds, it was brought down to the Hieron and then through the Stenon[3] to the City, and from there it reached the islands and came to Abydos, and it filled all the coast-line, bringing also different kinds of animals along which were stuck in it. Because of this, anyone who wanted to could pass on foot, as if on land, from Sophianai to St Mamas and into the City, and from there to Chrysopolis.[4] One of these large pieces crashed into the City wall, which resonated from its foundations together with the adjacent buildings on the inside and, when this piece was split into three, it surrounded the City from Mangana to Boosphorion[5] and reached much higher than the walls. On seeing this, the inhabitants of the City lamented inconsolably. **12** In the month of April, a swarm of stars passed in the sky, and they fell down to earth in such a way that those watching thought this was the end of the world. **13** The emperor went to

---

1 This is St Stephen the Younger, who lived at Mt Auxentios and also founded a monastery there. Whatever the truth was, later generations considered him one of the main victims of iconoclasm.

2 I.e. the Black Sea.

3 Stenon ('narrow') denotes the Straits of the Bosphorus, whereas Hieron denotes the beginning of the Straits at the Black Sea.

4 I.e. from the Asian side of the Bosphorus to the European, and from there to the City centre and over to the Asian side along the Marmara Sea.

5 I.e. round the coastline of the Acropolis, below present-day Topkapi (presuming that Boosphorion is the same as the Prosphorion harbour (cf. Mango/Scott 1997, p. 602, n. 14)).

war against the Bulgarians with the navy as well as the army, and he sent forces to Achelon.[1] However, a violent wind started to blow, and the ships were destroyed. On learning this, the Bulgarians join battle with them, and the emperor was terribly defeated and returned humiliated. For even until today the bones of those killed at Achelon bear evident witness to the defeat.[2] **14** This man, hated by God,[3] had the earthly remains of many saints burnt, and some of them he handed over to the sea. Among the latter was the body of St Euphemia and, since he was not able to stand the sight of how sweet oil gushed forth from it, he consigned it, coffin and all, to the depths of the sea. However, the body arrived safely at the island of Lemnos and was found there by the inhabitants through a divine revelation. The holy and all-praiseworthy woman's church he made into an *armamenton*[4] and a deposit for dung. During the reign of Constantine and Irene, the body of the same all-praiseworthy woman was brought back to the City with a great display of honour.[5] **15** This emperor promoted two of his sons to caesars, Nikephoros and Christopher, and his son Niketas to *nobelissimos*.[6] When Irene came from Athens to the imperial City accompanied by *dromones*, the emperor joined her in marriage to his son Leo, and he crowned them in the Church of St Stephen with the imperial crown as well as the crown of matrimony.[7] **16** The emperor had secretly made friends in Bulgaria, and these friends informed him about everything that their ruler planned. These men reveal to the emperor: 'The lord of Bulgaria sends people to imprison the inhabitants of Berzetia.'[8] The emperor made a show of going to war against the Arabs, and he sent messengers of peace towards Bulgaria. He then gathered the whole army together with the *tagmata* and, without having made a declaration of war, he fell upon the Bulgarians and routed them and achieved a great victory.[9] Then he returned to the City

1 Or: 'Anchialos,' present-day Pomorie in Bulgaria.
2 Another reference back from 'today' (cf. above, § 5). The battle took place in the 760s.
3 Or: 'God-hating.'
4 Probably 'stable' (cf. above, Chapter 108, § 6, where the same term seems to stand for an 'arsenal').
5 Yet another reference back from 'today' (cf. above, §§ 5 and 13). Constantine and Irene reigned, more or less conjointly, 780–797. Their rule saw a relaxation of iconoclasm (cf. below, Chapter 124, esp. § 10).
6 An honorary title given to members of the imperial family.
7 Here ends Nikephoros' *Short History* (cf. Introduction).
8 The territory, or city, of a Slavonic tribe living in Macedonia or Thessaly (see Mango/Scott 1997, p. 618, n. 6).
9 According to Theophanes (Mango/Scott 1997, p. 617) this was in 772/773.

and, wearing his armour, celebrated a triumph, and he called this war 'the noble war,' since no enemy had stood up against him and there had been no loss of Roman lives. **17** On learning that the emperor receives information from his own people about his plans, the Bulgarian chief, Telerichos, writes a deceitful letter to the emperor to the effect: 'I am planning to escape and to come to you, so that you with my help can subdue the whole of Bulgaria. Therefore send me a pledge of security and tell me who your friends here are, so that I can encourage them to come with me.' Being caught in stupidity and madness, the emperor wrote down the names of his informants and, having learnt them, Telerichos handed all of them over to a terrible death. On hearing this, Constantine pulled out his beard. **18** Setting out once again to campaign against the Bulgarians, the emperor was afflicted dreadfully by carbuncles in his legs and by a violent and burning fever. He returned to Arkadioupolis on a stretcher, and from there he came to Selymbria and, travelling by boat as far as the fortress of Strongyle,[1] he died there in body and soul, crying out and saying: 'While still alive, I have been handed over to the unquenchable fire because of the Mother of God, Mary. But from now on let her be honoured and hymned, for she is in truth the mother of God.' Shouting this and calling upon Mary, the Mother of God, and exhorting everyone else and expressing as his belief that the eternal virgin should be honoured and given special reverence as the Mother of God, he gave up his wretched soul in a terrible and painful way.[2]

123 Leo, the Son of the Chazar Woman

Leo, his son by the Chazar woman, reigned for five years.[3] **2** He started to lay hands upon the great riches left by his father. This he did in order to placate the ruling class and so as to appear pious in front of the people and as a friend of the Mother of God and the monks. He even made some monks metropolitans of episcopal sees.[4] **3** Then, the leaders of the *themata* entered

---

1 Selymbria (present-day Silivri), Arkadioupolis (Lüleburgaz) and Strongyle (or 'Round Castle,' also known as Kyklobion) are all in Byzantine Thrace (Kyklobion being at Hebdomon, only seven miles from the city centre).

2 This is a prime example of the bad death of an evil emperor.

3 Leo IV reigned 775–780. Cf. for his reign Theophanes (Mango/Scott 1997, pp. 620–626).

4 Thus, even though Leo promoted the careers of some monks, this hints at one aspect of iconoclasm, viz. as that of a conflict with monasticism.

the City together with a great crowd, and they begged him to make his son Constantine emperor. But he, who was afraid of his brothers, declared to them: 'I have only one son, and I fear to do so, lest death should come to me and you put him, who is only a small child, to death and appoint someone else instead of him.' But they assured him with terrible oaths that they would not accept any emperor other than his son. From Palm Sunday until Holy Thursday they kept asking for this, and on Good Friday he ordered them to swear on the Holy Cross. And those in charge of the *themata* and of the *tagmata* stationed in the City together with all the citizens swore not to accept any emperor but Leo and Constantine and their seed. **4** And on the Great Sabbath[1] he made his brother Eudokimos a *nobelissimos*, and he came in procession together with two caesars and three *nobelissimoi* and the young Constantine to the Great Church and, having made the customary ceremonies, he ascended the ambo together with his son and the patriarch. When the whole people entered and they had deposited their documents [with their signatures] on the altar, the emperor said: 'Behold! From the church and the hands of Christ you receive my son.' And the people cried: 'Son of God, be our witness that we receive the lord Constantine from Your hand to be emperor, and that we will guard him and die for him!' And on the following day, Easter Sunday, in the presence of all the people, Constantine was crowned in the hippodrome by his father and the patriarch. And the two emperors came to church in procession together with the two caesars and the three *nobelissimoi*. **5** The Arabs went out from their country, and the emperor sent armed forces against them and achieved a great victory, and he went out to Sophianai and made a *maioumas*[2] and celebrated the victory. For it was customary that the emperor should receive the spoils there. **6** When the patriarch Niketas, the Slav, had died, the venerable Paul, a worthy man, respected for words and deeds, was appointed. **7** The emperor Leo was informed that the *papias*[3] of the palace, Theophanes, together with three *koubikoularioi*, reveres and worships the holy icons. On hearing this, the emperor revealed the evil hidden in him, and he had them mercilessly flogged and made into confessors by having them killed in secret. **8** Aaron, the king of the Arabs, went out to the *themata* and seized several fortresses, and he took prisoners and returned home.[4] **9** The

1 Easter Saturday of 776.
2 A popular festival originating from Syria, see Mango/Scott 1997, p. 623.
3 Responsible for the security and maintenance of the palace.
4 I.e. Arab forces entered Byzantine territory. Aaron is the (fifth) Abbasid caliph Harun al-Rashid.

same Leo was obsessed with precious stones, and he took a fancy to the crown of Maurice, and he took it and wore it in a procession.[1] On his return [to the palace] his head was severely affected by carbuncles, and he was struck by a most violent fever from which he wasted away and died, earning the appropriate reward for his sacrilege.[2]

124 Constantine

Constantine reigned for ten years together with his mother Irene.[3] During their rule orthodoxy[4] and the proper ecclesiastical order were restored. **2** When Irene had reigned for forty days together with her son, some men in high office hailed the caesar Nikephoros, her husband's brother, as emperor. These people she had flogged and exiled to different places, with their property confiscated. But her husband's brothers, who were caesars and *nobelissimoi*, she had tonsured, and she forced them to take holy orders and administer communion to the people during the festival of Christ's birth. During this festival she also went forth in public in the manner of an empress together with her son, and she offered the Church the crown that had been taken away by her husband;[5] this crown had now been adorned with pearls. **3** A man who was digging at the Long Wall found a coffin and, when he opened it, he saw a large man lying in it, and there were letters carved into the coffin saying: 'Christ will be born from the Virgin Mary, and I believe in him. During the time of the emperors Constantine and Irene you, O sun, will see me again.' **4** Irene sent a message to Karoulos, the king of the Franks, to arrange the betrothal of his daughter to her son.[6] However, this came to nothing because of envy. Instead, Irene brought a girl from Armeniakon

1 On the crown cf. above, Chapter 107, § 10.

2 This is yet another example of the death of an evil emperor.

3 This refers to the ten years (780–790) of Constantine VI's regency council, headed by Irene, his mother, and Staurakios. Constantine then reigned in his own right until 792, and then jointly with Irene until 797, when he was dethroned and blinded. This chapter, such as it is, covers the whole period until Nikephoros I and his accession to the throne in 802 (i.e. Irene is not accorded a chapter of her own, and the years 790–797 are not accounted for in the overall chronology). Cf. for Constantine's and Irene's ten-year reign Theophanes, Mango/Scott 1997, pp. 626–640; for the years 790–797, Mango/Scott 1997, pp. 640–650; and for the years 797–802, when Irene reigned alone, Mango/Scott 1997, pp. 650–654.

4 εὐσέβεια.

5 I.e. the crown of Maurice, cf. above, Chapter 123, § 9.

6 The King of the Franks was Charlemagne, and the name of this daughter was Rotrude.

named Mary and united her in marriage to her son Constantine. This was against the express wish of Constantine because of the tie he had with Karoulos' daughter.[1] **5** Aaron, the leader of the Arabs,[2] came against the City with great forces and camped in Chrysopolis. But the emperor sent people and seized [the region of] Lake Van, and for this reason Aaron sues for peace. When journeying to Aaron over this matter, Peter the *magistros* and Staurakios the logothete and very many others in high office were seized for no reason and put in chains.[3] Because of this, the inhabitants of the City were forced to give a great amount of gifts, and so they received the hostages back, and the Arabs made peace and returned home. **6** Irene sent Staurakios the logothete with a great force against the Slav tribes and subdued them all and made them pay tribute to the empire. Accompanied by musical instruments, the emperor also went out to Thrace together with his mother and very many people. And he went as far as Beroia, and his mother had it rebuilt and she renamed it Irenopolis. She[4] also had Anchialos[5] rebuilt, and so they returned in good cheer. **7** The patriarch Paul fell ill and, since he had forebodings that he was about to leave this world, he left his throne and went to the Floros monastery and was tonsured. The emperor then came to him together with his mother, and he wanted to know the reason for his retirement. At this Paul, with many tears in his eyes, said: 'I wish I had never sat on the throne of the Church while it was in secession from the other holy thrones and subject to *anathema.*' On hearing this, the emperors returned home gloomy and downcast, but they sent *patrikioi* to Paul to hear what he had to say. **8** To these people Paul spoke freely and at the end of his explanation he said: 'Unless an ecumenical synod is convened and the error of your belief is corrected, you have no chance of salvation.' And they say to him: 'But why did you sign the document at your consecration, to the effect that one should not worship the holy icons?' He says: 'It is precisely for this reason that I cry and resort to repentance and pray that God may not punish me as a priest and a shepherd. For I have kept quiet until now and have not preached the truth out of fear of your madness.' On hearing this they left him, discussing at length amongst themselves. In this way, renouncing the abominable heresy and preaching the word of truth, he passed away peacefully, leaving the emperors and the pious people in great sorrow. For

---

1 They had not met, of course.
2 Harun al-Rashid.
3 The Greek text seems corrupt, and the translation is very hypothetical.
4 'She': or, possibly, 'he.'
5 I.e. the Achelon mentioned above, Chapter 122, § 13.

he was a most venerable man, adorned with every virtue. In his stead Tarasios, the former *asekretis*,[1] was elected. **9** By imperial command, which came into effect upon the suggestion and exhortation of Tarasios the patriarch, all bishops of Rome and the other holy thrones as well as those under the imperial City were gathered in the Church of the Holy Apostles in order to hold a synod on the worship of the holy icons. But, while they were reading out loud to the emperors and all the people the passages from the divine scriptures pertinent to the synod, the *scholarioi*[2] loyal to Constantine Kopronymos attacked them, drawing their swords and dissolving the gathering. At once the emperors had these men disarmed and removed from the City on pretext of a festival at Malagina,[3] and they were forced to return to their hometowns in dishonour. **10** The pious Tarasios is sent with the afore-mentioned bishops to Nicaea, and the synod is convened, and so the Church regained its old order.[4] For this second meeting 350 fathers convened in Nicaea, and they decreed that the icons and the Cross should be revered. **11** Being driven by envy and a desire to run the state on their own, some friends of the empress Irene estranged the mother from the son and persuaded her that 'it is not decided by God that your son should rule. It is really yours, the empire.'[5] By which she, being a woman, was fooled (she was also fond of power), and she was convinced in her own mind that this was so. But the emperor, who was twenty years of age and a very vigorous man, and able in military matters, fretted at his lack of power; and so he started to plot against his mother. On being told this by Staurakios, Irene had all the intimates of the emperor flogged and exiled. Peter the *magistros* and the *patrikios* Theodore Kamoulianos, and others in high office she had exiled in fortresses,[6] and she reproached her son greatly and isolated him, and she made all the army and the men in high office swear, that 'as long as you live, we will not accept your son as ruler.' **12** The people of Armeniakon were the only ones not to accept this, and they continued to hail Constantine together with Irene as before. Irene sent Alexios the *droungarios* of the *vigla*,[7] with

---

1 Secretary in the imperial chancery (here: former *asekretis*, Greek ἀπὸ ἀσεκρέτων).

2 Imperial palace guards (cf. *domestikos* of the *scholai* (see Chapter 130, § 22)).

3 Perhaps east of Nicaea (see Mango/Scott 1997, p. 636, n. 4, with further references).

4 This is the Second Council of Nicaea (or Seventh Ecumenical Council) that took place in 787 and restored the veneration of icons.

5 Or: 'the power.'

6 I.e. under maximum security, well away from the capital.

7 This *droungarios* was the commander of an elite unit (*tagma*) devoted to the protection of the emperor's person.

the by-name Mousele, to persuade them, but they detained him and made him their leader, keeping their own *strategos* imprisoned, and they hailed Constantine alone. On learning this, the people of the other *themata* did the same: it was the devil who suggested such denial and perjury to the people. **13** Irene was frightened by the people's impulsive action and so sent her son to the army. But the soldiers hailed him as emperor and renounced his mother, and they confirmed Alexios as the *strategos* of Armeniakon. On returning to the City, the emperor showed no mercy and had Staurakios and Aetios, the *protospatharioi*,[1] who were intimates of Irene, flogged and exiled, and did the same with the other eunuchs belonging to her entourage. But Irene he placed securely in the Eleutherios monastery,[2] which she had built herself and where she had also hidden a great amount of money. **14** There was also a fire, and the hall[3] of the patriarchate, the so-called Thomaitis, was burnt down, as well as the chambers beneath it, in which the originals of all the writings of John Chrysostom were stored. The fire went as far as the Milion[4] and the *quaestor*'s office, and it raged in all directions until it had burnt everything down. **15** The emperor went out against the Bulgarians and ravaged their country and defeated them and returned home. Likewise he went with a great army against the Arabs at Tarsos and took many prisoners and returned home. **16** Asked to do so by his mother herself and by many in high office, the emperor once again proclaims his mother empress, and he ordered everyone to hail 'Constantine *and* Irene,' as before. To this everyone agrees, except the people of Armeniakon; these rebel and ask for Alexios Mousele, whom the emperor had honoured with the title of *patrikios* and had kept with him. Because he was asked for in this way, and because of some rumour, which he had heard, to the effect that Alexios would become emperor, the emperor had Alexios flogged and tonsured and confined to prison. **17** Wanting to make Nikephoros, the former caesar, emperor, the *tagmata* and the *themata* gathered in the City. On learning this, the emperor sent for all[5] the sons of his grandfather Constantine and took them to St Mamas, and he had Nikephoros blinded in a terrible way, and had the tongues of Christopher, Niketas, Anthimos and Eudokimos cut out.

---

1 'first spatha-bearer' (*spatha* being a kind of sword): a dignity ranking below *patrikios*.

2 Or: 'house/institution' (Greek οἶκος), in the City; cf. below, § 24, where what should be the same is referred to as the 'Eleutherios palace.'

3 τρίκλινος.

4 A monument close to St Sophia from which distances in the empire were calculated.

5 'all': the Greek text has ἀμφοτέρους ('both'), which does not seem possible.

Together with these, he also blinded Alexios Mousele; this was upon his mother's advice. The people of Armeniakon he apprehended and, having routed their leaders in battle, he had them punished, tattooing in black on their foreheads: 'Traitor from Armeniakon'; and he exiled them to Sicily and other islands. **18** The emperor hated his wife Mary and, acting on the suggestion of his mother, who coveted the throne and who wished to make him hated, he forced Mary to become a nun. After this he was illegally betrothed to the *koubikoularia* Theodote, and he crowned her.[1] Plato, the *hegoumenos* of the Sakoudion monastery, and others split from the patriarch because of the emperor's second marriage, and on these people the emperor inflicted much sorrow.[2] But his mother protected them since they hated her son. **19** Kardamos, the lord of Bulgaria, wrote to the emperor: 'Either pay me tribute, or I will come to the Golden Gate.' The emperor put horse dung in a cloth and sent it to the Bulgarian lord with the words: 'I send you the tribute which is fitting to you. You are an old man, and I do not want you to exert yourself and come here. Therefore, I will come to you.' Then the emperor gathered a force and went out and chased Kardamos back to his country. **20** His mother flattered everyone and attracted people to her side by promising gifts to them, and she bided a suitable day for assuming absolute power. When the emperor went out against the Arabs, and the people had been prepared to seize him according to his mother's plan and because of the lawlessness of the woman[3] (for which she[4] became hated), the nobles convince him to return to the City; this they did on the instigation of his mother. Upon his arrival at the palace (his mother was not present), the nobles and his mother's counsellors shut him into the Porphyra,[5] in which he had been born, and they blind him in a terrible way, so as to be past healing, almost killing him.[6] Upon this, the sun was darkened for seventeen days, so

---

1 She was crowned with the crown of marriage and also proclaimed *augusta*.

2 This is the so-called Moechian controversy.

3 'the woman' (τῆς γυναικός): or 'his wife,' i.e. Theodote, in which case the intended meaning (although this is not clearly put in the Greek) may be 'because of the illegality of their marriage.'

4 'she': or, possibly, 'he.'

5 I.e. 'Purple (building, or chamber),' in which imperial children were born.

6 'almost killing him': or 'so as to kill him.' However, according to Chapter 125, § 3, he was alive early in Nikephoros' reign, and in Chapter 130, § 42, we are told where he lived after being blinded. Also, in Chapter 129, § 4, Thomas the Slav (whose rebellion took place 821–822) is said to have been able to claim to be none other than Constantine. On the problem of the actual date of Constantine's death see Mango/Scott 1997, p. 649f., n. 10, with further references.

that ships lost their way and everyone said that 'the sun was darkened because of the blinding of the emperor.' But behold God's inscrutable decisions! For, Constantine himself is blinded in the same month, on the very day five years after he had had his own uncles and Alexios Mousele blinded. **21** Thus Irene exercised power alone.[1] But her husband's brothers rebelled against her, and she exiled them to Athens. However, even there they made plans about regaining power, and therefore they were killed by the locals. In this way the family of the abominable Constantine[2] disappeared. **22** On the second day of Easter the empress went out for the customary procession to the Church of the Holy Apostles, and in the evening she showed herself riding in a chariot drawn by four white horses held by *patrikioi*, and she distributed a lot of largesse in the Mese. **23** While the empress was ill, it was announced to her: 'Staurakios is planning a rebellion against you.' At this, she held a *selention* in Justinian's *triklinos*, and decreed that none of the magistrates should have anything to do with Staurakios. Aetios, who was *paradynasteuon*[3] with Staurakios and who was jealous of him, managed to transfer Staraukios' power to himself. **24** In this situation, Nikephoros, *patrikios* and *genikos*, staged a coup against the empress relying on the counsel of the *patrikios* Niketas and Sisinios (these two were brothers, the treacherous and deceitful Triphyllioi), as well as of the *patrikios* Leo, called Sarantapechos, and the *patrikios* Gregory, called Mousoulakios, as well as some other people in high office. And having come to the Chalke Gate at the fourth hour of the night they greeted the guards by saying that they had been sent by the *augusta*, and they entered the palace and, while it was still night, they spread the word of Nikephoros' accession in all the City, and they placed guards at the Eleutherios palace[4] in order to keep Irene under surveillance. When the morning came, they sent for her and locked her up in the Great Palace, and so the wretched man [Nikephoros] came to the church in a procession in order to be crowned.

---

1 This was in 797. From this point, a chapter headed by Irene's name would have been expected.

2 Probably Constantine V, singled out, no doubt, for special mention as a kind of chief exponent of iconoclasm.

3 Vague title for a person with considerable influence with the emperor and chosen by him to assist him in ruling.

4 Cf. above, § 13.

125 Nikephoros

Nikephoros reigned for eight years.[1] The masses cursed the man who crowned[2] as well as the man who was crowned. **2** Feigning goodness, Nikephoros spoke words of consolation to the empress and said that he would give her any comfort if she revealed to him where her treasures were. But she gave a sensible answer, telling the treacherous slave of yesterday who had now become an usurper: 'I believe, my good man, that it was God Who promoted me to this empire, whereas I attribute my downfall to my own sins. In all this, may the name of the Lord be praised. However, you should not ignore the plots against you, of which I have been informed. If I did support these, I could easily have you killed. But I have decided to have nothing to do with all this, partly because I trust your oaths, partly in order to spare you, and I rather hand you over to God, through Whom emperors reign and rulers wield their power. And in the present situation, I make obeisance to you on the supposition that you are pious and have been made an emperor by God, and I ask you to spare me because of my weakness and, as a consolation for my incomparable misfortune, to let me have the Eleutherios palace which I have built.' But he said: 'If you want this to happen, you will have to assure me by oath that you will not conceal any treasure; then I will give you every comfort.' She assured him this and showed him great wealth. However, having got what he wanted, Nikephoros at once exiled her to the island of Prinkipos, where she had built a monastery. Seeing that all the people in high office were vexed at him because of his greed, Nikephoros became frightened and, even though it was very severe winter weather, he exiled the same Irene to the island of Lesbos to be kept under guard there. **3** He turned to Constantine, Irene's son,[3] who also showed him the treasure, which had been put behind marble slabs; this is the treasure which is now at the Sigma.[4] **4** The same Nikephoros had Niketas Triphyllios murdered by poison. **5** The *patrikios* Bardanes, *strategos* of the Anatolikon, named 'the Turk,' was proclaimed emperor by the overseas[5] *themata*.

1 Nikephoros reigned 1 November 802–26 July 811. Cf. for his reign Theophanes (Mango/Scott 1997, pp. 654–677).

2 I.e. the patriarch Tarasios.

3 See above, Chapter 124, § 20, on the question of the date of Constantine's death.

4 This could either be a place in the Great Palace (see Chapter 130, § 36) or the place of an intersection of one of the main roads leading out of the city (towards the Xylokerkos Gate). The former seems more likely.

5 Or: 'provincial,' or 'Asiatic' (τῶν περατικῶν θεμάτων).

He himself firmly refused to listen to this but, seeing that he could not avoid it, he went with an armed force to Chrysopolis; then, fearing before God that Christians would be slaughtered for his sake, he asked for, and received, a pledge of safe conduct from Nikephoros, and without the knowledge of his people he went in the middle of the night to the Herakleios monastery in the Katabolos,[1] and was made a monk without delay. Then, when he came in the imperial *chelandion*,[2] which had been sent for him, to the island of Prote[3] and to the monastery which he himself had had prepared, he is blinded by some men from Lycaonia acting at the behest of the emperor. When this had come to pass, the emperor, feigning, as the hypocrite he was, that he was struck with sorrow, assured everyone by oath that he was innocent of this deed. **6** During Nikephoros' reign the leader of the Saracens[4] went out to Amorion. Nikephoros advanced as far as Dorylaion[5] and made the following speech to the *protosymboulos*:[6] 'Why do you take pleasure in injustice and bloodshed, and why are you not content with your own country but transgress ancient boundaries, sanctioned by our fathers?[7] What divine prophet taught you to do this? Did not Muhammed, your prophet, encourage you to consider the Christian your brother and call him so? For, surely, God, the Creator of all, Who provides for both kinds,[8] does not delight in the unjust shedding of human blood?[9] May this not happen! Or is it because of a lack of silver and gold and the rest that you have marched out to do an injustice to those who have done no injustice to you? Yet you have in abundance the most beautiful and precious things—things that seem most desirable to us. But, if you are in need of anything that we have, we will at once give it to you as an act of friendship. Let us not, like immortals[10] or godless people, go to war with each other, and let us not out of envy

1 This is in Bithynia, at the Marmara Sea, not far from (present-day) Bursa (cf. Mango/ Scott 1997, p. 647, n. 6).

2 A galley warship.

3 One of the Princes' Islands close to Constantinople in the Marmara Sea, today Kınalıada.

4 This is Muhammed ibn Harun al-Amin, (sixth) Abbasid caliph (reigned 809–813).

5 In Anatolia, close to present-day Eskişehir.

6 I.e. the caliph.

7 This speech bears resemblance to that of Romanos I before Symeon the Bulgarian in 924 (see below, Chapter 136, §§ 35–36).

8 I.e. Christians and Moslems.

9 Or: 'For, surely, God, the Creator and Curator of all things, does not delight in the unjust shedding of anyone's blood?'

10 I.e. the ancient gods as depicted in pagan literature.

imitate the demons' war with the humans. For we know that in a little while, we will die and come before an impartial judge, who will give everyone retribution according to his acts.' The emperor Nikephoros sent this message to him together with some gifts, and the Arab was delighted and sent very many wondrous gifts in return and so went home in peace, in great admiration of Nikephoros' good sense.[1] **7** When Irene died of sorrow and despondency in exile in the island of Lesbos, where she had been kept under surveillance, the emperor had her body transferred to the monastery at Prinkipos, which she had built herself. For she was very pious and virtuous, and she built many guesthouses, and homes for the elderly, and monasteries, and she decreed the remission of taxes[2] and many other good deeds. **8** The emperor crowned his son Staurakios, who was an ugly and simple-minded person. **9** Also, the most holy bishop Tarasios departed from life and the most saintly Nikephoros is appointed patriarch instead of him.[3] **10** The emperor went to war against the Bulgarians and defeated them decisively. He even set fire to the so-called palace[4] of their leader Krum. And even though Krum pleaded for this ('let this be sufficient for you, emperor'), Nikephoros, because of his great greed, did not allow any discussion of a peace treaty. At this the barbarian was angered, and fenced off the entrances and exits to the land with wooden fortifications, and two days later he gathered people and attacked the emperor's tent and killed him and all the men who were with him. He cut off Nikephoros' head and put it on a stake. Afterwards, he laid bare the bone of the skull and plated it all around with silver and ordered the leaders of the Bulgarians to drink from it, and he triumphed over his enemy for being insatiable and for not wanting peace. **11** As some people said, Nikephoros killed many Christians because of his greed and love of money. For he augmented the taxes for his subjects, and he offered public office for sale to interested parties. And the man who paid the greatest sum in gold was considered worthy of being promoted to office. Nikephoros also invented what they call *chartiatika*.[5] In fact, it seems that almost everything that is evil and painful, it was he who devised it, in order to harm the Christians.

1 Even an evil emperor can show good sense—and does so occasionally, especially in a setting like this.
2 In contrast with Nikephoros, see below, § 11.
3 This was in 806.
4 τὴν λεγομένην αὐλήν.
5 An administrative tax, cf. Mango/Scott 1997, p. 669, n. 6.

126 Staurakios, his Son

Staurakios, his son, reigned for one year and two months.[1] **2** He had been wounded in his right thigh during the war, and returned to the City on a stretcher. Because of his wound he lay in the palace and was unable to go out. **3** He planned to blind his brother-in-law Michael, the *kouropalates*, and leave the throne to his wife. Then Michael, his brother-in-law, is suddenly proclaimed emperor in the hippodrome by the Senate and the *tagmata*, because Staurakios was already despaired of. **4** At once on learning this, Staurakios donned the monastic habit together with his wife Theophano, and he died in the monastery called [Ta] Braka[2] and was buried in the monastery of the Satyr.[3]

127 The Most Pious Michael Ragabe[4]

The most pious Michael reigned for two years.[5] He was crowned by the patriarch Nikephoros, and he gave fifty *litrai* of gold[6] to the patriarch and twenty-five *litrai* to the clergy. For he was a generous and magnanimous man, and he offered comfort to those to whom [the emperor] Nikephoros had done injustice by his greed. **2** He also crowned Prokopia, his wife, and he presented the Senate with many gifts, and he likewise crowned Theophylaktos, his son, on the ambo of the church, having offered very many holy objects to the Great Church. **3** Krum, the leader of the Bulgarians, wrote concerning peace, demanding much tribute. But the emperor listened to bad advice and did not embrace the peace. Michael was in every respect a good man and of a kindly disposition, but totally without guidance in matters of administration and a slave to the opinions of worthless people without military experience. Therefore, when he goes to war against the

---

1 Staurakios reigned 28 July–1 October 811. Cf. to his reign Theophanes (Mango/Scott 1997, pp. 674–677), and Skylitzes (Wortley 2010, p. 4).

2 Or: 'Hebraika'; it is not known where this is (see Mango/Scott 1997, p. 680, n. 3, and Wortley 2010, p. 4, n. 1).

3 On the Asian shore close to the Princes' Islands.

4 Or: 'Rangabe.'

5 Michael I reigned 811–813. Cf. to his reign Theophanes (Mango/Scott 1997, pp. 677–688), and Skylitzes (Wortley 2010, pp. 4–14).

6 One *litra* (pound) is equivalent in weight to seventy-two *solidi*, i.e. a little more than 300 g of gold.

Bulgarians and returns after a major defeat, Leo, a *patrikios* and *strategos* of the Anatolikon, is proclaimed emperor; this is done in the Kampos tou tribounaliou by the people and the leading men. **4** And, on hearing this, Michael dressed in the monastic habit together with his wife and children. He is confined to the island close to the City,[1] where he also died.

128 Leo, the Armenian and Apostate

Leo, the Armenian and apostate,[2] ruled for seven years and five months.[3] Having given a guarantee in writing of his own orthodoxy, he was crowned by the patriarch Nikephoros. **2** The new Senacherim,[4] Krum, was elated by his victory. He left his brother to besiege Adrianople, and six days after Leo's accession he descended upon the City and marched around it in front of the walls, from the Blachernai as far as what is called the Golden Gate, displaying his forces and making abominable offerings in the meadow in front of the Golden Gate. He challenged the emperor to conclude a peace treaty, should he [Krum] manage to plant his spear in the Golden Gate.[5] When the emperor refused to do so, Krum returned to his tent, marvelling at the walls of the City and the orderly ranks of soldiers at the emperor's disposal. Krum then turns to achieving a peace agreement using tempting arguments. The emperor seized upon this opportunity and tried to ambush Krum, but he was hindered from bringing his plan to pass because of the lack of skill of his subordinates, who struck at Krum but

1 The island of Prote.

2 παραβάτης, the word used to describe emperor Julian, in the fourth c. Perhaps the connective 'and' is significant here: it links the two facts together, i.e. that he was an Armenian and an evil person.

3 Leo V reigned July 813–December 820. Cf. to this chapter Theophanes (Mango/Scott 1997, pp. 685–688), Skylitzes (Wortley 2010, pp. 15–26), and Ps.-Symeon 603.1–619.3ff. Leo's reign is also covered by Joseph Genesios' *Chronicle* (book 1: see Kaldellis 1998), the so-called *Scriptor incertus de Leone Armenio* (unfortunately not readily available in a single, modern edition (or translation): see <http://www.paulstephenson.info/trans/scriptor. html>, accessed 19 July 2016), and *Theophanes continuatus* (book 1: see Featherstone/ Signes-Codoñer 2015).

4 Or: 'Sennacherib,' Assyrian king (705–681 BC) who attacked Judah and Jerusalem and, according to the biblical account (see 2 Kings 18–19, 2 Chronicles 32.1–23, etc.), was punished by God.

5 Or: 'he asked him to conclude a peace treaty if he [symbolically—so as not to use it] planted his spear.'

were unable to inflict a mortal wound. At this, the wretched man[1] [Krum] went mad, and he sent cavalry to St Mamas and burnt down the palace there, and he loaded onto carriages the bronze lion from the hippodrome,[2] together with the bear and the dragon from the aqueduct and also most beautiful marble works, and he retreated, besieging Adrianople and then seizing it. He brought many Macedonian nobles together with very many ordinary people over to the other side of the river Danube and settled them close to the river. 3 Having reigned for two years Leo went mad and exiled the saintly Nikephoros, who had crowned him, and he chose Theodotos as patriarch in his stead, a senseless man and 'dumber than fishes.'[3] And he started a relentless persecution of the Church.[4] 4 During Leo's reign a comet appeared in the form of two shining moons, which united themselves and split into different shapes. They even formed into the shape of a headless man. And there were also terrible earthquakes, famine, drought and fires during the reign of this man, hated by God. 5 Imitating the initiator of this abominable heresy, his namesake,[5] who was of the same disposition, the emperor now started the heresy and, on searching for fellow conspirators, he found John, called the Grammarian, who was rather another Jannes or a Simon,[6] famed for divination in dishes and for magic and shameful acts. He also found other associates. 6 He then invites Nikephoros, the famous patriarch, and his bishops to appear in front of the Senate, and he says: 'You know well that some have come forward to say that one should not revere the icons.' At once, St Euthymios, bishop of Sardis, spoke, and by extemporising from the Holy Scripture he silenced the wretched man. After him, Theodore, the eager champion of orthodoxy and the *hegoumenos* of Stoudios,[7] said: 'Do not, emperor, disturb the ecclesiastical order. For to you are entrusted the state and the army. Take care of these and let the Church remain in orthodoxy.' 7 On hearing this,

---

1 ἀλάστωρ.

2 A local hippodrome at St Mamas (see also Chapter 131, § 9, and Mango/Scott 1997, p. 686 and p. 688, n. 33).

3 This is a proverbial expression, stemming from Lucian (*Gallus* 1).

4 This inaugurates the second phase of iconoclasm, lasting until 842/43.

5 I.e. Leo III (see above, Chapter 121).

6 Jannes was one of two magicians who opposed Moses before Pharaoh (see 2 Timothy 3.8; cf. Exodus 7.11 and 22). Simon is the Magician who opposed Peter in Rome (see above, Chapter 52, § 4, and Chapter 53, § 5).

7 This is St Theodore, abbot of the Stoudios monastery and one of the most prominent opponents of iconoclasm.

the usurper boiled in anger, and the ape-like man roared like a lion[1] and drove all of them out with insults, and he removed the great Nikephoros from the City and banished him. He also sent Theodore from Stoudios into exile and established Theodotos Kassiteras in the patriarchate. **8** From this moment, the emperor poured out his anger and the guile of his soul, and he relied totally on his co-conspirators, those reckless people who, when they had become intimate friends with him, gave him three ideas which he promised to fulfil and which were to his liking: the denial of our orthodox faith, the destruction of the divine icons and the persecution of the pious. **9** Persuaded by these deceptions, being, as the wretch he was, excited by the miserable impulse, the weak-minded man first tears down every holy ecclesiastical monument. He then condemned to terrible punishment and to death everyone who was found to have icons of Christ or any saint, and he killed many respectable and famous people. Likewise, he sent an infinite number of monks to their death. **10** Michael, the leader of the *tagma* of the *exkoubitoi*, was accused in front of the emperor of plotting against him. The emperor kept him fettered and under surveillance in prison. When the birthday of Our Saviour came, the emperor decided to have Michael killed during the night. But he was prevented by his own wife on the grounds that it was a feast day, so he left him. On learning this, Michael, who was in prison, sent a message to all his counsellors and said: 'If you do not make an effort to get me out of prison quickly, I will denounce all of you to the emperor.' **11** Among these counsellors was the *papias* of the palace, who was one of Michael's relatives. The men armed themselves during the night, keeping their swords under their clothes and, when the *papias* opened up for them, they entered the palace as priests in ecclesiastical robes. When the emperor entered the church, they burst in and seized him and cut him into pieces, and he gave up his impious soul in the palace, [in a spot where][2] no emperor before him ever had been killed. **12** In the very same hour they go to the prison and bring Michael out from there and introduce him to the celebration—crowned and not in fetters, so that the word of the psalm is fulfilled with regard to him: 'In the evening the aulos will play in sadness, and in the morning in joy.'[3] **13** After this they dress the wretched Leo's

---

1 'ape-like ... lion': this is a rather absurd conflation of an insult ('to be ape-like') and a common expression ('to roar like a lion,' for which cf. above, Chapter 121, § 8).

2 Needless to say, many emperors had died, even been murdered, in the palace. The shocking thing in this case is that it takes place in the church.

3 Psalms 29(30).6.

limbs in shabby rags, and they put his most abominable body in a dinghy, and they bring it out to the island known as Prote and bury it. They also tonsured his children and made them live there.

129 Michael the Amorian

Michael the Amorian reigned for eight years and nine months.[1] 2 He relaxed to some extent the evil that had ruled until then, so that people in jail or subject to punishment or in exile could at least dream about freedom and relaxation. But then he secretly kindled the belief, hateful to God, of his impious predecessor. For, because of his extreme lack of sense and education he, too, became stuck on the same hook of the terrible heresy. Therefore he said during a *selention*: 'Those who prior to us have inquired into the correctness of position of the Church in these matters, will have to take responsibility about their opinions—whether they were right or wrong. However, we have decided to let the Church continue as it was at our accession.' 3 He had a child by Euphrosyne, by the name of Theophilos, and he crowned him in the Great Church.[2] 4 During his reign Thomas, the rebel,[3] who already had set out from the region of the Anatolikon *thema*,[4] dragging along vagabonds and a mixed crowd, moved against Byzantium in his unwarranted desire for the throne. Hailing from the land of the Romans, of low birth and of no importance, he came to Syria, where he renamed himself Constantine and claimed to be the son of Irene, the empress; and in this way he deceived many barbarians and Christians, and gathered an immense following and marched against Constantinople. His many followers made him over-confident, and he did not realise that 'an emperor's salvation is not dependent upon great force.'[5]

1 Michael II reigned 25 December 820–2 October 829. Cf. for this chapter Skylitzes (Wortley 2010, pp. 27–50), and Ps.-Symeon 620.8–624.14. Michael's reign is also covered by Joseph Genesios' *Chronicle* (book 2: see Kaldellis 1998), and *Theophanes continuatus* (book 2: see Featherstone/Signes-Codoñer 2015).

2 This is the emperor Theophilos.

3 The rebellion of Thomas the Slav, from early 821 to November 822 (cf., however, below, end of § 4, where the rebellion is said to have lasted for three years), was an extremely serious uprising against the ruling emperor. It has been attributed to various factors, such as social or religious unrest. Thomas himself claimed to be no less than Constantine VI, ousted from power by his mother Irene and of uncertain fate (cf. above, Chapter 124).

4 Or, more vaguely, 'the East's.'

5 Psalms 32(33).16.

Thus he ravaged Constantinople[1] for one year during which the citizens nobly resisted and fought from the walls and on the sea. For they set fire to most of the enemy ships and routed the enemy's picked men. Thomas lost the initiative, and he left the City and marched towards Thrace, which he pillaged. Discreetly, Michael left the City with a very great force, and he rushed against the enemy and, having besieged them for a short period of time, he captured Thomas without difficulty and mutilated his hands and feet and then impaled him. Thus he put an end to the harsh civil war that Thomas had started, which had lasted for three years. **5** While Michael was dealing with the rebel Thomas, because of his concern about him he disregarded everything else. Therefore, Crete and Sicily and the islands known as the Cyclades were taken away from the Roman state by the Africans and the Arabs. Recently the Arabs had begun to subdue and gain control over the Christian world. It was the first time that this happened, and it was because of the sins of the Roman people and the impiety of their leaders.[2] **6** In this political situation, Michael died a terrible death from difficult micturition and pain in the kidneys.[3] In his place, his son Theophilos held power together with his mother Euphrosyne.

130 Theophilos

Theophilos reigned for twelve years.[4] **2** His mother Euphrosyne sent to all the *themata* and had good-looking[5] girls brought in order to find a bride for Theophilos, her son. She brought these girls to the palace, and into the hall known as the Pearl,[6] and she gave Theophilos a golden apple and said to him: 'Give this to whoever catches your fancy.'[7] **3** Now, there was a girl

---

1 I.e. the City's hinterland.

2 To interpret the Moslem advance as punishment for the sins of Christians is not at all unusual. However, it is an interesting statement that this was the first time the Arab Moslems had gained control of parts of the Christian world.

3 No doubt considered just punishment for his religious policy (see above, § 2).

4 Theophilos reigned 2 October 829–20 January 842. Cf. to this chapter Skylitzes (Wortley 2010, pp. 51–81), and Ps.-Symeon 624.15–646.8. Theophilos' reign is also covered by Joseph Genesios' *Chronicle* (book 3: see Kaldellis 1998), and *Theophanes continuatus* (book 3: see Featherstone/Signes-Codoñer 2015).

5 Or: 'comely, suitable' (εὐπρεπεῖς).

6 Μαργαρίτης τρίκλινος; this is in the Great Palace.

7 The historicity of bride-shows is a long-debated subject; see, e.g., D. Afinogenov, 'The Bride-show of Theophilos: Some notes on the sources,' *Eranos* 95 (1997), pp. 10–18.

among these, called Ikasia, who was of good family and most beautiful. When Theophilos saw her, he was highly pleased with her beauty. He remarked that 'every base thing comes through a woman.'[1] At which she rather shyly responded: 'But the best things also spring from a woman.'[2] His heart was struck by these words, and he dismissed her.[3] Instead, he gave the apple to Theodora, who came from Paphlagonia. **4** He crowns Theodora in St Stephen's chapel[4] and was crowned, together with her, by the patriarch Anthony with the crown of marriage as well as that of emperor; this was at the Feast of the Pentecost.[5] From there they went in procession to the Great Church, and they gave great sums of money to the patriarch as well as the clergy and the Senate. **5** And the afore-mentioned Ikasia, on failing to gain the throne, founded a monastery and, having become a nun, she remained there until the end of her life, fasting and philosophising and living only for God. She also left behind a great number of her own writings.[6] Euphrosyne, the emperor's mother, left the palace by her own free will and lived quietly in her own monastery called Gastria.[7] **6** Theophilos arranged chariot races at the hippodrome, and he ordered Leo Chamodrakon, his *protovestiarios*,[8] to bring the candle-stand that had been cut in two with a sword when Leo the Armenian was murdered.[9] At the end of the races he invited all the members of the Senate into what is known as the *kathisma*, and he brought forth the candle-stand and showed it to them and said: 'He who enters the temple of the Lord and kills the Lord's anointed—what punishment is he liable to?' The Senate answered: 'He is liable to death, O Lord.' And at once he ordered the *hyparchos* to arrest those who, in association with his father Michael, had murdered Leo, and

---

1 Beginning with Eve.

2 And especially through the Virgin Mary.

3 One may wonder why. Perhaps he (or, rather, the author) thought that she would not know her place at court, or that her piety was too much, or that it, through her answer, was all too obvious that she did not share his iconoclast inclination.

4 In the Daphne wing of the Great Palace.

5 The date of this marriage is much disputed, with suggestions ranging from 821 until 830 or even later. If we believe in the historicity of the bride show or, at least, that Theophilos (who was born in 813) played an active role in choosing himself a wife, 830 seems suitable.

6 Ikasia (or Eikasia, or Kassia) is held to be the authoress of several hymns and also iambics.

7 Probably in south-western Constantinople, on the site of present-day Sancaktar Hayrettin mosque.

8 A palace eunuch immediately below the *parakoimomenos* in rank.

9 Cf. above, Chapter 128, § 11.

he ordered that their heads should be cut off in the Sphendone. At this, they protested very much and said that this decision was unjust: 'For,' as they said, 'had we not fought together with your father, O emperor, you yourself would not be ruling now.' And thus they had their heads cut off in the sight of all, on the pretext that they had dared to commit the murder in the temple of the Lord, but in truth because they had killed a fellow heretic and a man who shared his godless creed. 7 For the wicked[1] man clung to Leo's abominable heresy,[2] and he shunned the piety of the holy icons, some of which he tore down, others he plastered over, and monks who observed the true religion he either sent into exile or tortured. 8 To this Theophilos, Theophobos the Persian fled together with his father and 14,000 Persians. Theophilos distributed these amongst the *themata* and found places for them to live and divided them into *tourmai*; these *tourmai* still exist and are called the 'Persian *tourmai*.'[3] Theophobos himself he made his brother-in-law by marrying him to a sister of Theodora, the *augusta*. 9 This Theophilos was a man who loved luxury. From the head of the goldsmiths, who was a most accomplished man and a relative of patriarch Anthony, he commissioned the building of the *Pentapyrgion*[4] as well as of two exceedingly great[5] organs, totally of gold, which he had further embellished with different stones and glass. He had also a golden tree made on which birds sat and made musical sounds by means of some machinery. The emperor also made innovations in the royal robes, restoring them and adding gold embroidery to what is known as the *loros*[6] and all the other imperial vestments. 10 He pretended to care about worldly justice—he who more than earlier emperors had committed outrages against faith and religion. At one time a widow approached him in the Blachernai (it was his habit to go there) and cried that she had been wronged by Petronas, the *augusta*'s brother, who was a *droungarios* of the *vigla* ('he makes his buildings higher and changes them by adding structures, and overshadows my buildings, reducing them to nothing; no doubt, he treats me with so little respect because I am a widow'). Theophilos at once sent Eustathios, the *quaestor*,

---

1 ἀλιτήριος.

2 Presumably Leo V (see preceding §). However, the first Leo of abominable heresy was, of course, Leo III (see Chapter 121).

3 We may ask when it is that these Persian *tourmai* still exist. A tourma was a large sub-division of the armed forces of a *thema*.

4 'The Five Towers,' a cabinet for the display of valuable objects in the Great Palace.

5 Or: 'the two biggest' (τὰ δύο μέγιστα).

6 A long scarf to be worn around the torso by the emperor.

called Monomachos, who lived in Oxeia, together with Leo, the son of Symbatios, and Demetrios Kamoulianos, to see if indeed the construction work was causing problems to the woman. They went there and saw the damage, and they were convinced that the woman was telling the truth; and so they returned and told the emperor about it. And, in the presence of the emperor, the same Petronas was questioned by them and, in the middle of the road, he was stripped of his clothes and had his back severely beaten. Then the *quaestor* and the secretaries[1] were ordered to go and raze his houses to the ground and turn the property over to the woman. **11** Alexios the Armenian, also called Mousele, who was a valiant and strong man, the emperor made his son-in-law by marrying him to Mary, his beloved[2] daughter, and he made Alexios a *patrikios* and after a short time also a *magistros*.[3] Then, having come to suspect that Alexios was coveting the throne, he sent him away to be a *stratelates* and *doux* of Sicily. But envy gave birth, and some Sicilians came and accused Alexios before the emperor, saying: 'He betrays Christian interests to the Arabs, and he plots against your Majesty.' **12** In the meantime Mary, the emperor's adored daughter, had died,[4] and he had her coffin embellished with silver (this silver was later taken from her grave by the emperor Leo[5]), and he issued an edict of amnesty to those seeking asylum for some crime. He also sent for the archbishop Theodore, with the by-name Krithinos, who had resided in the City at the time when Alexios was accused, and he gave him his personal seal and sent him to Sicily to give a guarantee of immunity to Alexios and to bring him to the emperor. So the archbishop went there and, with his characteristic good sense, he persuaded Alexios to come with him, and he brought him to the emperor. But the emperor had him beaten as a rebel and put into prison, and confiscated all his belongings. **13** On seeing this, the archbishop went to the prison and donated all his possessions to Alexios and said, that 'it is because of me that you have suffered all these terrible things.' And when the emperor, as was his custom, went to Blachernai, the archbishop anticipated him and, clad in liturgical dress, he placed himself

---

1 ἀντιγραφεῖς, i.e. 'copyists.'

2 Or: 'favourite' (cf. § 12).

3 This Alexios may be a son, or grandson, of the Alexios Mousele mentioned in Chapter 124, § 12ff.

4 Mary died in 839. Her marriage to Alexios Mousele may have taken place around 836, and Alexios' expedition to Sicily ca. 837–839.

5 This is a reference to emperor Leo VI (886–912), proving that this part of the text is no older than the late ninth c.

within the sanctuary;[1] and when the emperor together with the Senate approached the *solea*,[2] the archbishop cried out loudly: 'For what purpose, O emperor, do you exert yourself and provide guidance and exercise rule?' Embarrassed by the presence of the Senate, the emperor said: 'For the sake of truth and meekness and righteousness.'[3] And the archbishop said: 'And what justice is there in you, if you give a written guarantee to Alexios through me but do not keep it?' On being censured the emperor was provoked to anger and irrepressible fury, and he drove the archbishop out of the sanctuary with violence, and he subjected him to an immoderate beating and had him exiled. This he did not only because he was criticised by the archbishop, but because he realised that the archbishop honoured and worshipped the holy icons and secretly accused the emperor of impiety. **14** Shortly after, on coming to the Great Church and being criticised by the patriarch because of what had happened with the archbishop, the emperor summoned him back. But since the archbishop, because of what had happened to him, considered himself unworthy of[4] priestly duty, the emperor made him an *oikonomos* of the Great Church. He also released Alexios from prison and gave him back all his belongings and treated him with respect. **15** There was also Manuel, the most notable *stratelates* of all those in the East, a man held in honour by the emperor. This Manuel had a quarrel with Myron, who was *logothetes tou dromou*[5] and an in-law of Petronas. At Myron's instigation, Manuel was slandered before the emperor, who was told that Manuel was coveting the throne and laying terrible plans against him. But Leo the *protovestiarios*, who stood up for Manuel and was concerned about him, assured the emperor that what was said about Manuel was untrue. **16** On learning about the matter, Manuel evaded the emperor's rage and the accusations, and left the City in secret. Having gone to the City gates he entered a public carriage and went in flight to the passes of Syria, hamstringing the horses as he went. And he said the following to the Arabs: 'I flee the fury of the emperor and, if you do not intend to force me to leave my faith, I take refuge with you. But even if this is so, and you receive me on these conditions, send me a guarantee of immunity.' The Arabs heard this with great joy, and they sent him a guarantee and received him as the

---

1 I.e. in the Church of the Most Holy Mother of God at Blachernai.
2 An elevated walkway in front of the iconostasis in a church.
3 Cf. Psalms 44(45).5. The words by the archbishop function as a cue to the emperor.
4 Or: 'unfit for.'
5 'logothete of the course': official in charge of ceremonies and foreign affairs; also head of the imperial post, etc.

emperor of the Romans. **17** On learning that Manuel had joined the Arabs, the emperor was deeply distressed and grieved. He discussed the matter with John the *synkellos*, who said to him: 'If you very much wish that Manuel should come to you, emperor, I am ready to bring that about myself. Give me money and send me to the emir[1] on the pretext that I should visit those in prison and in chains. And I will take a written guarantee[2] from your Majesty, by which I will convince Manuel when I come into his presence. For I think that I will achieve this by the written guarantee and by my skills of persuasion and because of his piety, and because it is reasonable that he should love his country.' **18** The emperor gave John a very large sum of money and gifts for the emir and sent him on his way. He came to Arab country with all the money and all kinds of luxurious objects, so that even the Hagarenes were amazed at his wealth. Having visited the prisons and seen the *protosymboulos*,[3] he was even able to talk to Manuel in private and to give him the written guarantee with the emperor's seal. **19** Having done this, John returned and announced to the emperor what he had done. Manuel asked the emir to be allowed to go out against a certain hostile tribe. Being granted the request, he took the emir's son and a great number of people with him, and he achieved a glorious victory. As a result of this, he was held in [even] greater esteem than before, and he could get whatever he asked for from the emir. **20** He then thought carefully about going to Romania and, after some time, he said to the emir's leading men: 'If you give me the emir's son and an army, I will go out and subdue Romania.' This made them very glad, and they hoped to get this in addition to the earlier advantages brought by him, so they armed him and sent him out against Romania at once. **21** When he came close to the Anatolikon *thema*, he called his subordinates to him and the emir's son, on the pretext that he was going on a raid or a hunt. At some distance from the enemy, he embraced the emir's son and kissed him and said, that 'I will now go to the emperor and to my own country, for nothing in life is more important to me than my faith and my kinsmen. You, however, may return with your men to your own people. Do not fear that you will suffer any harm from us.' And so, shamefacedly and in tears, the emir's son returned home, whereas Manuel, who had sent

1 This must be the Abbasid caliph of the time, probably the eighth caliph, al-Muʻtasim (reigned 833–842).

2 I.e. a letter with the emperor's official signature (and, see the following, seal), so as to make it clear that the emperor himself was the sender (Greek λόγον ἐνυπόγραφον).

3 Probably the emir of the preceding, i.e. the caliph (similarly the titles of emir and *protosymboulos* are confused below, § 32).

someone in advance to announce his arrival, went to the emperor. **22** The emperor considered this messenger a bearer of very good tidings, and he rewarded him with money and office. He also received Manuel in a fitting way, making him at once a *magistros* and a *domestikos* of the *scholai*;[1] he also became a godfather of his children. **23** Elated by this, the emperor, together with Manuel and the Senate and all the army, went out against the Hagarenes, and with ease he captured Zapetra and Samosata[2] (Samosata was famous at that time for its riches and its power, since the emir stemmed from there), and he returned boasting with his victory and the spoils.[3] And having come as far as Bryas, he ordered that a palace should be built there and that gardens should be planted and water be brought[4]—which indeed happened. **24** From there he came into the City, and he paraded the spoils and held chariot races in the hippodrome, and he gave the signal for the first heat and, being dressed in blue,[5] he rode on a white[6] chariot and, on winning, he was crowned and the factions cried: 'Welcome, incomparable faction leader!'[7] **25** On the death of the patriarch Anthony, John the *synkellos* was appointed in his stead, or to be more precise, the new Jannes and Jambres.[8] He was famous for sorcery and divination with dishes and every [other] kind of impiety. He also turned out to be a suitable vehicle for the emperor's impiety and [evil] inclination, and he worked together with the emperor in every way to achieve destruction. But the basilisk of impiety, which he conceived but contained, was brought forth and given birth to by the emperor, who ordered that the holy icons should be either painted over or erased. **26** Outside the City, this John built a house of carved stone, known even in our days[9] as *Troullos*. There, with the aid of certain sacrifices, he conversed with demons and predicted the future to the emperor. This house

---

1 Commander of the *scholai* (imperial palace guards).

2 This is on the Euphrates.

3 This expedition took place in March–April 837.

4 I.e. that an aqueduct should be built. What may be the foundations of the Bryas palace have been found on the Asiatic shore of the Bosporos. Skylitzes (see Wortley 2010, p. 60 (also with further references with regard to the palace)) gives a somewhat fuller description of the building project.

5 'blue' (βένετος): the colour of one of the circus factions.

6 'white' (λευκός): the colour of another of the circus factions.

7 φακτωνάρης.

8 This is John VII, the Grammarian, mentioned already above, Chapter 128, § 5 (with references to 2 Timothy 3.8 and Exodus 7.11 and 22: in Timothy, the two magicians opposing Moses before Pharaoh are named Jannes and Jambres).

9 Yet another reference to a point in time later than the narrated time.

remained uninhabited afterwards because of the demonic hauntings that had occurred at that time. **27** When matters stood thus, the Arabs went out against Romania with a great force. The emperor marched against them together with the Persian refugees and the *tagmata* and Manuel, the *domestikos*. When battle was joined, the emperor was defeated and went into hiding in a crowd of Persians, thinking that they would save him.[1] When Manuel, looking around, saw that the emperor was among the Persians and understood that these now were inclined to betray him to the Arabs and, by doing so, be reconciled with the Arabs, he cut a way through them and seized the bridle of the emperor's horse and pulled him out. This he did against the emperor's will, and he did it because he considered it an intolerable shame for the Romans if the Arabs should take their emperor prisoner. Now the emperor was out of his mind because of fear, and he wanted to join the Persians again. But Manuel drew his sword as if to strike him. This frightened the emperor so that he followed, although he did so unwillingly, and he was saved only with difficulty. From there he shamefacedly returned to Dorylaion, having suffered a terrible defeat. **28** Having shown proof of much bravery against the Hagarenes, Manuel was wounded in the war, and he was taken ill and died. His body was brought to the monastery that he had founded, and he was buried there; this is the Manuel monastery close to the cistern of Aspor.[2] **29** As a consequence of this, many accusations against the Persians were voiced in front of the emperor, as well as threats against Theophobos, who was said to be a rebel and a traitor and a man of ill will. On hearing about this, Theophobos gathered the Persians and went down to Sinope, and he occupied this city and ruled it harshly. When the emperor heard of this, he was deeply troubled (for he feared that the Persians might join the Arabs), and he went as far as Paphlagonia and gave the Persians a promise that they would not suffer in any way. From there he took Theophobos with him and, accompanied by him, returned to the City, and the rest of the Persians came and settled at the same place as before. Because of his orthodoxy Theophobos was loved by the citizens no less than by the Persians. **30** At this time a child is born to the emperor by Theodora.[3] The emperor named him Michael. **31** When the emperor went to Blachernai,[4] as was his custom, a man came

---

1 This is the battle of Anzen (Dazimon), in the Armeniakon *thema*, 22 July 838.

2 Or: 'cistern of Aspar,' in the City.

3 This is the future emperor Michael III, perhaps born 19 January 840.

4 These travels from the Great Palace to the Blachernai were among the best opportunities for anyone who wanted to accost the emperor (cf. also below, § 42).

forward to him and said: 'The horse that your Majesty is riding is mine.' Because of the sudden approach of the man, the horse shied, but the emperor managed to check it, and he asked the *komes* of the stables: 'To whom does this horse belong?' He said: 'The *komes* of Opsikion sent it to your Majesty.' The next day, the emperor brought in the *komes* of Opsikion, who happened to be in the City, together with the man who had approached him, and he asked: 'Tell me the truth. To whom does this horse belong?' The answer was, that 'it is mine, but the *strategos* sent for it and took it from me by force, neither paying me for it nor giving me any office in return.' The emperor then said to the *komes*: 'Tell me if this is so and why you sent me the horse without having paid for it.' The *komes* said, that 'he wanted to become a *scholarios*.[1] But, since I did not know if he was man enough, I offered him a hundred *solidi*.[2] But he refused to take them.' The emperor: 'But why did you not finish the affair with him in a proper way before you sent me the horse?'[3] After this, the emperor made an investigation and was informed that the *komes* had taken the man's horse by force. He then had the *stratelates*[4] chastised with the proper corporal punishment,[5] and he returned the horse to the man who had approached him. However, the man did not wish to receive the horse back, so he accepted two *litrai* instead as payment for it. It was also decided that the *strategos* should put him to the test and, if he turned out to be man enough, to make him a *scholarios*. But on going to war, when battle was joined, he turned out to be a coward, and he was found amongst those fleeing, and he was killed by the enemy. **32** When the emperor attended a procession at the Bryas, a message was brought to him from the *strategos* of Anatolikon, to the effect that the *protosymboulos* had gone out with an army in order to destroy Amorion. The emperor paid what was due to the soldiers and their leaders and then went in haste to Cappadocia. The emir[6] detached 50,000 people together with Soudee, who had the greatest reputation among the Hagarenes for courage and good sense, and he gave them their individual payment and sent them against the emperor. When they met in battle, the emperor was defeated and had to flee, and he

---

1 Member of the *scholai*.

2 I.e. as payment for the horse, instead of accepting the horse as payment for office.

3 Or: 'Why did you send me a horse that had not been properly paid for?'

4 The *strategos* mentioned above.

5 μαγλαβίοις (cf. below, Chapter 131, § 38).

6 This emir is probably the same person as the just mentioned *protosymboulos* (i.e. the Abbasid caliph, al-Mu'tasim: for this kind of confusion, cf. above, §§ 17–18).

returned ignominiously, saving his life with difficulty.[1] The emir came with a great force to Amorion, and he surrounded it by a palisade. But, although he fought several battles, he did not manage to destroy it; for the people on the inside fought bravely and relentlessly. **33** There was a pupil of Leo the philosopher in the fortress.[2] When the emir wanted to retreat, this man, who was an astronomer,[3] conveyed a message to him through someone and said: 'If you can last for another two days at the fortress, you will be able to take us by storm.' And so it happened. For the fortress was betrayed by a man called Voiditzes and by Manikofagos. And a number of well-known men of good family[4] were captured and had to go to Syria as prisoners. These were: the *patrikios* Theophilos, the *strategoi* Melissinos and Aetios, Theodore the *protospatharios*, who was a eunuch and also called Krateros, Kallistos the *tourmarches*,[5] Constantine the *droungarios*, Vasoes the *dromeus*[6] and some of the commanders of the *tagmata*. These were put under pressure by the *protosymboulos*, in order to make them renounce their faith. On refusing to do this they had their heads cut off by the sword; for they preferred eternal life to the short life on earth. **34** But, exchanging shameful delivery for the better salvation,[7] the pupil of Leo the philosopher had joined the emir. On being asked by the emir about his scientific knowledge his answer was that he was a pupil of the philosopher Leo. On learning about Leo and what kind of a man he was, the emir wanted to meet him. Therefore, he gave a letter for Leo the philosopher to one of the prisoners and sent him to Constantinople, assuring him that, if Leo himself came out, he would be held in honour by the emir. **35** When Leo received the letter, he was afraid that the matter would become known, so he brought it to emperor Theophilos. When the emperor became aware of Leo's knowledge, and that he had such a learned man in his state,[8] he accommodated him in the Magnaura palace and gave him

---

1 This is probably the battle already mentioned above, § 27. Amorion was besieged in early August 838 and eventually captured 12 August.

2 This Leo (ca. 790–after 869), also called the Mathematician, was a well-known character at the time of the Macedonian Renaissance.

3 I.e. an astrologer.

4 'a number ... family' (τῶν ὀνομαστῶν ἄνδρες οὐκ ἀγεννεῖς): perhaps ἀγεννεῖς is wrong for ὀλίγοι ('not a few well-known men').

5 The commander of the *tourma* (cf. above, § 8).

6 I.e. 'the runner.'

7 With other words, so as to save his life at the price of his soul.

8 πολιτεία.

permission to teach and also furnished him with pupils, putting every necessary convenience at his disposal. This Leo was later even made metropolitan bishop of Thessalonica. **36** The same emperor builds the Trikonchos in the palace and the building known as the Sigma[1] and the scaffolding on which the factions of the people stand,[2] and he also erected an open courtyard with a fountain[3] where what is called the *saximod-eximon* is performed, during which the horses of both sides pass by,[4] wearing golden saddles. Below the Trikonchos, on a lower level, he made by an ingenious construction what is called the Mysterion, [a room] in which everything said in one corner can be heard in the other. **37** On learning that Theophanes, the poet, and his brother Theodore, who lived by themselves,[5] derided the emperor's impiety and exposed it, Theophilos sent for them in anger and had them brought into his presence and said the following: 'Where are you from?' They said: 'From Palestine.' And the accursed man: 'So why did you leave your country and come to ours, but still do not obey our authority?' When they did not answer this, he allowed their faces to be severely beaten. **38** Later, he had them flogged until they were at the brink of death, and he said in a roaring rage to the *hyparchos*: 'Take them to the *praitorion* and inscribe their foreheads, and engrave the following verses on them.' And he added: 'Never mind if they are not good!' This he said since he knew that the brothers were very accomplished and very well trained in the details of different kinds of versification. Someone even added: 'Anyhow, they are not worth being inscribed with good iambs.' But the brothers said: 'Write, just write, emperor, whatever you want to!' For, they intended[6] to read it before the fearsome and righteous judge. The *hyparchos* brought them to the *praitorion*, and after two days he had them tied down by their hands and feet and had the verses tattooed on their faces, and then they were exiled. **39** The blessed Theodore died in exile,[7] whereas the glorious Theophanes, the poet,

---

1 This is not the same as the Sigma in the city (cf. Chapter 125, § 3), but part of the same complex as the Trikonchos exedra in the Great Palace.

2 I.e. during ceremonies.

3 φιάλη (cf. above, 114, § 5, where the same kind of fountain is built for the same purpose, i.e. the ceremony of the *saximodeximon*).

4 Or: 'pass by on both sides.'

5 'by themselves': perhaps 'as hermits.' These are the famous Graptoi (i.e. 'inscribed,' or 'tattooed') brothers, enemies of iconoclasm in its last phase.

6 'they intended': or 'for the emperor would have.'

7 St Theodore died 28 December 840.

lasted until the reign of Michael and Theodora, having laboured very hard during the reintroduction of orthodoxy. He was also made a metropolitan of Nicaea; this was at the time when the religious situation already had changed for the better.[1] **40** During Theophilos' reign the golden crest on the statue of Justinian, the one on the column called Augusteus,[2] fell down. Everyone was at a loss and wondered how it could be possible to climb up [the column and the statue]. Then a professional acrobat was found. He climbed the roof tiles of the Great Church and threw a projectile tied to a rope onto the equestrian statue of Justinian, which was made of bronze. And when the projectile stuck on it, the acrobat, to the admiration of the onlookers, went on the rope over to the other side and fitted the crest into place. Thus he earned the emperor's gratitude and achieved great fame for his art and his prowess, and he was rewarded with a hundred *solidi* by the emperor. **41** Theophilos crowned Michael, his son, in the Great Church and, as the custom was, he gave gifts to everyone at the coronation.[3] **42** He also prepared a hospice, which is now called the Theophilos [hospice]. The building had belonged to Isidore, the *patrikios*, who came from Rome with Olybrios in the time of Constantine the Great. After some years it had been given to the *kourator*[4] in order to accommodate women of the nobility who did not know how to live in chastity. During the reign of Leo the Isaurian it was made a guest-house by the emperor from having been a brothel. Later it became the house of Constantine, son of Irene; this was after he had been blinded by his mother.[5] When he died, his wife took monastic robes and made it a monastery and called it [the monastery of] 'Repentance.'[6] This house was extremely large and worthy of admiration. But a beam in the main hall[7] hung loose and threatened to fall down. The nuns asked the emperor for help with this when he was on his way to Blachernai,[8] but he refused. However, it made him aware of the house, and he came to like it, and so he removes those same nuns to another monastery, and he embellished the

---

1 πρὸς τὸ εὐσεβέστερον.
2 This is the statue already mentioned in Chapter 104, § 10.
3 This was perhaps 16 May 840.
4 An administrator of imperial estates. Cf. Chapter 136, § 8, where a *kourator* of the Mangana palace is mentioned.
5 This refers to Constantine VI. See Chapter 124, § 20, and Chapter 125, § 3.
6 τὰ Μετανοίας.
7 Or: 'in one of the halls (τρικλίνων).' The text appears to be slightly corrupt here.
8 Cf. above, § 31.

house in every way and made it into a hospice, and he donated a great lot of valuables and money to it and estates, and he called it the Theophilos [hospice]. **43** Before his death, this emperor, hated by God, made a secret concord with his sympathisers about Theophobos the Persian. For he said: 'The Persians under my command love Theophobos greatly and have much faith in him, as do not a few other people in high positions as well. Therefore, should I die, I fear they may rebel against my son, who is just a baby, and against my wife.' He then sent for Theophobos and brought him to the palace and kept him at his side. When he was worn down by his illness, he confined Theophobos to the prison chambers at the Boukoleon[1] and, when the Persians started to ask what had happened to him, the emperor sent the *augusta*'s brother, Petronas, with the logothete in the night, and had Theophobos' head cut off. However, they made the Persians believe that Theophobos was in the palace with the emperor. **44** When the emperor had died a terrible death from dysentery,[2] his wretched body was brought to the Church of the Holy Apostles, whereas the body of Theophobos was brought in secret from the Boukoleon and taken to safety at a place close to the Narses monastery, in the monastery now called Theophobia,[3] and there they deposited it.

131 Michael and Theodora

Michael reigned together with his mother Theodora for fifteen years, alone for ten years, and together with Basil one year and four months.[4] **2** Theodora was such a faithful and orthodox person that even while her husband was still alive she honoured and revered the holy icons in secret. It was on her decision, but at the suggestion and with the encouragement of Theoktistos,

---

1 This palace was to the south of the Great Palace and with its own harbour at the Marmara Sea.

2 Theophilos died 20 January 842. This is another example of a bad death of an impious emperor.

3 I.e. 'Fear of God,' alluding to the man's name.

4 Michael III was formally emperor from the death of Theophilos 20 January 842; he assumed real power 15 March 856 (see below, § 22), and reigned together with Basil I from 26 May 866 (see § 39) until his death, 23/24 September 867. Cf. to this chapter Skylitzes (Wortley 2010, pp. 82–115), and Ps.-Symeon 647.3–686.10. Michael's reign is also covered by Joseph Genesios' *Chronicle* (book 4: Kaldellis 1998), and *Theophanes continuatus* (book 4: see Featherstone/Signes-Codoñer 2015).

the *kanikleios*[1] and logothete, that the patriarch John, who had been raised together with the empress,[2] was driven out of the Church and the City; the empress then had him confined to the place known as Kleidion in the Stenon. She brings in the blessed Methodios, a monk, and installs him as patriarch. And she brought together all the monks and bishops who had been exiled by Theophilos and, on the first Sunday in Holy Lent, she confirmed the orthodox creed and gave peace to the Church.[3] **3** Theodora sent Theoktistos the logothete on an expedition against Crete.[4] When he came with many men and a great naval force, he put fear into the Hagarenes who soon could not resist his attack any longer. But when he learnt that the *augusta* had made another person emperor,[5] he was even more upset himself and was happy to flee. This hit him through Saracen deceit and the venality of his men, and it convinced him that he should return to the City and leave the army to be slaughtered by the Cretans.[6] **4** Having made such a bad impression in Crete, Theoktistos appeared even worse and even more unsuccessful on his return. For at that time Amer went out against Romania and pillaged and destroyed everything in his way, and Theodora and Michael[7] sent this same Theoktistos, who was considered the most reliable person to them and their foremost intimate, against Amer.[8] When Theoktistos arrived and went into battle with Amer at the place called Mauropotamon, he was defeated.[9] He returned to the City, while many of his men had been killed, whereas others fled to Amer because of the harsh and hateful behaviour of the logothete. One of these was Theophanes from Phargana, who excelled in courage and strength;

---

1 The *kanikleios* (or, as here, *kanikles*) was one of the secretaries to the emperor. He had the duty of guarding the inkstand with coloured ink and was thus invested with symbolic power that could sometimes be converted into actual power.

2 Or: 'baptised together at the same ceremony' (σύντεκνον αὐτῆς ὄντα), an act creating a symbolic bond.

3 This was 11 March 843, and it marks the formal end of the iconoclast controversy.

4 This was in 843.

5 This was not true at the time. See, however, below (especially from § 19 onwards) on the subsequent career of Bardas.

6 This sentence is difficult. I would like to thank Constantin Zuckerman for suggesting the interpretation adopted here.

7 This was in 844 (see below), and it may be kept in mind that Michael was only about four years old at the time.

8 This is the relatively independent emir of Melitene (Malatya), Umar ibn Abdallah ibn Marwan al-Aqta.

9 This was the battle of Mauropotamon, in Cappadocia (still in 844).

some years later, he received a pledge of security and fled back to the Christians. **5** On returning to the City from Crete, Theoktistos endeavoured to be close to the *augusta*. Once, on meeting with Bardas, the brother of the *augusta*, he came into a dispute with him and blamed him for the defeat, which he attributed to him by saying that the Roman army had turned to flight at his instigation and on his decision. Theoktistos thereupon manages to get Bardas removed from the City, following a decision by the *augusta* Theodora. The same Theoktistos, the *paradyn-asteuon* under the *augusta*, had houses and a bath and a garden built in that which is now called the Apsis.[1] This he did in order to be close to the palace. But in order to guard himself and for his own security he had an iron gate built at Daphne,[2] and he ordered that a *papias* should keep guard there. **6** When the emperor now had grown into a man, he spent his time at hunting and competing in chariot races on the double circuit at the hippodrome, and at all other kinds of impure actions. Now the *augusta* Theodora, together with the logothete Theoktistos, decides to give a wife to her son Michael. For she had noticed that he had become friendly with Eudokia, the daughter of Inger, a girl whom the logothete and the *augusta* hated intensely because of her rudeness.[3] Therefore, they join him to Eudokia Dekapolitissa, and they crown him together with her in the Church of St Stephen at Daphne.[4] The banquet was held in the Magnaura, and the Senate dined in the Hall of the Nineteen Couches. **7** After a short time the *strategos* of the Boukellarioi[5] brought a high-spirited, fine horse to the emperor. Thinking about using it in the races at the hippodrome, the emperor first wanted to take a look at its teeth (from which the age of a horse can be gathered) and get to know its temper. But the horse was out of control and bucked, and the emperor was vexed by this, for he did not have anyone who by natural ability or knowledge could calm or even control the horse. When he was venting his annoyance, Theophilitzes,

---

1 This 'now' refers to a time, possibly in the tenth c., later than the time narrated. The exact location of this Apsis is unclear.

2 Daphne was one of the wings of the Great Palace.

3 It has been supposed that this Inger was of Scandinavian extraction (cf., e.g., the present-day Norwegian male name Ingar). Later on, Eudokia Ingirina married Basil I, became the mistress of Michael III, and played a prominent role as a party animal (see below, § 32, etc.).

4 I.e. they are joined in marriage. This took place in 855, in the same church in which Theodora herself had been joined with Theophilos (see above, Chapter 130, § 4).

5 This is one of the *themata* (administrative and military provinces).

who belonged to the *noumera*[1] and who was *komes* of the Wall at that time, came up. When the emperor said, that 'I do not have anyone who is man enough to cope with my horses,' Theophilitzes replied: 'My Lord, I have a young man who is extremely experienced and capable with horses, just the man your Majesty wants; his name is Basil.' The emperor ordered that Basil should come to him at once, so a *koitonites*[2] was sent to the Iron Gate[3] where he found Basil, and he brought him to the emperor without delay. Being ordered to hold the horse, Basil held the bridle with one hand and with the other he touched the horse's ear and so reduced it to the mildness of a lamb. At this the emperor was pleased and comforted, and he handed Basil over to Andreas, who was a *hetaireiarches*,[4] so that he should belong to the *hetaireia*[5] and work with the emperor's horses. **8** I have considered it necessary to tell the story of this Basil, about his early life and where he came from, up to the time when these things happened.[6] Basil is born in Macedonia, in the area around Adrianople, during the reign of Michael Ragabe,[7] the father of Ignatios the patriarch and the son-in-law of the emperor Nikephoros through his daughter Prokopia. **9** During his reign Krum, the ruler of Bulgaria, went out against the Christians and, when Michael was routed and Leo the Armenian rebelled against him and usurped the imperial power, Krum came after him[8] and surrounded the City. But having been ambushed by Leo the Armenian, he turned back to Bulgaria, and he sent people to St Mamas and took away the bronze statues there. He also went to Adrianople and occupied it,[9] and he moved 10,000

1 Probably some kind of military unit.

2 A chamberlain (servant appointed to the emperor's bedchamber); the distinction between this and *koubikoularios* (see Chapter 105, § 4) is unclear.

3 Cf. Chapter 135, § 6.

4 A commander of the *hetaireia* (cf. following note).

5 The exact function of the *hetaireia* is uncertain, but it seems to have been a guard force fairly close to the emperor's person. It is interesting to note that the term is only in the singular in this text, although it has been supposed that the changes that turned diverse *hetaireiai* into one force, occurred as late as the eleventh c. There was probably also at some time a change as to how the members of the *hetaireia(i)* were recruited, going from mainly foreigners (which could be suitable in the case of Basil) to the noble youth of Constantinople.

6 This is the future emperor. It should be noted that this text does not at all hint at an elevated ancestry to Basil, as suggested by the *Vita Basilii* and other texts, according to which he was of royal Armenian descent.

7 I.e. 811–813 (cf. below, n. on § 13).

8 'him': Leo, or possibly Michael. The author makes a simple story less than clear. The story about Krum's attack is told above, Chapters 127, § 3, and 128, § 2.

9 Adrianople fell in June 813.

people, not counting the women, and settled them on the other side of the Danube. **10** In the days of the emperor Theophilos, there was a *stratelates* in Macedonia called Kordyles.[1] He had also a son called Bardas who was very valiant, and this son he left to govern the Macedonians[2] on the other side of the river Danube in his stead. Kordyles himself came by some device to Theophilos, who received him with pleasure and who, having learnt what he wanted, sent ships to take these people and bring them to the City. **11** The ruler of Bulgaria was Valdimer, the descendant of Krum, father of Symeon who ruled afterwards.[3] Now, the people[4] decided to come to Romania with women and children. When Michael the Bulgarian had arrived in Thessalonica, they started to come over with all their belongings. On learning this, the *komes* went against them in order to fight them. At this the Macedonians despaired and made Tzantzes and Kordyles their leaders, and they joined battle and killed many, while they made some of them their prisoners. But those Bulgarians who were not able to come over attached themselves to the Hungarians,[5] and they informed them about everything concerning the Macedonians. There also came ships belonging to the emperor to take them and bring them to the City. At once an infinite number of Hungarians turned up. On seeing these, the Macedonians shed tears and cried: 'God of St Adrian,[6] help us!' And they drew themselves up to join battle. But the Turks said to them: 'Give us all your possessions and go wherever you want to!' **12** But the Macedonians did not accept this, and they remained prepared for battle. This they did for three days, but on the fourth day they started to embark on their boats. On seeing this, the Turks joined battle, and this lasted from the fifth hour until evening. At this, the heathen were routed, and the Macedonians pursued them. On the next day, when the Macedonians wanted to retreat, the Huns turned up again to fight them. Then a fairly young Macedonian who later became a *hetaireiarches*,

1 The events of §§ 10–12 seem to have taken place in 836.
2 'Macedonians' are in the following the Christians belonging to the Byzantine province of Macedonia (as opposed to the Bulgarian pagans).
3 This seems to be confused: Symeon's father was Boris/Michael, who reigned 852–889. The first Vladimir(-Rasate) reigned 889–893 and is not relevant for this narrative. The Bulgarian ruler during the events depicted here must be Omurtag (reigned 814–831), Malamir (831–836) or Presian I (836–852). It was Malamir who was Krum's grandson (if the Greek word, ἔγγονος, can be taken to mean precisely this, not just 'descendant').
4 I.e. the Bulgarians.
5 Hungarians: in the following also referred to as Turks, or Huns (or pagans).
6 This is probably St Adrian of Nicomedia, Christian martyr in the early fourth c. and protector of Christians under persecution from pagans.

called Leo, from the family of the Gomostoi, came forward. He, together with other Macedonians of good family, routed the enemy and drove them away. On returning [from the war] they embarked upon the ships and came safely to the emperor. There they were lavished with gifts by him and then returned to Macedonia, their own country. **13** Basil was a young man at this time and had recently returned from captivity. He spent time as a prisoner during the reign of Leo, the emperor, and Michael the Amorian, and he came to the City during the time of the emperor Theophilos, when he was about twenty-five years old.[1] When he was resettled in his own country, he attached himself as a servant to a *strategos* of Macedonia called Tzantzes,[2] and it was because he was not favoured by him in any way that he came to the City and the Golden Gate. He arrived exhausted by the journey (it was a Sunday and towards sunset), and he lay down on the pavement at St Diomedes; this was a public[3] church at the time, and it had a *prosmonarios*[4] called Nicholas. **14** During the night a divine voice called the *prosmonarios* with the words: 'Rise and bring the emperor into the chapel!' The *prosmonarios* rose, but could not find anyone except Basil lying there like a beggar, and he returned to bed. But again, for a second time, the same voice came to him. He went out and looked around but did not find anyone, so he went back and closed the gate and returned to bed. Then suddenly someone hit him in the ribs with a sword[5] and said: 'Go out and bring in the man you see sleeping outside the gate; that is the emperor.' So he went out, eager and terrified, and he found Basil with his pouch and his staff, and he brought him into the church. And on the following day[6] he went to the bath with him and gave him new clothes. And he went to the church and adopted him as his brother, and they rejoiced together. **15** The

---

1 Basil's date of birth is a matter of debate, with suggestions ranging from 811 to 835 at least. This text expressly advocates a date around 811 or slightly later (cf. §§ 8 and 13). This, however, is problematic in the other end: it makes Basil arguably too old to play the role as young friend of Michael III (see below, § 16), and it makes him seventy-five years at the time of his death during a hunting expedition (see Chapter 132, § 27). More seriously, perhaps, there is then (see the following §) a gap in Basil's biography of around twenty years—years supposedly spent in the city (Basil cannot have come into Michael's life to play a role of the kind indicated in the sources any earlier than around 855 (Michael was born in 840)).

2 See above, § 11.

3 Greek καθολική.

4 A church caretaker, or warden.

5 Greek ῥομφαία: this is a very particular word, and it is also used for the Flaming Sword watching the road to paradise (see above, Chapter 21).

6 Or: 'on Monday' (τῇ δευτέρᾳ ἡμέρᾳ).

same Nicholas had a brother who was a doctor and who worked for Theophilitzes. Coming by chance to his brother, the doctor saw Basil and was struck by his stature and his manly looks, and he said to his brother: 'Where does this man come from?' Nicholas then tells him everything, but then asked him to keep it a secret. However, when the doctor was sitting at the table together with Theophilitzes and Theophilitzes was talking to himself and at last said: 'I cannot find a suitable man for my horses,' the doctor rose and told his master about Basil's manliness and said: 'He is just the man you desire and are looking for.' So Theophilitzes eagerly sent for him, and when he saw that Basil had curly hair and a big head, he gave him the nickname Kephalas[1] and set him to take care of his horses. Thus, in the manner described and for this reason it came to pass that Theophilitzes gave Basil to Michael. Up to this point is the story of Basil's early years. **16** The emperor introduced the same Basil to his mother and said joyously: 'Look here, mother, what a boy I have hired!' But she came out, looked at Basil and then turned away, saying to her son: 'This, my child, is the man who will destroy our family.' But Michael did not believe his mother at all when she said this, and he did not pay any attention to it. **17** The blessed Methodios, the patriarch, died and Ignatios, son of Michael the *kouropalates*, is appointed in his place.[2] **18** Since the Bulgarians made raids in Thrace and Macedonia and pillaged these *themata*, Theodora made a levy of men and, emerging from the fortresses in small scattered groups, these attacked the Bulgarians who were ravaging the country, and they killed them or made them prisoners.[3] Thus the Bulgarians were subdued and forced to remain in their own country. **19** Caesar Bardas became friendly with Damianos the *patrikios* and *parakoimomenos*. Damianos seized the emperor and persuaded him that Bardas should be allowed to enter the City.[4] Having brought the emperor's intimates over to his side by gifts, Bardas was then ordered to come to the palace together with the *parakoimomenos*. Having made friends also with Theophanes the *protospatharios*, called Phalganos, a valiant man, they, together with Damianos, decide to kill Theoktistos the *kanikleios*. The emperor too was won over to this plan by Damianos and gave his approval to it. For Bardas kept saying to Damianos: 'As long as Theoktistos is with the *augusta*, the

---

1 '(Big-)head.'
2 This was in the summer of 847. Michael the *kouropalates* is emperor Michael I Ragabe.
3 This is of uncertain date, perhaps 846 (or later).
4 On Bardas' exile, see above, § 5.

emperor will never rule or be free to act.' **20** Theoktistos, as was his habit, went to the bath in the Areovindos district.[1] He then went to the *asekreteia*[2] carrying the reports, and from there he entered the Lausiakon.[3] Looking around, he saw Bardas, who was sitting there occupied with something,[4] and he was very upset and said: 'I am going in to the *augusta* and I will have him chased away.' When he had come as far as the Horologion,[5] he met Michael himself together with Damianos, and he was not allowed to go in to Theodora. Instead, he[6] furiously asked Theoktistos to open his reports and read them in front of him. And when he was unwilling to do so, he was forced to turn round and leave, and so he left, weeping and wailing bitterly. In the Lausiakon Bardas came up to him and started to beat him in the face and tear his hair. On seeing this, the *droungarios* of the *vigla*, Maniakes, rose and protested and told Bardas not to beat the logothete. But Bardas replied that he was doing so by the emperor's orders. On Damianos' instigation also the emperor turned up and, on seeing him, Bardas and Theophanes Phalganos take hold of the logothete and slaughter him and cut him into pieces fit for dogs, displaying the cruelty and brutality of wild beasts. **21** Having been told about this by the *papias*, Theodora went out and, as is reasonable, vented her fury against Michael and those who had carried out the murder. And although the emperor tried in every way to placate his mother, she remained entirely unimpressed and with undiminished anger, and she did not let anyone console her; when she was spoken to, she let herself be consoled and conciliated just as much as a wave of the sea.[7] When this became evident, it was as if the emperor changed soul and mind, and as much as he had earlier tried to serve the empress, he now, by his demeanour and his actions, tried to hurt her. He even forced his sisters Thekla, Anastasia and Anna to leave the palace, and he brought them to the monastery in the Karianos district. But Poulcheria,

1 The murder of the logothete Theoktistos, described in this section, took place 20 November 855.

2 Department of imperial administration (in this case probably archives).

3 A hall at the southern end of the Great Palace complex, close to the Chrysotriklinos.

4 Or: 'looking busy' (Greek ἔμπρατον).

5 Another hall ('Sun-Dial Hall') in the Great Palace (and not identical with the well-known Horologion of St Sophia, cf. Wortley 2010, p. 214, n. 53). Cf. also below, § 31, and Chapter 136, § 43, where the same Horologion as here must be intended.

6 Michael, or possibly Damianos (the Greek has the passive ἐκελεύσθη).

7 This harks back to Euripides' *Medea*, lines 28–29: ὡς δὲ πέτρος ἢ θαλάσσιος κλύδων ἀκούει νουθετουμένη φίλων / 'She is as deaf to the advice of her friends as a stone or a wave of the sea' (transl. D. Kovacs).

who was the favourite of his mother, he sent to the monastery of Gastria. Shortly afterwards, he had them all united in the monastery of Gastria and made into nuns, donning the monastic garb. **22** Being unanimously acclaimed by the Senate Michael starts to rule on his own, and he makes Bardas a *magistros* and *domestikos* of the *scholai*.[1] But because of what he had done to hurt her and because of the unjust murder of Theoktistos, his mother refused to be reconciled with him, and there was open hostility between them. Therefore, he removed her from the palace and sent her to the monastery called Gastria. She was very much upset by this and unable to think clearly because of the shock, and so, in a manner unworthy of herself, she makes a plan against Bardas. For this plan she took the emperor's *protostrator*[2] and many others into her confidence, and she decided that Bardas should be killed when he returned from his estate at Kosmidion. **23** Their plan was exposed before it was put into practice, and the evil was turned against the planners themselves. For they were found out and apprehended and had their heads cut off in the Sphendone. And so Michael makes Basil a *protostrator* in the place of the one who had died, and he also makes his uncle Bardas a *kouropalates*. At this time thick dust with the colour of blood[3] fell from heaven and down upon the roof tiles, and many people found stones red as blood in the streets and in gardens. Michael promotes Antigonos, the son of Bardas, to *domestikos* of the *scholai*. To Bardas' other son[4] he had given a wife. But he was deceived by her. So the emperor makes him *monostrategos*[5] of the Western *themata*; he then died there. After a short while, on the Tuesday of the *Diakinesimos*,[6] Michael promotes his uncle Bardas to caesar, and Bardas rode in a chariot and distributed largesse in the Mese. **24** Also Amer went out, and he came down as far as Sinope[7] and, having pillaged all Roman territory, returned without being caught by the Roman army. **25** Michael goes out

---

1 This was 15 March 856.

2 First of the *stratores*, imperial grooms with a duty to accompany the emperor when on horseback.

3 This is a reference to Saharan dust. The Greek (κόνις ... αἱματῶδης πλήρης) is a little odd. αἵματος πλήρης, as in some MSS, would do, but there seems to be an error in the transmission.

4 The name of this son (and his wife) is unknown.

5 This title occurs only here in this text but a couple of times elsewhere, e.g. in Theophanes. It is of somewhat uncertain meaning: by Mango/Scott 1997 it is translated as 'commander-in-chief,' or *generalissimo* (see in particular p. 550, n. 4).

6 This was 26 April 862, the week after Easter ('New Week').

7 This expedition of the emir of Melitene took place in 863.

with an army together with Caesar Bardas, and he moves against Michael,[1] the ruler of Bulgaria, on land and sea. This he did since he had learnt that the Bulgarian people were suffering famine. On learning of his approach the Bulgarians retreated as at the sound of thunder and, even before the action and the battle had begun, they despaired about their chances for victory, and they asked to become Christians and to subject themselves to the emperor and the Romans. Thus the emperor had their leader christened and received him and gave him his own name. He also had all the Bulgarian noblemen brought to the City and christened there.[2] From this moment there was profound peace. **26** Amer went out again against Romania, and Petronas, who was *stratelates* of the East, and Nasar of the Boukellarioi lay in ambush for him at the road where he had to return. They met with Amer at Lalakaon, and there is a skirmish, and they rout him and, when he flees, he is hunted down by one of the *komites*, who cut off his head and brought it back to Petronas the *stratelates*.[3] When the *strategoi* came to the City with the spoils, they made a triumphant display of them in the hippodrome. After this, because of the killing of Amer there was total peace also in the East. And to others belonged the toil and the valiant deeds against the enemy, but the emperor's love for Basil grew, and he considered him to be the only one who could really serve him. **27** Michael built a stable for his horses and embellished it with marble slabs, and he had water fountains constructed in it and made it very beautiful. Now, there was a man in the City called Peter, who was witty and given to mockery, also called Ptochomagistros.[4] When the stable was finished, Michael invited this man to the stable and showed him the unreasonable splendour of the building. This he did because he wanted to be praised by Peter, and he also said, 'I will always be remembered by this building project.' But Peter said to the emperor: 'Justinian built the Great Church, and he had it decorated with gold and silver and precious marble, and nobody remembers him nowadays. And you, emperor, who have made a dung-deposit and a resting-place for

---

1 Still called Boris at this time (cf. following n.).

2 The expedition against Bulgaria, leading to the christening of this nation, took place in 864–865. Michael III acted as godfather to the Bulgarian prince Boris, who took the name of Michael.

3 Amer was killed 3 September 863 in the battle at the river Lalakaon, in north-western Anatolia.

4 '(the) poor *magistros*'; cf. the sobriquet Ptochoprodromos for Prodromos, author of satirical verse.

horses,[1] you think that you will be remembered by this?' Failing to receive the expected praise, the emperor was infuriated, and he had Ptochomagistros kicked out and beaten. **28** There was a rumour going around that Caesar Bardas was sleeping with his fiancée.[2] On hearing this, the patriarch Ignatios repeatedly pleaded with him to abstain from this scandalous act and not become a stumbling block for many people, he who, instead, should be an example of virtue and a chaste way of life. But Bardas did not obey this, but violently attacked the patriarch who was accusing him and entreating him to be chaste. At one time, when Bardas was about to receive Holy Communion, the patriarch turned him away for not obeying the ecclesiastical canons and the recommendations given to him. Bardas was struck with anger in his soul, and he chased the man who exhorted him away from the church and called him lawless and corrupt, and he subjected him to endless, brutal torture, which made the patriarch resign. However, he does not give in,[3] and he appoints Photios patriarch instead of Ignatios, Photios who was a *protasekretis* at that time and a very learned man.[4] **29** Having left Ooryphas, a *hyparchos*, in the City to guard it, the emperor went on an expedition against the Hagarenes.[5] But before the emperor had achieved anything that he planned and had in mind, Ooryphas announced the arrival of the godless Russians; the emperor was already at Mauropotamon[6] when this happened. So the emperor turned away from the road on which he was travelling. Nor[7] did he achieve anything worthy of an emperor, or noble, while he was travelling on the road back to the City. But the Russians had already arrived inside Hieron,[8] and they had murdered many Christians and shed

1 Or: 'senseless animals' (Greek ἀλόγων).

2 I.e. they were suspected of having pre-marital sex.

3 τοῦ δὲ μὴ πεισθέντος: this is vague, but taken here to refer to Bardas. Otherwise, Ignatios is intended, meaning that he had an opportunity to apologise and stay patriarch after all.

4 With other words, Photios was a layman. The change of patriarchs took place in October 858.

5 The events of §§ 29–30 (the war against the Arabs and the simultaneous attack by the Rus on Constantinople) took place in 860. This is the first recorded attack of the Rus (whether they be Russians proper or Scandinavians). See also Wortley 2010, pp. 107–108.

6 This is in Cappadocia.

7 The text is difficult at this point and may be corrupt.

8 I.e. they were already travelling down the Bosphorus. The remains of the fortress of Hieron still stand on the north-eastern shore of the Bosphorus, overlooking the Black Sea.

much innocent blood. Two hundred ships were surrounding the City and causing great fear to those inside. **30** When the emperor arrived at the City, he came through [the blockade] with difficulty. Together with the patriarch Photios he came to the Church of the Mother of God at Blachernai, where they try to placate and propitiate the Divine. They took out the holy *omophorion*[1] of the Mother of God, and they brought it to the shore and dipped it into the water. And, although there was a calm, winds suddenly came up and, although the sea was still, successive waves rose against each other, and the ships of the godless Russians were broken into pieces, and few of them escaped the danger. **31** When Caesar Bardas, dressed in a silk *skaramangion*,[2] came to the Horologion in procession, Damianos the *patrikios* and *parakoimomenos*, who was sitting there, did not rise in his honour.[3] On seeing this, the caesar was extremely angered and, going into the Chrysotriklinos[4] and seating himself close to the emperor, he wept in fury and rage. The emperor asked for the reason, and he said: 'At your Majesty's behest, I have been considered worthy of great honour. But in disrespect of me and of your Majesty, Damianos the *parakoimomenos* did not rise to me in front of the Senate.' This infuriates the emperor and at once he orders a certain Maximianos, a *koitonites*, to apprehend Damianos and to bring him to the emporium of St Mamas and tonsure him as a monk there and order that he should be kept under guard. And on the same day he promotes Basil the *protostrator* to the rank of *parakoimomenos*. But the caesar became envious on hearing this, and from this time on he wanted to kill Basil. **32** Michael divorced Basil from his wife Mary and gave him Eudokia Ingirina as wife, and he ordered him to have her as his official wife. She was the emperor's concubine, and he loved her dearly because of her beauty. But to Basil's former wife Mary he gave gold and other things, and he sent her home to Macedonia. His own sister, Thekla, Michael attached to Basil as his mistress. **33** From this time on, the caesar and Basil watched each other with suspicion, and both looked for an opportunity to kill the other. Basil slandered the caesar in private and said that he plotted against him.[5] But the emperor considered

1 I.e. robe or veil. Cf. Chapter 136, § 32, where Romanos I Lekapenos employs the *omophorion* against Symeon the Bulgarian.

2 A long tunic, worn by emperors but also by others (in this text only mentioned for Caesar Bardas and for Basil on becoming emperor).

3 Cf. above, § 20, and the similar setting for the murder of Theoktistos.

4 A reception hall in the Great Palace.

5 I.e. that Caesar Bardas plotted against Basil, or possibly against the emperor.

this nonsense. In his eagerness to furnish information to the emperor, Basil becomes friendly with Symbatios, the *patrikios* and *logothetes tou dromou*, the son-in-law of the caesar. By oaths they guaranteed each other that they would be of one mind and in constant affection. Basil also told Symbatios under a terrible oath: 'The emperor has great affection for you, and I too work for your sake. He thinks about making you caesar but, because of your father-in-law, he cannot do that.' Deceived by Basil's oaths Symbatios became the enemy of Caesar Bardas, his own father-in-law, and he went in to the emperor and told him under oath: 'The caesar wants to kill you'; and he told everything about the plan. The emperor believed what Symbatios said under oath and, being confirmed in his belief by what Basil said, he secretly began to make plans against the caesar. **34** Knowing that everything was well prepared against the caesar but not being able to put any plans into practice in the City, Basil persuades the emperor to deploy a fleet and an army against Crete. When this happened, Leo the philosopher entreated Caesar Bardas to keep calm and to watch out for Basil. And, for his part, the caesar begged the emperor once again to protect him from Basil. On the day of the Annunciation[1] a procession was made to the Chalkoprateia and, when the entry had taken place[2] and the gospel had been read, the patriarch Photios and the emperor, together with the caesar and Basil the *parakoimomenos*, went up to the catechumens,[3] and the patriarch held the honourable body and blood of Our Lord Jesus Christ in his hands. And the emperor and Basil dipped their hands in holy water and made the sign of the Holy Cross, and they reassured the caesar by oaths[4] that he could make the expedition together with them without fear. For Leo the philosopher had told Bardas explicitly that he should not set out with them, saying that, if he did so, he would not return. **35** After the celebration of Holy Easter the emperor set out with a great army, and he arrived in the *thema* of Thrakesion.[5] When they came to Kepoi,[6] Basil the *parakoimomenos* proceeded with his plan to kill the caesar. Marianos, his brother, was involved in this plan, and Symbatios and Bardas, [also][7] his brothers, and Asyleon, his cousin, and

---

1 Greek εὐαγγελισμός: this was 25 March 866.
2 I.e. into St Sophia.
3 I.e. into the galleries.
4 Thereby, as we shall see, committing a kind of perjury (*ante factum*).
5 In western Asia Minor.
6 A mustering point for the military forces at the Meander river (in western Asia Minor).
7 This is a little oddly put. However, on Basil's brothers see also below, § 50.

Peter the Bulgarian and John the Chaldean and Constantine Toxaras. John Neatokometes understood what was going on, and therefore he went down to the caesar's tent at sunset. There he met with Prokopios, the caesar's *protovestiarios*, and he told him in earnest: 'Tomorrow our lord caesar will be cut down and slaughtered.' Prokopios entered the tent and informed the caesar about this. But on hearing this, the caesar said to Prokopios: 'Go and tell Neatokometes: "You are talking nonsense; you know that you are a young man, and the office of *patrikios* does not suit you. This is the reason why you stir up these tares."'[1] **36** Having spent a sleepless night, Bardas gathered all his men together before daybreak, and he revealed to them what he had been told, and he asked for their advice. Philotheos, the *protospatharios* and *genikos*, and a personal friend of his, said to the caesar: 'Tomorrow, my Lord, dress in your golden[2] coat and show yourself to your enemies; and they will flee from your sight!'[3] **37** At sunrise Bardas mounted his horse and arrived at the emperor's camp with a splendid display of men surrounding him; his *protostrator* was the noble Eustathios Argyros. But at Basil's behest Constantine Toxaras came forward to meet him, and he knelt in front of Bardas and then turned back and announced the caesar's arrival to Basil. Basil too went out and knelt in front of him and took him by the hand and brought him to the emperor. The caesar sat down with the emperor and said: 'All the people, my Lord, are gathered together. Now order them to cross to Crete.' Behind them stood Basil. With his hand he made a threatening sign against the caesar. Suddenly, the caesar turned around and saw Basil who threatened him. At that instant Basil struck Bardas with his sword, and the others who were there cut him limb from limb while the emperor watched in silence. **38** This was at the third hour of the day. Immediately afterwards, the emperor and Basil turned back towards the City. When they came as far as the emporium of Akritas, a lot of people had gathered together to see the emperor. Among these there was a man dressed in monastic habit standing on a high cliff and shouting to the emperor: 'A splendid expedition, indeed, O emperor, that you have killed your own kinsman and your paternal blood by the sword. Woe unto you, woe unto you, for what you have done.' This infuriates the emperor, and he and Basil send Morotheodoros, the

---

1 'stir up these tares': this is Matthew 13.25.

2 'golden': the text has χρυσοπερσικόν, which is difficult (it is unknown from other texts). Perhaps χρυσοπερίκλειστον ('with golden rims'), known from *De Cerimoniis*, is the required word.

3 This is Deuteronomy 28.7.4 (cf. Judith 14.3.5).

manglabites,[1] to kill the monk with a sword. But the people closed in upon him who had been sent,[2] and they pleaded for the monk, saying that he was mad and possessed by a spirit; and so, although with difficulty, he escaped punishment. **39** Late on the Saturday of Pentecost, the emperor, through his *protovestiarios* Rentakios, commanded Photios the patriarch to make announcement of Basil's ascent to the throne.[3] And on the following day two sedan chairs were brought out [from the palace]. This troubled the people: how could it be that two chairs were brought out when there was only one emperor? When the emperor went in the procession, Basil walked behind him wearing a *skaramangion* with a sword, as is the custom for the *parakoimomenos*. When the emperor came to the imperial doors, he did not, as is the custom of emperors, put down his crown. Instead, he kept it on until he came to the holy gates,[4] and he turned aside, and still with the crown on his head he ascended the three steps of the ambo. Just below the emperor stood Basil the *parakoimomenos*, and below Basil, Leo the *kastor*[5] and *asekretis*, who held an imperial *tomos*[6] in his hands, and Michael the *praipositos*,[7] called Angouris, and the demarchs[8] together with the demes. **40** Thus Leo the *asekretis* started to read, saying that 'Caesar Bardas plotted against me in order to kill me, and for this reason he lured me away from the City and, if this had not been announced to me by Symbatios and Basil, I would not be among the living. Bardas died as a consequence of his own sin. Now I want Basil the *parakoimomenos*, who is faithful to me and who guards my imperial power and who has saved me from my enemy and loves me dearly, to be the guardian of my power and to take care of me, and I want him to be universally hailed as emperor.' At this, Basil's eyes were filled with tears. The emperor took the crown from his own head and gave it to Photios, the patriarch. Photios took the crown to the altar[9] and prayed

1 Or: '*maglabites*,' a kind of police officer responsible for corporal punishment (cf. above, Chapter 130, § 31).

2 I.e. Morotheodoros.

3 Basil was crowned 26 May 866.

4 Of St Sophia.

5 The meaning of this is uncertain: perhaps the title of quaestor is hiding here; otherwise it might be a personal name.

6 A roll (or, at least, document) containing a decree.

7 Earlier the title of the head chamberlain (cf. above, Chapter 103, § 3), at this time it probably entails a ceremonial function in the palace (see, e.g., the following paragraph where *praipositoi* assist at the crowning ceremony of Basil I).

8 Perhaps the leaders of the circus factions.

9 I.e. into the hidden, holy area.

over it. And the *praipositoi* brought a *divitision*[1] and *tzangia*[2] and dressed Basil in them. Having donned the *chlamys*[3] he fell before the emperor's feet. And the patriarch came out and[4] took the crown from the emperor's head and handed it to him in his hands. And when the sceptres fell, Michael crowned Basil in the customary way, and everyone cried in acclamation: 'Long live Michael and Basil!' **41** The *kastor* and *asekretis*,[5] who had read the *tomos* out loud, came to Nicomedia and went to a monastery for men, built in the middle of a swamp, where he remained. There was a well there, and the man fell into it and was drowned, and he was buried there.[6] **42** When Symbatios, who was the son-in-law of the caesar, was not given the office of caesar, he realised that he had been deceived by Basil, and he started to hate him, and he agreed with George Peganes, the *stratelates*, that on the next day he should ask to be made a *stratagos*. Instead of him Goumer, who also was *komes* of Opsikion, was made *logothetes tou dromou*. And Symbatios and Peganes went out together and started to ravage and burn cornfields and vineyards (for it was harvest time), and rejecting Basil they hailed Michael alone. On learning this, the emperors ordered the rest of the *stratelatai* to overcome them. Nikephoros Maleinos made a plan: he threw written documents everywhere among the people, telling them to apprehend the men secretly and not fight them openly and so risk a civil war. And so everyone let the men alone.[7] **43** Peganes was apprehended, and they took him and brought him into the City. On the orders of the emperor, the *eparchos* Constantine Myares blinds him, and they placed him at the Milion and put a vessel in his hands, and everyone who passed by could throw into it whatever they wanted to and happened to have handy. And thirty days later Symbatios the Armenian was seized by Maleinos in a guest-house in Keltzene,[8] and Maleinos brought him to the emperor who was at St Mamas. And on the orders of the emperor they bring Peganes to meet Symbatios, and they put a pottery censer in Peganes'

---

1 A silk tunic dress.

2 Shoes, in this case of the elegant kind and in the colour (red/purple) reserved for the emperor.

3 A cloak.

4 There may be a short lacuna here, and perhaps we should read something like: 'and the patriarch came out, put the crown on the emperor's head (uttered a prayer), took the crown, etc.'

5 I.e. Leo (see above, § 39).

6 This bad death is obviously thought to be the just punishment for the man's participation in the promotion of Basil.

7 I.e., presumably, withdrew all support from them.

8 A fortified city on the Euphrates, in eastern Anatolia.

hands with sulphur as perfume, and they blind the same Symbatios in one eye and cut off his right hand. Then they put him at Lausos[1] and gave him a vessel in his lap so that whoever was inclined to do so, could throw him something. And three days later they brought the men to their own houses and kept them under surveillance there. **44** The emperor Michael sent an engineer[2] called Lamaris and had Constantine Kaballinos taken out of his grave.[3] He found the body in good shape, but when he wanted to put him in a bag, Constantine Kaballinos did not fit into it, so he had to be wrapped up in a cloth. Likewise, he took the patriarch Jannes[4] from his grave together with his *omophorion*. And these were, on the orders of the emperor, locked into the *praitorion* for two days by the *hyparchos*,[5] and on a day with races in the hippodrome the *hyparchos* had them taken out and stripped of their robes and corporally punished, and he sent their bones to the Amastrianos[6] to be burnt. The emperor had Kopronymos' sarcophagus, a wondrous work out of green stone, sawn up, and he had it made into a balustrade for the church that he built in the palace at Pharos.[7] **45** The emperor Leo was born to Michael and Eudokia Ingerina.[8] This was while Michael was still alive, on the first of the month of September, in the fifteenth[9] year of the indiction.[10] **46** The

---

1 I.e. they were placed where a lot of people were bound to pass by: Lausos (chiefly the name of a palace) was probably located between the hippodrome and the Mese, and close to the already mentioned Milion.

2 μηχανικός.

3 This is Constantine V, also nicknamed Kopronymos. The reason why Constantine is picked out for this bizarre punishment *post mortem* could, perhaps, be his status as an ideological leader of iconoclasm (cf. also above, Chapter 124, § 21). According to *Theophanes continuatus* and Skylitzes (see Wortley 2010, p. 107), the tomb was put to new use as a prison for Patriarch Ignatios.

4 I.e. John the Grammarian, the prominent iconoclast patriarch (see Chapter 128, § 5, etc.).

5 Perhaps wrong for *eparchos*, an official more likely to be responsible for punishments.

6 This was an open space to the west of the Forum Bovis.

7 The Church of the Virgin in the Great Palace.

8 It is a very surprising statement that Leo VI was the natural son of Michael III. A parallel, also pointing at the promiscuity of Michael and Basil (and of Eudokia Ingerina), is constituted by the case of Prince Constantine (see chapter 132, § 18), where, conversely, it is hinted (with less conviction) that Basil, rather than Michael, was the biological father.

9 This would be 1 September 866. Sometimes his birth is put at 19 September (so V. Grumel (*Echos d'Orient* 35 (1936), pp. 331–333)).

10 An indiction is originally a period for taxation. The term is used in Byzantine times for a fifteen-year cycle. That the term is used occasionally from here on (often, as we shall see, erroneously), may point at a change of authorship, or main source, of the text.

emperor also arranged horse races at St Mamas and drove for the Blue party. Constantine the Armenian (he was the father of Thomas the *patrikios* and of Genesios[1]), *droungarios* of the *vigla*, drove with white colours, and Agallianos drove with green colours, and Krasas with red. When the emperor had won and had sat down to dinner together with Basil and Eudokia,[2] Basiliskianos the *patrikios* praised the emperor for driving his chariot so skilfully. At this the emperor ordered him to stand up and to accept the emperor's *tzangia* as a gift and to put them on.[3] When Basiliskianos hesitated to do so and looked towards Basil, the emperor ordered him in fury to do it. Now Basil nodded assent, and Basiliskianos put the shoes on. But the emperor cursed loudly and said to Basil: 'They suit him better than they suit you! And should I, who made you an emperor, not have the power to make also another man emperor?' And he vented his fury against Basil openly. But Eudokia wept and said to the emperor: 'The imperial office, my Lord, is very grand and we, too, have been honoured undeservedly, and it is not right to treat it with contempt.' But the emperor said: 'Do not worry about that. For I want to make Basiliskianos an emperor, too.' **47** Basil was greatly angered and distressed by this. When the emperor went out to the *kynegion*,[4] a monk came towards him and gave him a piece of writing which described Basil's plot against him. On reading this, the emperor became angry and started, in his turn, to plot against Basil. On being invited by his mother Theodora to Anthemios[5] the emperor sent Rentakios, his *protovestiarios*, together with other men, who were his intimates, to do some hunting and to send the catch to his mother.[6] **48** Basil prepared himself against Michael and was in a terrible mood.[7] When the emperor sat down to dinner, he called upon Eudokia and Basil to sit close to him and to dine

1 This may be Joseph Genesios, the historian (cf. Kaldellis 1998).
2 This is Eudokia Ingerina, at this time Basil's wife and the alleged mistress of Michael.
3 This is, of course, most inappropriate, since shoes of this type could only be worn by an emperor.
4 Perhaps the hunting park mentioned in Chapter 69, § 2.
5 This was a place in Chrysopolis with a monastery.
6 Perhaps in order to pave the way for reconciliation?
7 This elaborate description of the murder of Michael III is very different from that of the *Vita Basilii* and Skylitzes, etc., where Basil is said to be under a very real threat from Michael. The description of the present text is also by far the most graphic and detailed, leaving no doubt about Basil's active participation in the deed and his guilt.

with him.[1] Now, when the emperor had drunk a lot of wine, Basil rose with the excuse that he needed to perform a private function, and he went to the emperor's bedchamber and bent its key (he was a strong man) so that the door could not be locked. He then returned and continued to dine with the emperor. **49** When Michael had done even more drinking—with Ingerina, as usual, contributing to his enjoyment—he rose and, supported by Basil, went to his bedroom, and Basil kissed his hand and left.[2] In the bedchamber there was Basiliskianos, who on the emperor's orders slept in Rentakios' bed, so as to be able to protect the emperor. Ignatios the *koitonites* went to lock the door of the bedchamber but found that it[3] had been twisted. This disconcerted him, and he sat down on the bed tearing his hair. **50** Now the wine-sozzled emperor was sleeping a sleep similar to death. When Basil suddenly arrived, with some other men, and opened the door, Ignatios came out and in terror entreated Basil not to enter. But Peter the Bulgarian passed under Basil's armpit and went straight to the emperor's bed. There he was apprehended by Ignatios who tried to plead with him, at which the emperor woke up. At once John the Chaldean struck the emperor with his sword and cut off his hands. And Jakobitzes ...[4] the *apelates*,[5] the Persian—these men wounded Basiliskianos with the sword and threw him off his feet. Marianos and Bardas, the father of Basil the *rector*,[6] and Symbatios, Basil's brothers, and Asyleon, who was Basil's cousin, and Constantine Toxaras—all these stood on guard outside, and none of Michael's men understood what was happening. **51** Then Basil and his men gathered together to discuss the situation. Asyleon said to Basil, that 'even if we have cut off his hands, we have still left him alive and, if he lives, what can we say in our defence?' And as a favour to Basil he turned back and found Michael lying on his couch, without hands, and wailing pitiably against Basil. Showing no mercy Asyleon planted his naked sword in the heart of the emperor, and he cut

---

1 This dinner and the subsequent murder took place in the Anthimos palace.

2 This, with the act of kissing, could be a kind of allusion to Judas Iscariot.

3 I.e., presumably, the key.

4 There seems to be a lacuna in the text at this point: comparing with Chapter 132, § 2, we have reason to be believe that Jakobitzes and the Persian *apelates* were two different individuals. § 52 below shows that there were several Persians (or rather: Armenians) involved in this episode.

5 An *apelates* was a lightly equipped irregular soldier on frontier duty or engaged in brigandage, often of foreign origin.

6 A high-ranking palace official.

through his intestines. He then went back to the others and bragged about the matter in front of Basil—as if he had done a most valiant deed. **52** There was a storm at sea [that night], and Basil's men gathered together and went down to Perama[1] and crossed over to the house of Eulogios the Persian, and they took him with them and went to the Marina neighbourhood[2] and up through the wall and to the palace. There was a slab, which supported[3] the wall. Basil took two of his men with him and kicked the slab and brought it down, and so they were able to get through and to the palace gates. Eulogios the Persian spoke in his own tongue[4] to Artavasdos the *hetaireiarches* and said: 'Michael has been killed by the sword, so open for the emperor!' **53** And Artavasdos ran to the *papias* and took the keys from him by force and opened up for Basil who, when he came inside, took personal control of the palace keys; on the following morning he made Gregory, with the by-name 'of Philemon,' *papias*. At once Basil sends a messenger to St Mamas, and so he brought Eudokia, daughter of Inger, to the palace with great ceremony. He also sent John the *praipositos* to take the Dekapolitissa[5] and bring her to her parents. **54** Basil sent Paul the *koitonites* to bury Michael. Arriving there, Paul found him wrapped in the saddlecloth of the right horse that he drove,[6] and he found his intestines hanging out. He also found Michael's mother and sisters there, weeping and lamenting over him. And he put Michael on a barge and crossed over to the monastery of Chrysopolis[7] and had him buried there.

---

1 On the Golden Horn, about at the site of the modern Galata bridges.
2 Ta Marines: around the palace of the same name.
3 περιφράσσουσα.
4 I.e., presumably, in Armenian.
5 I.e. Eudokia Dekapolitissa, wife of Michael III.
6 Presumably one of a chariot pair used for circus games.
7 Michael was buried in the Philippikos monastery in Chrysopolis.

132 How Basil Achieved Imperial Power[1]

Basil reigned for one year and four months together with Michael, and for nineteen years alone.[2] He ordered the *hyparchos* and[3] Marianos, son of Petronas, to go up to the Forum and proclaim him sole emperor in the presence of the whole people. 2 I have considered it necessary to write also about God's vengeance upon those who laid hands on Michael and to tell what happened to each of them respectively.[4] Jakobitzes went hunting with the emperor in the Philopation[5] when, dropping his sword and getting down to pick it up, before his foot had reached the ground, and while his other foot was still stuck in the stirrup,[6] his horse was frightened and dragged him through gullies and hollows and caused him to be torn to pieces. John the Chaldean, who had become *stratelates* in Chaldea,[7] was detected plotting against the emperor and, on the emperor's orders, was impaled by the *stratelates* Andreas. The emperor's cousin, Asyleon, was forced by the emperor to go into retirement at his estate called the Chartophylax and, since he was cruel and brutal towards his slaves, he was murdered by them with daggers during the night. The emperor seized these people, and had them cut to pieces and burnt them in the Amastrianos.

---

1 This is a slightly unsuitable and anomalous heading (Greek Ὅπως ἐκράτησε τῆς βασιλείας Βασίλειος). The chapter does not deal with Basil's road to power (this is dealt with in the previous chapter) but is rather the normal kind of chapter about an emperor's reign.

2 Basil I reigned, as a co-emperor to Michael, 26 May 866–23 September 867 and, as senior emperor, until 29 August 886. Cf. to this chapter Skylitzes (Wortley 2010, pp. 116–164), Ps.-Symeon 686.11–699.22, and *Vita Basilii* (Ševčenko 2011). The story told here (starting in the previous chapter), painting an indifferent or negative picture of Basil, stands in stark contrast with *Vita Basilii* in particular.

3 There are two textual problems involved here: first, whether the title should be *hyparchos* or *eparchos* and, second, whether one or two persons are implied, i.e. whether Marianos is the *hyparchos/eparchos* himself or if he is rather accompanied by such an official. Ps. Sym 687.6 mentions no active person but Marianos ('Marianos, the *hyparchos* and son of Petronas'). However, the MSS of this text unanimously state that two different persons are meant.

4 This excursus recounts the typical bad death of evildoers. For the formula ('I have considered it necessary'), cf. Chapter 109, § 10, and Chapter 131, § 8.

5 Philopation was a region outside the City walls, opposite the Blachernai, with a palace and a garden complex. It was favoured by several emperors, including Basil.

6 'stirrup': the translated Greek word is σκάλα. This could be either a stirrup in the modern sense or a contraption such as a ladder, from which a horse could be mounted.

7 'Chaldea' (or 'Chaldia'): (at this time) a Byzantine *thema* in north-eastern Anatolia.

The *apelates*, the Persian,[1] became infested with worms and thus lost his life. Constantine Toxaras died by the sword in the Kibyrrhaiotai. Finally, Marianos, the emperor's brother, broke his leg when falling from his horse, and, developing gangrene, died infested with worms. **3** On Christmas Day, the emperor went forth in the procession to the Great Church, and had his son, Stephen, baptised.[2] He came in a chariot drawn by white horses, and he sat with the *augusta*, and the *praipositos*, Baanes, was with them and held the child all the way to the palace, while the emperor was distributing largesse in the street. **4** There was a very great earthquake at St Polyeuktos, and the earth trembled for forty days and forty nights.[3] On this occasion, the globe of the statue at the Forum[4] also fell down, as well as the Church of the Most Holy Mother of God, the one at what is known as the Sigma, and all those who were chanting there at the time were killed. Leo the philosopher,[5] who happened to be there, told the chanters and all the people present to get out of the church, but they did not obey him, and they all perished. The philosopher himself stood by a pillar under a beam and was saved with two other people; along with five others, who remained under the ambo, these were the only ones to be saved. **5** When the emperor came to the church in order to receive Holy Communion, Photios, the patriarch, called him a robber, a murderer and unworthy of divine communion. This infuriated the emperor, who sent a messenger to Rome and had an edict [from the pope] brought by Roman bishops, and he had Photios ousted from the throne, and made the blessed Ignatios patriarch for the second time.[6] **6** The emperor Alexander was born from Eudokia, daughter of Inger.[7] He was a legitimate child of Basil's.[8] **7** The emperor went to war against the Hagarenes of Tibrike, and

1 There is a slight textual problem here, and the transmitted text reads as '*apelates of* the Persian' (Greek ἀπελάτης τοῦ Πέρσου). Cf., however, above, Chapter 131, § 50.

2 Stephen was born in November 867 and was baptised on Christmas Day of the same year.

3 This earthquake took place 9 January 869.

4 I.e. the statue of Constantine the Great.

5 Cf. Chapter 130, § 34–35, where the same Leo becomes famous, and Chapter 131, § 34, where he warns Caesar Bardas to beware of Basil.

6 Photios was forced to abdicate 23 September 867, and Ignatios was made patriarch 23 November of the same year.

7 Alexander was born perhaps 23 November 870.

8 Cf. Chapter 131, § 45, where it is said explicitly that Leo was the son of Michael III.

he joined battle but was defeated.[1] He often joined battle with the Hagarenes, and he lost many Roman lives. When the emperor was fleeing and was almost captured by the Hagarenes, he was saved by Theophylaktos Abastaktos, the father of Romanos who later became emperor. After this, the emperor searched for his saviour, and he found him and recognised him (there were many people who told the emperor: 'I am the one who saved you'). But Theophylaktos refused to accept the reward offered him but asked for a place in the succession, which he also received.[2] On returning to the City, the emperor sent Christopher, his son-in-law, to Tibrike, and he achieved a very great victory, destroying the city and razing it to the ground. **8** Ignatios, the patriarch, had a most beautiful church built in the emporium of Sator;[3] it was named after the Archistratege, the Rising One. The same patriarch also had a male monastery built, in which his body is resting. **9** Thekla, the sister of the emperor,[4] sent a certain member of her household called Metrios to the emperor [Basil] in order to deliver a message, and the emperor asked him: 'Who has your lady?'[5] He said: 'Neatokometes.' The emperor at once sent for Neatokometes, and had him beaten and tonsured and clad in monastic garb. Likewise, he sent his *protovestiarios* Prokopios and had Thekla beaten. Prokopios also took all Thekla's money and brought it to the emperor. Later, the emperor made Neatokometes *oikonomos* in the Great Church. **10** The same emperor also had all the Jews of his realm baptised, and all those in high positions took part in receiving them,[6] and the emperor treated the Jews kindly and gave them much support and many gifts. **11** The afore-mentioned Nicholas, the one called Androsalites, who was also *prosmonarios* of St Diomedes, and to whom, as has been said

1 This is the fortress Tephrike in north-eastern Cappadocia. Having become a Paulician stronghold ca. 850, it was captured and ultimately destroyed by the Byzantines in the 870s, although there is some dispute as to the exact date of this (perhaps 878, see Ševčenko 2011, Chapter 50.1–2).

2 The claim that Theophylaktos, father of emperor Romanos I (for Romanos see Chapter 135, §21ff., and Chapters 136–37), had saved Basil and so provided a justification for the aspirations of the Lekapenoi goes well with the supposition that this part of the work contains Lekapenian propaganda.

3 This should refer to the Satyros complex, already mentioned above, Chapter 126, § 4 (cf. Ps.-Sym 690.14–16 and Theophanes Cont. 1, § 10).

4 In fact, she was the sister of the former emperor, Michael III.

5 I.e. approximately: 'Who is your lady's man?'

6 I.e. they acted as godfathers at the baptism.

earlier, the witness about the emperor had appeared,[1] the emperor honoured with the offices of *oikonomos* and *synkellos*. He also made one of his brothers, John, *droungarios* of the *vigla*, and his other brother, Paul, [was given a post] at the *sakellion*,[2] and the other, Constantine, [he made] *logothetes tou genikou*. When Nicholas the *synkellos* dies, they bury him in Arkadianai,[3] in his own house, the place where there is now[4] the *metochion*[5] of St Constantine. **12** Having expropriated many houses, the emperor started to excavate near the Great Palace in order to build the Nea Ekklesia.[6] Then it was announced to the emperor that Syracuse was being besieged by the Hagarenes. However, since the navy personnel were occupied in the construction and excavation of the Nea Ekklesia, there was some delay in [preparing] the fleet and the people, and Syracuse surrendered shortly before the fleet arrived, and the emperor wept and lamented much because of this.[7] **13** Niketas Xylinites, the *epi tes trapezes*,[8] was accused of being the *augusta*'s lover, and for this reason the emperor had him tonsured and made a monk. In the emperor Leo's reign, Niketas became *oikonomos* in the Great Church and, when he died, he was laid to rest in the monastery he himself had built. Basil also made his sisters into nuns. **14** The emperor had many bronze objects taken down to be used for the Nea Ekklesia, but he also took pieces of marble and mosaic tesserae and pillars from many churches and other buildings in order to build it. Among these was a bronze statue in the form of a bishop which stood in the Senate building;[9] the figure was holding a staff in its hand around which curled a snake. This statue they took away and put in the imperial *vestiarion*.[10] The emperor went down to the place where the statue had been erected, and he put his finger into the snake's mouth. A real snake lived there, and it bit the emperor's finger. Although he received an

1 Cf. above, Chapter 131, § 13ff.
2 'purse,' or 'treasury' (cf. the term *vestiarion* used below, § 14).
3 In Constantinople.
4 This is a case of a reference to a point in time later than that of the narrative.
5 I.e. a monastic dependency.
6 I.e. the 'New Church.'
7 The works on the Nea Ekklesia in the city, one of the most prestigious building projects of Basil's reign, may have started in the autumn of 877. Syracuse fell to the Arabs 20–21 May 878.
8 Responsible for the emperor's table.
9 Greek ἐν τῷ σενάτῳ (the word *senaton* occurring only here in the text). It is unclear where this was at this time. Perhaps the Magnaura is intended.
10 'treasury' or, possibly, 'state warehouse' (cf. above, § 11, *sakellion*).

antidote, the emperor barely escaped alive, and everyone wondered at this. Also, he had the statue of Solomon in the largest basilica[1] taken down, and ordered that it should be given an inscription with his name and be placed in the undercroft[2] of the Nea Ekklesia, as if he were offering himself in dedication for this building project and to God. **15** Once more, the emperor went to war, against Melitene, and after having taken many prisoners and fought many battles he returned home.[3] **16** St Ignatios the patriarch dies and, in his place, the emperor once again, for a second time, puts Photios on the patriarchal throne.[4] When later Photios died in exile, his body was laid to rest in the Eremia monastery in Merdosagari; this was earlier a public[5] church, but it had been made into a monastery for nuns by Photios himself.[6] **17** Once again the emperor goes to war, this time against Germanikeia in Syria, and having pillaged this city and taken prisoners he returned home.[7] **18** Constantine, the son of the emperor Michael by Eudokia, but according to rumour the son of Basil, dies.[8] Basil, who had loved him dearly, was deeply afflicted, and Constantine's body was put to rest in the imperial mausoleum. **19** On the first of May the church, which the emperor had built and embellished elaborately, is inaugurated and consecrated by the patriarch Photios. And the emperor wore a *loros* at the inauguration and bestowed much money on the church and named it the Nea.[9] **20** Prokopios the *protovestiarios* was sent out by the emperor with all the Western *themata*.[10] At this time Eupraxios was *stratelates* in Sicily,

---

1 Or possibly: 'very big statue of Solomon in the basilica.' The MS tradition gives different readings and is not reliable.

2 Or: 'foundations.'

3 This expedition is variously dated: perhaps 879 or 873.

4 Ignatios died 23 October 877. Photios was reinstalled directly after this, whereas the approbation by the pope and the synod came in the autumn of 879.

5 καθολική.

6 Photios died sometime after 893. This is in the Mardosangaris district of Constantinople.

7 The expedition against Germanikeia took place in 879.

8 Constantine died 3 September 879. The text of this paragraph is at odds with § 21 below, where Basil's paternity is taken for granted. Cf. also Chapter 131, § 45, where it is claimed that Michael III, not Basil, was the father of Leo VI. The rationale for casting doubt upon the paternity in cases such as these seems (apart from the general promiscuous behaviour of Michael, Basil and their wives and girl-friends) to be signs of affection or hatred too obvious to conceal. Thus, as seen here, Basil's love of Constantine is explained and, Chapter 131, § 45, Basil's hatred of Leo.

9 The inauguration of the Nea Ekklesia took place 1 May 880.

10 The events recorded in this paragraph took place in 882 or 880.

Mousilikes in Cephalonia, Rabdouchos in Dyrrachion and Oiniates and Apostoupes in the Peloponnese. Having accomplished many feats and valiant deeds, it at last came to open war and, when all his men were betrayed by Apostoupes, Prokopios was killed. **21** Leo Salibaras introduces the monk Theodore, archbishop of Euchaita, to the patriarch Photios and tells him that Theodore is a pious man and able to perform miracles and see into the future. Photios, in his turn, introduces him to Basil, the emperor, and the emperor came to like him (for the man agreed with his inclinations) and held him in high esteem. When the emperor was depressed on the death of his son[1] Constantine, for he had loved him dearly, the Santabarene[2] deceived him and promised to show him his son alive, which he did. For, when the emperor was passing through a thicket, he was confronted by an apparition on horseback, dressed in gold and in the shape of Constantine. On seeing this with his own eyes, the emperor embraced it and kissed it and, when it disappeared, he believed he had seen Constantine and did not realise that he had been deceived. Therefore, he also founded a monastery there and named it St Constantine's. By this and very many other similar devices, the Santabarene, who was very well versed in magic of the type practised by Apollonios,[3] made the emperor acquire great faith in him. **22** The emperor brought the daughter of Martinakios as wife to the emperor Leo.[4] He also crowned her,[5] celebrating the marriage in the Magnaura and the Hall of the Nineteen Couches.[6] **23** The Santabarene denounced Leo the emperor to his father and said: 'He carries a dagger around and wishes to kill you.' But it was the Santabarene himself who by his treacherous advice had made Leo procure himself this dagger and wear it in his leggings; he had said to him: 'Your father often asks for a knife for some need or other; why don't you keep one ready for him?'[7] Having procured this dagger, Leo the emperor was denounced by the Santabarene and, having been found out to actually be carrying a

---

1 Cf. to this above, § 18 with note.

2 This is the monk Theodore mentioned at the beginning of the paragraph. He is called 'the Santabarene' because he stemmed from Santabaris, a place in Asia Minor that cannot be located with certainty (perhaps Bardakçı by Eskişehir).

3 Apollonios of Tyana, also mentioned above, Chapter 60, § 4.

4 The bride's name was Theophano.

5 With the wedding crown, but perhaps also as empress.

6 This was perhaps in September 882.

7 This is a strange and highly improbable episode as far as human psychology is concerned.

dagger in his leggings, he was not believed although he protested his innocence eagerly. As a consequence of this, Niketas Helladikos,[1] his *protovestiarios* (the man who was made *papias* during the time of emperor Romanos[2]), was flogged as well as others with him and, after being punished terribly, they were sent into exile. **24** The emperor imprisoned Leo in the Pearl Hall and intended to have him blinded. This would have happened had not Photios, the patriarch, together with Stylianos Zaoutzes, who was *mikros hetaireiarches*[3] at the time, made the emperor change his mind by appealing to him constantly.[4] Leo spent three months[5] away from the public eye, wailing and lamenting and writing countless letters with pleas to the emperor. Now, the emperor had great faith in St Elijah, and Leo the emperor was reconciled to him on St Elijah's day. When the procession took place and the people saw Leo in it, they shouted: 'Glory to you, God!' But the emperor (Basil) turned to them and said in his own defence: 'Do you praise God for my son? You will have a lot of troubles to endure and hard days to go through because of him!' **25** Andreas, the *domestikos* of the *scholai*, was accused by the Santabarene in front of the emperor for being a supporter of Leo. And therefore he was removed from his office and, in his place, Stoupiotes was made *domestikos*.[6] Stoupiotes then went with many people to Tarsos but was defeated there and lost all his men.[7] And thus, Andreas is made *domestikos* again by the emperor. **26** A plot was hatched against the emperor by John Krokoas, who was a *domestikos* of the *hikanatoi*,[8] and it was supported by the prisoner in the Blachernai.[9] Many of the senators and other people in leading positions (in fact, as many as sixty-six[10] people) were found to be on his side. There was Michael the *hetaireiarches*, and Katoudares, and Myxares, and Baboutzikos, and others. When this plot had been revealed to the emperor

---

1 I.e. from the province of Hellas.

2 I.e. emperor Romanos I, see below.

3 The title of *mikros hetaireiarches* ('lesser hetairiarch') is not attested elsewhere, and the meaning is uncertain. It may be that there was a *Lesser Hetaireia* (in addition to the *Great* and the *Middle Hetaireiai* that we know of). There is also the possibility that Stylianos was heading the barbarian regiment of the *Third Hetaireia*.

4 Photios had been Leo's private teacher.

5 According to some MSS: three years.

6 Known as Kesta Stoupiotes (or Styppiotes).

7 This is the battle of Chrysoboullos at Tarsos 14 September 883.

8 The leader of the *hikanatoi*, one of the *tagmata*.

9 Perhaps Leo.

10 This is a surprisingly precise number.

by Krokoas' *protovestiarios*, and everyone had been caught, the emperor went out to the hippodrome and sat there and examined everything concerning them; he had them flogged, and what hair they had left[1] cut off and burnt. After this, the emperor went out in the procession for the Annunciation,[2] which was the day when they had planned to carry out their coup. They walked behind him naked and in fetters to the Forum, as he had ordered. He then had everyone's belongings confiscated and the people sent into exile. **27** The emperor went out to hunt, and a huge deer appeared unexpectedly and, when the emperor pursued it, it turned upon the emperor and seized him by his belt and dragged him from the horse with its horns. The first to arrive on the spot drew his sword and cut off the emperor's belt, and so saved him. After his return the emperor ordered that the man who had cut off his belt should have his head cut off for having drawn his sword against the emperor. The man protested wildly and said: 'I did this for your sake.' But to no avail. Basil dies having contracted an infection from being mangled by the deer.[3] He leaves Leo as emperor together with Alexander.[4]

133 Leo, Son of Basil

Leo, son of Basil, reigned for twenty-five years and eight months.[5] His brother Stephen, who was a cleric and a *synkellos*, lived together with Photios the patriarch and was fostered and educated by him.[6] **2** After he became emperor, Leo sent the *stratelates* Andreas with many candles and with clerics and senators to Chrysopolis. And they took Michael from the tomb and put him in a coffin of cypress wood and put this on a stretcher

---

1 In other words, an old men's plot.

2 This was 25 March, probably in the year of 886.

3 Basil died 29 August 886.

4 The word here used (instead of *basileus*) for emperor, *autokrator*, is unusual. If 'senior emperor' is meant, it might be implied that Alexander was also emperor at the time (for the question of his status see below, Chapter 133, § 63). If, however, *autokrator* means no more than *basileus* (and Alexander was an emperor at the time), the sentence appears awkward.

5 Leo VI reigned 29(30) August 886–11 May 912. Cf. to this chapter Skylitzes (Wortley 2010, pp. 165–187), and Ps.-Symeon 700.6–715.18.

6 Since in the first paragraph of each chapter dynastic matters are usually set out and persons with a direct claim to the throne are mentioned, one may wonder why Stephen is mentioned here and not Alexander (on the possibility that Alexander had no status as emperor at this time see above, Chapter 132, § 27, and below, Chapter 133, §§ 47 and 63).

and covered it in a way befitting royalty, and they honoured him with hymns and many tokens of respect (Michael's siblings also followed them there), and they took him to the Church of the Holy Apostles and put him in a sarcophagus.¹ **3** After this, the emperor despatched Andreas, *domestikos* of the *scholai*, together with John Hagiopolites, a most learned man and a former *logothetes tou dromou*, and they ascended the ambo of the church and read accusations against the patriarch Photios and forced him from the throne and confined him to the monastery of Armonianai, the one called Bordon's.² And the emperor promoted Stylianos Zaoutzes to the offices of *magistros* and *logothetes tou dromou*. And he brought the *synkellos* Stephen, who was also his brother, to the patriarchate, and before Christmas Stephen is made patriarch by the *protothronos*³ Theophanes and the rest of the bishops, and he remained patriarch for six years and five months; on dying he is buried in the monastery at Sykai.⁴ **4** During Leo's reign the fortress called Hypsele was betrayed and captured by the Hagarenes, and all the people who lived there were made prisoners.⁵ **5** There was also a great fire close to Sophi(an)ai,⁶ and the Church of the Holy Apostle Thomas also burnt down, which the same Leo had renovated in a lavish manner. **6** The emperor sent a messenger to Euchaita and brought Theodore of Santabaris to the City. For Andreas the *domestikos* and Stephen the *magistros*, of Kalomaria, who had been subject to much slander by the Santabarene in the days of Basil, suggested to the emperor (they had made up a story to this effect) that Photios the patriarch and Theodore of Santabaris were planning to make one of Photios' men emperor. The emperor ordered that Photios the patriarch and Theodore of Santabaris should be brought to the palace of Pegai, and he demanded that they should be kept under surveillance separately. **7** Stephen the *magistros* and Andreas the *domestikos* and Krateros and Gouber, who were *patrikioi*,

1 This episode describes Leo's attempt to reach an understanding with the family of Michael III. It may be one of the reasons why Leo was thought by some to be Michael's natural son. It is one of several examples of actions taken by Leo in stark contrast to the policy followed by Basil I.

2 Or: 'Gordon's' or 'Kordon's,' an otherwise unknown institution.

3 This title is used in different contexts to denote the person highest in rank among bishops. In this case it is the bishop of Caesarea.

4 This was at Galata/Pera, over the Golden Horn from Constantinople proper.

5 This was in 887. The fortress was close to Sebasteia (Sivas) in north-eastern Cappadocia.

6 This is possibly the same palace as that mentioned in Chapter 105, § 3, or a part of the city, or another palace (named Sophiai), or a bath.

and John Hagiopolites, were sent by the emperor to investigate the accusations against them. And they brought in the patriarch and placed him on a throne, showing him signs of respect, and they sat down themselves, and Andreas the *domestikos* said to the patriarch: 'My Lord, do you know father Theodore?' He answered: 'I do not know any 'father' Theodore.' Andreas said: 'Don't you know father Theodore of Santabaris?' The patriarch answered: 'I know the monk Theodore, who is the archbishop of Euchaita.' **8** At this stage they brought the Santabarene in to them, and Andreas the *domestikos* says to him: 'The emperor says to you: "Where are the belongings of my empire?"' He said: 'Where the emperor of the day had them placed—there they are. But, if the emperor wants them back, he can take them.' Then Andreas said to him: 'Tell me: who did you plan to make emperor when you cooked up that story and suggested to my father that he should have me blinded—one of the patriarch's men or one of your own?' He answered: 'I have no idea what you are talking about accusing me like this.' At this point Stephen the *magistros* says to him: 'And how come that you asked the emperor: "Shall I question the patriarch on this matter?"' **9** At this the Santabarene fell at the patriarch's feet and said: 'By God I swear to you, my Lord: have me deposed first; then, when I am stripped of the priesthood, they may punish me as a simple criminal. For I did not say anything like this to the emperor.' And the patriarch said in front of everyone: 'By the salvation of my soul, Lord Theodore, you are archbishop in this world as well as in the world to come.' At this Andreas was angered and said: 'So you did not, father, make me ask the emperor on your account: "Shall I question the patriarch on this?"' But he denied any knowledge of the matter. **10** On their return they informed the emperor about their conversation. The emperor was overcome with anger and uncontrollable wrath since he had not found any valid accusation against the patriarch. He sent people and had the Santabarene severely flogged and exiled to Athens. He then sent people after him and had him blinded and exiled to the East. Many years later, however, the emperor acted on a petition and had him returned to the City and ordered that he should receive a pension from the Nea Ekklesia. The Santabarene died during the joint reign of Constantine and Zoe, Constantine's mother.[1] **11** During Leo's reign it also happened that Aiulf, who was *exarchos* and *doux* of Lombardy and the son-in-law of the king of France, rebelled against the emperor and enslaved the whole region and subjected it to his own

1 I.e. somewhere in the period 914–919.

regime.[1] On learning this, the emperor sent Constantine the *epi tes trapezes* with all the Western *themata* to defeat Aiulf. And when battle was joined, Constantine's men were defeated and slaughtered, and he himself barely escaped alive. **12** There was a solar eclipse, so that there was night at the sixth hour and stars became visible.[2] There were also thunder and strong winds and lightning, and seven people were burned to death on the flight of steps to the Forum. And the Hagarenes besieged the fortress of Samos, and Paspalas, the *strategos* in command, was taken prisoner. **13** Leo the emperor appointed Zaoutzes *basileopator*.[3] He had already fallen in love with Zaoutzes' daughter Zoe, whose husband, Theodore Gouzouniates, had died by poison of some kind. **14** When Stephen the patriarch left this world, Anthony, known as Kauleas, was made patriarch in his stead.[4] **15** There was also a message from the *strategos* of Macedonia, to the effect that the leader of Bulgaria, Symeon, is planning to go to war against Romania.[5] The reason why Symeon was angry was the following. Zaoutzes the *basileopator* had as his slave a eunuch by the name of Mousikos. This Mousikos was befriended with Staurakios and Kosmas, two traders from the province of Hellas who were very greedy. With a view to their own sordid gain and by the mediation and influence of Mousikos, these men had removed the Bulgarian market from the City to Thessalonica, and they treated the Bulgarians badly as far as their trading interests were concerned. The Bulgarians reported this to Symeon, and he informed the emperor Leo about it. But the emperor, who was hindered by the *basileopator* who liked Mousikos, treated all of this as of no consequence. **16** At this the Bulgarian loses his temper and goes to war against Romania, and on learning this, the emperor sends Krinites as *stratelates* in command of a heavily armed military force against the Bulgarians; this force included many leaders

1 This is a reference to Aiulf II (Greek Ἀγίων), prince of Benevento 884–891, who tried to counteract the Byzantine ambitions in Calabria, southern Italy, in the 880s by capturing Bari.

2 The solar eclipse took place 8 August 891. It may be that all occurrences listed between the solar eclipse and the death of the patriarch Stephen (§ 14) occurred in the time between these exactly datable occurrences (so Jenkins 1965: see Introduction); however, it is also possible that a number of catastrophes are bunched together, although they in reality were further apart in time.

3 It has been suggested that this was a new title, invented for the occasion, in which case its use above (Chapter 95, § 4) is an anachronism.

4 Stephen died 17/18 May 893, and Anthony Kauleas was made patriarch in August of the same year.

5 These wars with Bulgaria (§§ 15–21) can be dated to around 894–896.

from the City who were negatively inclined against Symeon.[1] When battle is joined in Macedonia, the Romans are routed, and Krinites and the Armenian Kourtikes and all the rest are killed. But some of the Chazars, who were Leo's followers, were apprehended, and their noses were slit so as to bring shame on the Romans, and they were sent back to the City by Symeon. **17** On seeing these, the emperor was infuriated and he sent Niketas, also known as Skleros,[2] with *dromones* into the river Danube to give gifts to the Turks[3] and to incite them to war against Symeon. And Niketas went there and met with the Turkish leaders, Arpades and Kousanes, and they agreed to go to war, and Niketas received hostages and returned to the emperor. And again the emperor sent Eustathios the *patrikios* and *droungarios* of the fleet by sea, and by land he sent Nikephoros Phokas the *patrikios*, who was also a *domestikos*, with the *themata*, and they entered Bulgaria. **18** After this, the emperor embraced a peaceful solution and he also sent Konstantinakes the *quaestor* to Symeon in order to discuss the peace. However, on seeing the movement against him on land and sea Symeon locks the *quaestor* up in a fortress thinking that he has come with foul intentions. At this time (Symeon was occupied with the expedition of Phokas), the Turks passed through Bulgaria, and they enslaved the entire country. On learning this, Symeon moves against the Turks who make a counter-move and join battle with the Bulgarians, and Symeon is routed and barely gets himself safely to Distra.[4] **19** The Turks asked the emperor to send representatives and buy the prisoners' freedom from the Bulgarians. This the emperor did, and he sent citizens who paid for their freedom. But Symeon sued for peace through Eustathios the *droungarios*, and the emperor yielded to this and sent Leo Choirosphaktes to negotiate the peace while Nikephoros together with the *droungarios* Eustathios accepted the task of returning home with the men. However, Symeon did not pay Leo any attention but kept him safely under arrest. Thereupon, Symeon went on an expedition against those Turks, who did not have any protection from the Romans but were left without attention,

---

1 'this … Symeon': this is a somewhat free translation of Greek which is not necessarily corrupt but somewhat loose in its structure.

2 I.e. 'the hard one': this is the name of a well-known family in Byzantine politics and administration. Known since the early ninth c., it reached its highest prominence through Bardas Skleros (died 991).

3 I.e. Magyars.

4 Or: 'Dristra,' a fortress on the Danube, also known as Dorostolon (present-day Silistra in north-eastern Bulgaria).

and he slaughtered them all and became even prouder and more boastful than before. **20** On his return he encountered Leo in Moundraga[1] and he said to him: 'I will not make peace if I do not receive all my prisoners back.' The emperor then decided to return the prisoners, and Theodore the Bulgarian, who was an intimate of Symeon's, came with Leo, and they were handed over to him. On the death of Nikephoros Phokas, Symeon looked for a reason to dissolve the peace, and he went out against the Romans with a view to taking prisoners once more. **21** Leo the emperor appoints Leo Katakalon to the office of *domestikos* of the *scholai* (Leo had his house in Rabdos[2]) and, together with him, he sends Theodotos, the *patrikios* and *protovestiarios*, on an expedition. And they transfer[3] all the *themata* and the *tagmata*, and a battle was fought at Boulgarofygon and the Romans were routed en masse and everyone perished, including the *protovestiarios* Theodotos (on whose account the emperor was more than usually distressed).[4] During[5] Leo's reign, the soldiers of the fortress at Cherson murdered their *strategos* Symeon, son of Jonas, and the fortress Koron in Cappadocia was taken by the Hagarenes.[6] **22** The emperor made a procession to the Damianos monastery[7] at which Zaoutzes the *paradyn-asteuon* accompanied the emperor, as did also Zaoutzes' daughter Zoe. Theophano, however, who was the emperor's wife, was not present there but remained in prayer in the Church of the Holy Soros in Blachernai. And when the emperor decided to remain there overnight, the relatives of Zaoutzes, including his son Tzantzes and the rest of them, decided to kill the emperor during the night.[8] However, Zoe, who was sleeping at the emperor's side, heard a noise and looked out through a window and asked for quiet. But when she realised the seriousness of what was happening, she woke the emperor who immediately embarked on a boat and crossed to Pegai,[9] leaving Zaoutzes and everyone else behind. In the morning the

1 Site of yet another Bulgarian fortress.

2 In the Ninth Region of Constantinople, on the Marmara Sea (present-day Etyemez).

3 I.e. to Europe from the Asian side of the empire.

4 The battle at Boulgarofygon (or Boulgarogefyron) was fought in 896. This is at the site of present-day Babaeski in Thrace (north-western Turkey).

5 There is no connection between this and the previous account of the wars against the Bulgarians (a new paragraph would therefore have been called for in my edition).

6 Koron was captured 5 August 897.

7 In Constantinople.

8 The attempt at Leo's life described in this paragraph cannot be dated with any exactitude.

9 A city on the southern shore of the Marmara Sea.

emperor returned quickly to the palace and removed John the *droungarios* of the *vigla* and appointed Pardos, son of Nicholas the *hetaireiarches*, in his stead. For this Nicholas, who had become a personal friend of the emperor, had revealed to him all the machinations of Zaoutzes. And from this time the emperor did not enter Zaoutzes' cell until the reconciliation between them brought about by the *magistros* Leo Theodotakes.[1] **23** The *augusta* Theophano dies having reigned for twelve years.[2] Just a few days later God showed her as a wonderworker; this happened because of her generous and forgiving character and because she was constantly showing her love for God and the holy churches by good deeds and prayers. Leo the emperor crowns Zoe, the daughter of Zaoutzes, and, together with her, he is blessed by a cleric, nick-named Sinapes, who belonged to the palace.[3] The cleric who blessed them was ousted from office, and Zoe reigned for one year and eight months. When this same Zoe had died they found a sarcophagus in which to lay her body to rest, and on the inside of this sarcophagus there was the following inscription: 'The wretched daughter of Babylon.' **24** Mousikos and Staurakios were accused in front of the emperor Leo of taking gifts from *strategoi* and civil servants and of communicating with the *basileopator*. And it happened once that Staurakios entered the palace with a letter to Zaoutzes from one of the *strategoi*, and the emperor, who was standing at the *heliakon*,[4] saw him and, on the pretext of asking him about the *strategoi*, went up behind him and took him by the arm and led him out. He then brought him to a window and took the letter from him and threw it away, and he handed him over to the first people he saw, with the instructions that they should remove him from the palace; he also ordered that he should be tonsured. On learning this, Mousikos fell into deep despair. The emperor entered the place where Mousikos was standing close to Zaoutzes and he took him by the neck and pushed him out and handed him over to Christopher the *koitonites* to take him to the Stoudios and make

---

1 Leo seems to have had an indulgent attitude towards Zaoutzes. One reason could be that he was afraid of him, but perhaps it was because Zaoutzes' daughter Zoe was the love of Leo's life.

2 Theophano almost certainly died 10 November, but it is uncertain in which year: suggestions range from 893 to 897. See also above, Chapter 132, § 22.

3 The marriage between Leo and Zoe probably took place in May or July of the year 898. Zoe died somewhere between December 899 and March 900.

4 This could also be understood as a proper name. It was either an open place flooded with sunlight, such as a sun balcony, or a sundial (see also Chapter 135, § 26, where a *heliakon* is located at Boukoleon).

him a monk. **25** A short time later, Zaoutzes dies in the palace, and they carried him out through the Boukoleon[1] and brought him to the Kauleas monastery[2] and buried him there. After[3] the death of Zaoutzes, Basil Epiktes, the son of Nicholas the *hetaireiarches*, made friends with Samonas the *koubikoularios*, who was a Hagarene by descent. This he did because he coveted the imperial throne. He assured Samonas: 'Since our saintly Zoe is dead the emperor is bound to take another wife and he will make away with all of us. But give me a written guarantee and I will confide all my plans to you.' And Samonas gave him a written guarantee, and Basil confided everything to him. **26** However, Samonas went in to the emperor and said to him: 'My Lord, I am going to say something to you in private that may be my death; however, it will kill you if I do not tell you.' He then told the emperor all about Basil's plot. The emperor was not convinced by what Samonas said, so he asked: 'It is not that someone suggested to you to say this and that you have accepted bribes to do so?' But Samonas said: 'Send the people you want, whom you trust, my Lord, and let them hide in my cell, and let them write down whatever they hear from Basil and me.' **27** At once the emperor sends the *protovestiarios* Christopher together with Kalokyros the *koitonites*, and they came up and hid in Samonas' cell. Thus Basil took the bait, and he received an oath from Samonas at his place of prayer, and he told him everything about the plot and about those who had participated in it. While they were having breakfast, Christopher and Kalokyris went down and read everything to the emperor as they had written it down. The emperor at once called for Basil and gave him 24,000 *miliaresia*, said to be for the soul of his holy Zoe, as if she had decided this, and he sent him to Macedonia. In this way he removed Basil from the City. The rest of those who had taken part in his plan or had known about it, he handled as follows: Pardos the *droungarios* of the *vigla* he sends to Stypiotes, purportedly to fetch him to the City; Stypiotes, however, had been warned in advance by an imperial letter that he should apprehend Pardos. The emperor made a pretext of going away to St Lazaros, in the descent to the polo-ground,[4] to dine, and he placed John Garidas together with the rest of the *hetaireia* in the emperor's private quarters,[5] and when

---

1 Which had its own harbour.

2 Zaoutzes died in 899. The monastery, situated in the City, belonged to the patriarch Anthony Kauleas, who had enjoyed Zaoutzes' patronage.

3 The attempted coup by Basil Epiktes cannot be dated more exactly than ca. 900.

4 τζυγκανιστήριον.

5 κουβουκλεῖον.

the emperor was on his way down, John and his men seized Nicholas the *hetaireiarches* and removed him from the City. He[1] then brought Basil from Macedonia and subjected him to investigations and had him beaten and his hair burnt and paraded him in the Mese and exiled him to Athens, where he died miserably. Further, as far as the rest is concerned, that is, Nicholas the *hetaireiarches*, Stylianos, John, and all the relatives of Zaoutzes—some he had tonsured and some exiled, and he confiscated the possessions of all of them. Thus the whole clan of Zaoutzes was wiped out because of Samonas. **28** The emperor called together all the *magistroi* and the men in high positions, and he read out to them what Samonas had reported. They commended Samonas very highly for taking care of the emperor's life, and they said that Samonas was worthy of the greatest honour. And the emperor honoured Samonas with the office of *protospatharios*, and befriended[2] him. **29** The patriarch Anthony died and in his stead Nicholas, the emperor's *mystikos*,[3] was made patriarch.[4] **30** Damianos the Hagarene captured the Demetrias fortress in the *thema* of Hellas.[5] **31** The[6] emperor Leo crowns Anna, the daughter of the Zoe who was the daughter of Zaoutzes, for he was not able to perform the prescribed ceremonial banquets without the presence of an *augusta*. **32** The emperor brought a most beautiful girl from the Opsikion *thema*, called Eudokia, and he crowned her and proclaimed her empress and married her.[7] He had a male child by her at whose birth both she and the child died. **33** The emperor Leo bought buildings close to the Church of the Holy Apostles and he had a most beautiful church built there in the name of his former wife, St Theophano. He also had a church built in the place known as Topoi,[8] which he named after St Lazaros and made into a monastery for male eunuchs. He then conveyed the bodies of St Lazaros and Mary Magdalene and deposited

---

1 In this and the following sentence, the acting subject is presumably the emperor.

2 'befriended' (προσῳκειώσατο): or, possibly, 'made him a member of the hetaireia.'

3 This was an assistant to the emperor with secretarial duties, in particular with regard to juridical matters. In the case of Nicholas, it can be seen as a kind of surname.

4 Anthony II Kauleas died 12 February 901 and Nicholas I Mystikos was made patriarch on 1 March.

5 Demetrias is close to Volos in Thessaly. There is some dispute as to the date of its capture, with guesses ranging from 897 to 902.

6 The crowning of Anna cannot be independently dated but must have taken place while Leo was a bachelor, i.e. between the death of Zoe and his remarriage with Eudokia Baiane (see § 32).

7 This was perhaps in the summer of 900. Eudokia Baiane died 12 April 901.

8 This, too, is in the City.

them there, and also conducted the inauguration of the church. **34** While the navy was occupied with the construction of these churches, the Africans seized Taormina in Sicily.[1] This happened through the negligence, or rather, the treacherous behaviour, of Eustathios, the *droungarios* of the fleet, and Karamalos was also there, and Michael Charaktes,[2] and there was a great loss of Roman lives. When they returned to the City, they were questioned by the emperor and the patriarch, and they were condemned to death for treason by Michael Charaktes. But the patriarch pleaded with the emperor, and the death penalty was lifted and they were only flogged and had their belongings confiscated and were tonsured, Karamalos at Pikridion, and Eustathios in the Stoudios monastery. **35** The island of Lemnos was also occupied by the Hagarenes, who took many prisoners.[3] **36** In the procession in the middle of Pentecost[4] the emperor Leo went to St Mokios, and when he entered the church and approached the *solea*, someone stepped out from under the ambo and struck him on the head with a thick and powerful stick, and if the momentum of the stick had not been diminished by a candle-stand, which came in its way, the emperor would have been killed then and there.[5] At this there was a panic and, while a lot of blood was streaming from the emperor's head, officials fled, and many perished in this. **37** During all this, the emperor's brother Alexander had claimed to be ill, and he had not come down to the church, and because of this he came under suspicion of being behind the attack himself. Nor was Samonas there; he had gone to bring Zoe to the palace to be with the emperor. The man who had struck the emperor was apprehended and interrogated and was for many days subjected to many kinds of torture and punishment, but since he did not name anyone responsible, they finally just had his hands and feet cut off and burnt him at the Sphendone in the hippodrome. From this date this procession was cancelled. **38** However, some time later Markos, the most wise *oikonomos* of the same church, came up to the palace. It was he who had completed the *tetraodion*[6] of the Great Sabbath, originally written by lord Kosmas, and dining at the emperor's table he entreated the emperor not to cut out the feast. When the

1 Muslims from northern Africa captured Taormina 1 August 902.

2 The Greek text is a little problematic. From the following it is clear that Karamalos but not Michael Charaktes had a responsibility for things going wrong.

3 The capture of Lemnos took place in 902.

4 I.e. in the middle of the fifty-day period between Easter and Pentecost.

5 This may have been 11 May 903 (see also below, § 38).

6 A hymn consisting of four parts.

emperor seemed unwilling to talk about the matter, Markos said: 'It was written already by the prophet David that you should suffer this, my Lord. For he prophesied the following: "Such evil the fiend perpetrated against your sacred person. And those who hate you were elated in the middle of your feast."[1] And you, my Lord, are bound to reign for another ten years after this.' This indeed happened.[2] For, on the same day on which he received the blow, he also dies. **39** Zoe was the fourth wife of the emperor and she lived with the emperor in the palace without having been crowned.[3] **40** When the emperor was occupied by a procession at the emporium of Boutios (this was in order to inaugurate the monastery of his *protovestiarios* Christopher), there came a message that the navy of the Hagarenes with the Tripolitan[4] in charge was coming up against Constantinople. Therefore, the emperor sends Eustathios, the *droungarios* of the fleet, with all the navy and the *strategoi* against the Tripolitan but, since the Romans were not able to match the Hagarenes, they returned having achieved nothing. Instead, the Tripolitan came in behind them and proceeded inside of Abydos as far as Paraion.[5] On learning this, the emperor became very depressed and worried and he sends Himerios the *protasekretis* as head of a fleet against the Tripolitan. This fleet the Hagarenes did not dare at all to approach and, by the will of God, Leo of Tripoli had to turn away and so went to Thessalonica, which he besieged and captured together with its *strategos*, Leo Chatzilakios; and he killed many and took many prisoners. **41** A certain Rhodophylles, a *koubikoularios*, had been sent to Sicily on some duty and was carrying with him 100 *litrai* in gold. Happening to fall ill during the journey, he entered Thessalonica in order to restore himself by bathing; and he was captured by Leo. When Symeon the *asekretis* (who later became *patrikios* and *protasekretis*) passed through the country, he took the gold and the gifts that Rhodophylles had simply left along the road; for doing so Rhodophylles was severely beaten and died. On learning that the Tripolitan planned to

1 Psalms 73(74).3–4.

2 Leo died 11 May 912. If the attack on his life (see above, §§ 36–37) is correctly dated to 11 May 903, he died at the very beginning of the tenth year after this attack.

3 Cf. below, § 49: she had not been made an empress at this time nor was she even married to him (i.e. given the crown of marriage).

4 This is Leo of Tripoli (Rasiq al-Wardami, or Ghulam Zurafa), a convert to Islam who became a successful admiral of the Arabs. His expedition against the Byzantines took place in 904, Thessalonica falling 31 July of that year.

5 I.e. they continued into the Marmara Sea.

destroy the city of Thessalonica, Symeon asked him to take the gold and leave the city alone. He even persuaded him to do so and he received a written guarantee, and so he agreed to give the Tripolitan the gold for leaving the city alone.[1] And so it happened. **42** On the pretext of going out to his monastery, named Ta Speira, the one at Damatrys,[2] Samonas fled with his money and his horses, having hamstrung the public horses at the respective stations.[3] On learning this, the emperor sends Basil Kamateros, the *hetaireiarches*, and George Krinites after him to overtake him. And when Samonas was about to pass the Halys river, Nikephoros the *droungarios*, the one called Kaminas, caught up with him and stopped him from crossing. At this, Samonas came up with many promises, but on failing to persuade Nikephoros, he took refuge in the Holy Cross at Siricha, pretending that he had made the journey because of his faith in the Cross. **43** Then Constantine Doukas arrived and took Samonas with him and returned to the City. The emperor ordered that Samonas should be kept under surveillance in the house of Caesar Bardas. The emperor asked Constantine Doukas about Samonas and, having learnt that he really had tried to escape to Syria, he told Doukas not to say so in front of the Senate; when asked about this, he should just say that Samonas had gone to Siricha to pray. For the emperor wanted to be reconciled with Samonas. **44** Hence, the emperor called Constantine Doukas in front of all those in authority and said: 'By the name of God and by my head: did Samonas flee or not?' Earlier, however, Constantine had said to the emperor, that he would not say what he was told to say if he had to take an oath. When he now heard the oaths, he said frankly and in front of everyone that Samonas had fled to Syria. This made the emperor furious, and he sent Constantine away. Samonas had to spend four months in the house of Bardas but was reconciled while the emperor was still reigning. **45** At this time a comet also appeared, which sent its rays in an easterly direction, and was visible for forty days and nights.[4] **46** Samonas was made *patrikios* after his flight. **47** Leo had a son, named Constantine, by

1 This passage is somewhat tautological and it may be that the Greek text is not sound.

2 This is probably modern-day Samandira, actually within the boundaries of present-day Istanbul (cf. Mango/Scott 1997, p. 531, n. 11). The point, however, is that it was on the Asian side, and beyond the City walls, and that Samonas, having come that far, could hope for further escape towards the East and the Arabs through a laxity of control. The most difficult thing for a person like Samonas was presumably obtaining an excuse to get out of the palace.

3 The flight of Samonas took place in the spring of either 904 or 905.

4 This comet was probably visible in late spring 905.

Zoe, his fourth wife.[1] At Epiphany, this son was baptised by Nicholas the patriarch in the Great Church, and was received by[2] Alexander the emperor and Samonas the *patrikios* and all those in high office. **48** Also at this time Kyphe was made a home for the elderly, and the prostitutes were chased away. **49** After the feast,[3] Leo the emperor was blessed together with Zoe by Thomas the *presbyteros*, who was later ousted from office.[4] Leo also proclaimed Zoe *augusta*, and for this reason the patriarch prevented the emperor from entering the church. Instead, he had to go from the right side as far as the *metatorikion*,[5] and was not able to walk through the church in the usual way. **50** Samonas was appointed *parakoimomenos* because of his support for the emperor in every lawless and evil action, and he began to plot against the Church. On the first of February they invited Nicholas the patriarch to court and entreated him earnestly to accept the situation.[6] When they did not succeed in this, they took him from the banquet hall through the Boukoleon and put him in a small boat and ferried him over to Hieria. From there he had to accomplish a laborious march on foot through deep snow[7] in order to get to Galakrenai.[8] In his stead, Euthymios the *synkellos* is made patriarch, a pious man showing both self-discipline and discretion. They say that he accepted the office after a divine revelation, which told him that the emperor planned a heresy and to issue a law that would allow a man to have three or four wives and that many most learned men would support the emperor in this.[9] **51** In the month of June, Leo the

1 This is the future emperor Constantine VII Porphyrogennetos. He was born at an uncertain date in 905 and baptised 6 January 906.

2 Greek δεξαμένων: this should mean that all these people became his godparents. The question may be asked how many godparents there could be.

3 'After the feast': this must refer to the story told in § 47. The information contained in § 48 looks like a secondary insertion into the text.

4 This is the inception of the tetragamy controversy, triggered by Leo's insistence to legalise his relationship with Zoe Carbonopsina. Leo and Zoe married in spring/summer of 906.

5 The *metatorikion/mitatorion* was a room, or suite of rooms, in St Sophia where the emperor could change clothes, take meals, etc. Cf. also below, § 60.

6 I.e. to accept the marriage of Leo and Zoe as legal and their offspring as the rightful heir to the throne. This was 1 February 907.

7 Or: 'in heavy snowfall.'

8 This was on the Asiatic side of the Bosphorus (as is also Hieria).

9 The logic would be that Euthymios thought that he would be able to exert some moderation over the emperor if he accepted office as patriarch. It is an interesting question whether the four marriages of Leo were associated in some people's minds with Muslim practices and Leo was suspected of being a crypto-Muslim.

emperor was invited by Constantine Lips to his monastery situated in Merdosagari,[1] in order to inaugurate it and have lunch. But then the wind called Lips came up, which blew until the third hour,[2] shaking and disturbing houses and churches, so that everyone fled into the open air and said that it was the end of the world, if God's love of humanity did not stop this destruction through rain.[3] **52** The emperor made Himerios, the *logothetes tou dromou*, head of all the naval forces; for the fleet of the Hagarenes had taken to the sea against the Romans.[4] Andronikos Doukas also received the command to embark on the ships together with the logothete Himerios and to fight the Hagarenes. Now, Samonas was the irreconcilable enemy of Andronikos and he was constantly and in many ways scheming against him, and he tried to harm Andronikos by every method and with great energy; this he did after returning from his flight. He made someone secretly write to Andronikos: 'Do not embark on the boats; if you do, you will be apprehended by Himerios. For Samonas has suggested to the emperor that you should be apprehended and blinded by him.' **53** Himerios entreated Andronikos earnestly to embark on the ships against the Hagarenes but he did not comply, although the Hagarenes were pressing on. Therefore, on St Thomas' day[5] Himerios alone joined battle with the Hagarenes and achieved a great victory. On learning this, Andronikos despaired and, together with his relatives and men, he went away and seized the fortress of Kabala.[6] At this open act of rebellion, Samonas said to the emperor: 'Did I not tell you, my Lord, that Doukas was your enemy?' **54** At once the emperor sent Gregoras, the *domestikos* of the *scholai*, also named Iberitzes, an in-law of Andronikos, to defeat him. When Andronikos learnt this, and also that the patriarch Nicholas had been ousted from the Church, he fled, together with his relatives and children and friends, to the Hagarenes, who at that time had gone out against the Romans, and he was received with great honour by the emir.[7] **55** Leo the

---

1 The monastery is today the Fenari Isa Camii.

2 'third hour' (Greek τρίτου): this is unclear and the translation not certain.

3 This is an odd story, and its function in this context hard to grasp. Also the connection between the family name of Constantine and the wind is unclear.

4 This was in 905 or 906.

5 I.e. 6 October (for the year, see previous note).

6 This is in Asia Minor, not the Kavalla in northern Greece.

7 Andronikos' flight must have taken place shortly after Nicholas' abdication from the patriarchate in February 907. The emir mentioned is presumably the Arab naval commander (or the seventeenth Abbasid caliph, Al-Muktafi).

emperor was very distressed on account of Andronikos and he often thought about sending him a written guarantee, in the way Theophilos had done with Manuel.[1] Some people suggested to the emperor that he should make friends with one of the Saracens employed at the *praitorion* and send him to Syria with such a letter. This the emperor did, and he wrote in red ink and sent it with a *chrysobull*[2] concealed in a small wax candle. **56** When the Saracen came out from the audience with the emperor, Samonas called after him and said: 'Do you know what you are carrying?' (he was alluding to the wax candle) 'The ruin of Syria.' And he gave him money and gifts and entreated him to give these into the hands of the vizier. And this the man did when he came there. But Andronikos was apprehended [by the vizier] and fettered together with all his relatives, and on learning that this had happened to him because of the guile of Samonas, and being subjected to torture,[3] he renounced his Christian faith and became a Moslem, and so did all his men. **57** A short while after this, on knowing that it would be impossible for Andronikos ever to escape, his son Constantine and others fled on their own (this they did on Andronikos' suggestion)—a truly remarkable flight by which they escaped from the middle of Syria and arrived in Romania fighting their way;[4] only a few, and with great difficulty, were thus saved, including Andronikos' son Constantine. **58** Abalbakes the Old and the father of Samonas came to the City from Tarsos asking for a treaty, and the emperor received them in the Magnaura with dignity and tokens of respect and esteem.[5] They even embellished the Great Church with costly adornments and showed all the holy vessels to the Hagarenes—an act unworthy of the empire and the Christian state, namely that the Gentiles should see God's holy vessels. Samonas' father wanted to be with his son and to stay in Romania. But Samonas spoke kindly to him and said: 'Keep the faith which you have; instead, if I can, I will rather come to you.' **59** On the day of Pentecost Leo the emperor has his son Constantine crowned by Euthymios the patriarch.[6] **60** Samonas offered one of his men to work for the *augusta* Zoe. This man was named Constantine and he had previously worked for Basil the

---

1 See above, Chapter 130, §§ 17–18.
2 I.e with an actual golden seal (although the term *chrysobull* also is used for solemn documents in general).
3 'torture': or 'put under pressure' (Greek ἀναγκασθείς).
4 'fighting their way' (καταπολεμούμενοι κατὰ χώρας).
5 This was perhaps in the spring of 908.
6 Probably 15 May 908.

magistros and *kanikleios*. This Constantine became very dear to the emperor Leo and the *augusta*, and for this reason Samonas grew very jealous of him and started to slander him, saying that he had an improper relationship with the *augusta*. The emperor thought this might be true, and by the agency of Samonas he had Constantine sent to the monastery of St Tarasios and tonsured there. But some time later he ordered Samonas to receive him into his own monastery of Ta Speira, with the intention of having him accepted at court again. Then it happened that the emperor went on a procession to Damatrys, and he had lunch in Samonas' monastery. There he saw Constantine, and at once he gave an order to Samonas, and Samonas had Constantine dressed in secular clothing, and Constantine served the emperor at the table and returned with him to the palace. Seeing, however, that the emperor's affection for Constantine is growing, Samonas contrives a conspiracy together with the *megistos koitonites*[1] and Michael, son of Tzerithon. They set up a document full of slander aimed at[2] the emperor; the document is formulated by Rhodios, the *notarios*[3] of Samonas, and written in his hand. When the emperor came to the Great Church he found this document in the place where he used to pray, in the *mitatorion*,[4] and he took it and read it and was highly distressed and wanted to know who had done this. **61** There was also a lunar eclipse and the emperor ordered the astronomers of the day to tell what would come of it.[5] When the metropolitan Pantoleon, who was a friend of Samonas, came and was on his way in to the emperor, Samonas asked him: 'Who will suffer from this?' Pantoleon said to him: 'You will, but if you can make it past the thirteenth of June, you will not suffer any harm.' But to the emperor they said that the moon meant harm to the second [in rank], and the emperor supposed this to refer to his brother. Later, however, Tzerithon told the emperor in private that Samonas had made up the document,[6] and at once the emperor has Samonas removed to his own house and has him tonsured and taken to the monastery of the

---

1 'chief *koitonites*.'

2 'aimed at the emperor' (κατὰ τοῦ βασιλέως): this is a little unclear, since it would seem that the sole purpose of the conspiracy was to get rid of Constantine. For the development of the story see following §.

3 In this case this title seems to denote the private secretary of an individual. In other cases (see Index of terms and concepts) it is the title of a government official.

4 Or: *metator(ik)ion* (cf. above, § 49).

5 This eclipse took place 20 March 908.

6 See above, § 60.

patriarch Euthymios. But after this he became once again the subject of slander, and they removed him to the monastery of Martinakios. Leo made Constantine *parakoimomenos*, and he built him a monastery in Hosiai, and he went out together with Euthymios the patriarch and inaugurated it. **62** In the month of October[1] a naval battle was fought between the logothete Himerios and the Hagarenes Damian and Leo; Romanos, who later became emperor, was a *strategos* at Samos at this time.[2] Himerios was defeated in this and barely escaped, and almost everyone who was there came into danger.[3] **63** The emperor Leo began to suffer from an ailment of the stomach[4] so that he was not able to come out to the Magnaura and make his public speech at the beginning of Lent.[5] There was also a fire in the candle storage room of the Great Church, and all the boxes and bags containing documents, including those of the *sakelle*,[6] were destroyed by the fire. On the eleventh of May the emperor Leo dies having named his brother Alexander emperor.[7] It is said that Leo, on seeing Alexander entering his room, uttered: 'Beware, the bad time will come in thirteen months.'[8] And he begged and entreated Alexander to take care of his son Constantine.

---

1 This was in October 911.

2 I.e. Romanos I Lekapenos.

3 'danger' (κινδυνευσάντων): perhaps a euphemism for actually dying ('succumb to danger').

4 The explicit mentioning of the whereabouts of his illness could be a hint that this should be considered a death befitting a person having committed the kind of sins that Leo had (i.e. sins of sexual indulgence, having married four times). Cf. the fate of Zeno (Chapter 101, § 4) and of Leo III (Chapter 121, § 19).

5 This was 4 March 912.

6 Or: *sakellion* (cf. above, Chapter 132, § 11). In this case (as, perhaps, opposed to above, Chapter 132, § 11) it is probably a question of the *sakelle* of St Sophia only (and not of the imperial administration).

7 This would seem to imply that Alexander had not the title of emperor until this moment. However, § 47 above would seem to state implicitly that he was emperor earlier. Cf. also Chapter 132, § 27, which is ambiguous.

8 Alexander died after a reign of thirteen months (see below). Cf. also above, § 61, and the prophecy made after the lunar eclipse.

134 Alexander, Son of Basil

Alexander reigned for one year and twenty-nine days, together with Constantine, son of Leo.[1] 2 He sent for Nicholas and brought him from Galakrenai, and, deposing Euthymios, he enthroned Nicholas for a second term.[2] Alexander held a *selention* and a synod[3] in the Magnaura, and brought Euthymios from the Agathos monastery of the Stenon, and, seating him with Nicholas the patriarch, they dethroned Euthymios [formally], and they tore off the priestly and admirable man his honourable beard in an unworthy manner and subjected him to other kinds of outrage and punishment, which the honourable and holy man bore quietly and without complaint. And thereupon he was once again exiled to the Agathos monastery, where he died; he was buried in his own monastery, at Psamathia,[4] in the capital. 3 Because of the suspicions which his brother Leo had entertained against him when he lived, this man Alexander had been busy with hunting and had resided in palaces outside the capital, and he had not accomplished any deed worthy of an emperor but had led a life of constant luxury and licentiousness and drunkenness. For this reason he did not do anything noble when he became emperor. Instead, his first decision in office was to make the priest John, called Lazares, a *rector*; after the death of Alexander, this man met with a bad end while playing ball[5] in Hebdomon. 4 Alexander did, it is told, also greatly enrich Gabrilopoulos and Basilitzes the Slav with treasures from the palace. They also say that he planned to make Basil[6] emperor (he was childless himself) and have Constantine, Leo's son, castrated. He had often expressed this intention, but he was always

---

1 Alexander reigned 11 May 912–6 June 913 (however we count, this is a little less than one year and twenty-eight days). Cf. for this chapter Skylitzes (Wortley 2010, pp. 188–190, with further bibliography), and Ps.-Symeon 715.19–718.2.

2 I do not think that the text is sound at this point, and I think it likely that it actually was Leo who called Nicholas back (see S. Wahlgren, 'The Return of Nicholas I Mystikos to the Patriarchate: the evidence of the Chronicle of the Logothete once more,' *Classica et Medievalia* 52 (2001), pp. 217–222).

3 I.e. a convention of the Senate and of bishops, for the purpose mentioned below.

4 This is present-day Samatya (in the Fatih district), on the shore of the Marmara Sea.

5 Probably during a game of *tzykanion*, or polo (cf. below, § 9, the similar death of Alexander himself). It has been suggested, not very plausibly in my opinion, that there is a confusion here and that the death of John was transferred to Alexander (P. Karlin-Hayter, 'The Emperor Alexander's Bad Name,' *Speculum* 44:4 (1969), p. 590).

6 Basil and Basilitzes here denote the same man (it may be especially fitting to use such a diminutive as -tzes to a Slav man, considering the tendency in Slavonic to use diminutives).

diverted by those who had been helped by Leo who either said that, anyhow, Constantine was just a child, or, as they sometimes did, suggested that he was in poor health. **5** During the reign of this emperor, a comet appeared from the West for fifteen days. This they said was called Xiphias and that it signified bloodshed in the City.[1] **6** This emperor delivered himself into the hands of frauds and magicians. These even convinced him that 'the statue of the boar in the hippodrome is dedicated to[2] you and your life,' thereby implying that the foolish man lived the life of a swine. He was deceived by these, and he had the boar's genitals and teeth, which were missing,[3] renewed and, trusting to the same deception, he organised games at the hippodrome, and he took holy vestments and candle-stands from the churches and decorated the hippodrome with them, and he made a light-show in honour of the statues. Because of this, God's Hand was removed from him, for he had given to the idols the honour due to God. **7** When Himerios the logothete returned after the defeat by the Hagarenes, Alexander sent him into exile in the monastery at the Palatine called Kalypa,[4] and he threatened him and said that he had been his enemy in the days of his brother Leo.[5] Himerios was taken ill because of his great grief, and he died after six months in exile. **8** Symeon, the ruler of the Bulgarians, sent an embassy to Alexander with a message of peace and friendship and reverence, just as he had done in the days when Leo was the emperor. Alexander, influenced by folly and thoughtlessness, dismissed the envoys dishonourably, hitting out at Symeon with threats. Therefore, the peace was dissolved at this time, and Symeon began to prepare himself to take arms against the Christians.[6] **9** One day during the heat of the Dog Star[7] Alexander had lunch and got drunk and went down to play ball,[8] and he was struck by a God-driven sword, and he returned to the palace with

1 'The Sword Fish (Sword-Bearer)': presumably Halley's Comet, which was visible in the summer of 912.

2 Ancient statues and monuments as well as places (especially the hippodrome) were viewed with distrust by some and thought to have voodoo-like properties.

3 Or: 'since they were defective in his own case.'

4 I.e. in the Great Palace itself.

5 Himerios may have returned to Constantinople at the end of May 912 and died in November of the same year.

6 Symeon and the other Bulgarians were, of course, also Christians at this time.

7 This is at least a little imprecise: Alexander died 6 June 913, and by any definition the heat of the Dog Star (Sirius) should be later than this.

8 This is presumably a game of polo, and the manner of death the well-deserved, violent death of an evil person (cf. above, § 3, the similar fate of John Lazares).

much blood running from his nose and from his genitals. He died two days later, leaving as guardians the patriarch Nicholas, the *magistros* Stephen, the *magistros* John Helladas, John the *rector*, Euthymios, Basilitzes and Gabrilopoulos. He left the throne to Constantine, the son of Leo. They laid Alexander to rest in the mausoleum next to his father Basil.

135 Constantine, the Son of Leo

Constantine, who was still a child when his father Leo died (he was then in his seventh year), was left to rule by his uncle Alexander, under the charge of guardians.[1] Thus he reigned with his guardians and his mother for another seven years; and he reigned together with Romanos, his father-in-law, being subordinate to him, for a further twenty-six years; and he ruled as sole ruler for fifteen years. Consequently the total duration of his rule amounted to fifty-five years.[2] 2 Now, when the patriarch Nicholas gained control of the palace (for he, too, was one of the guardians), together with the *magistros* Stephen and John Helladas, who was also a *magistros*, he took care of the common good and paid daily attention to the matters of importance to the reign. 3 In this political situation, some leading men of the City suggest to Constantine Doukas, a *domestikos* of the *scholai*, that he could enter the City and that he would be able to bring it under his control without effort; they did so because they held him in esteem for being courageous and of good sense and well able to govern the empire.[3] At this, Constantine, who even before this had been dreaming about becoming emperor and was coveting the crown, travelled at the greatest speed possible to the capital with a large number of the elite troops under his command.

1 Cf. to this chapter Skylitzes (Wortley 2010, pp. 191–205). See also ps.-Symeon 718.3–727.4.

2 Fifty-five is probably the correct number for the years of his life, not for his reign. Constantine was born (probably) 2 September 905 and was crowned co-emperor 15 May 908, and his father, Leo VI, died 11 May 912—i.e. when Constantine was in his seventh year. After Alexander's death (6 June 913) there was a caretaker government for around seven years until the rise to power of Romanos Lekapenos (crowned 17 December 920). There was then joint government with the Lekapenoi until the dethronement of the younger Lekapenoi on 27 January 945 (this could account for the twenty-six years mentioned: Romanos himself had been ousted in December 944). After this, and until his death on 9 November 959, Constantine reigned as supreme emperor, i.e. for around fifteen years. Needless to say, this part of the text must have been finished after the death of Constantine.

3 The rebellion of Constantine Doukas (described in §§ 3–9) took place in 913.

And during the night, he entered the City by the side-gate, which was under the control of the *protovestiarios* Michael (this is close to the Acropolis), and, together with his men, spent the night awake in the house of his father-in-law, Gregoras. **4** Niketas, the *asekretis* who later became *protonotarios*,[1] announced Constantine's arrival to the *patrikios* Constantine and to a monk, Helladikos,[2] and both of these visited Constantine Doukas in the course of the same night, and they held a discussion and, even before day broke (while it was still dark), they went, heavily armed, to the hippodrome gate with torches and many people, and they hailed Constantine as emperor. **5** Constantine's groom was ambushed and killed there by people standing on the inside of the gates of the hippodrome. Then, when he was not accepted by the people there but was rejected, Constantine, in his desire for power, behaved as though in a frenzy caused by some demon and as if he was out of his mind, and retreated into[3] the hippodrome in a despondent and dispirited mood, considering the killing of his groom a bad omen. **6** From there, he proceeded amidst acclamations to what is known as the Chalke and, having entered through the Iron Gate of this Chalke, he came to the *exkoubitoi*. At this, the *magistros* John Helladas picked men from the *hetaireia* and some wagon drivers and sent them armed against Doukas. When these came to the Chalke, a battle ensued and many fell victim to the sword on both sides—in fact, so many that the place was flooded with blood that flowed like a river. Gregoras, the son of Doukas, was also killed, and Michael his cousin, and that Kourtikes,[4] who was of Armenian descent. **7** On learning this, Constantine Doukas charged on horseback while the greatest confusion ensued. But the horse slipped on the paving slabs there and threw its rider to the ground and someone, who saw him there, thrown to the ground and alone (for all the others had dispersed), cut off his head with his sword. **8** When this had happened, Gregoras, the *magistros* who was his father-in-law, together with Leo, whom they called Choirosphaktes,[5] took refuge in the Church of the Holy Wisdom of God.[6] But they were torn

---

1 Chief notary (for *notarios* see Chapter 133, § 60).

2 A personal name is lacking (Helladikos probably denoting origin only ('from the province of Hellas') or being a family name). One MS gives the name of this monk as Michael.

3 'into the hippodrome': perhaps there is a textual problem here (depending upon whether we find it likely or not that he went further into the hippodrome at this moment).

4 Cf. Chapter 133, § 16.

5 I.e. 'Pig-killer.'

6 I.e. St Sophia.

away from there by force and were tonsured in the Stoudios monastery. Also, Constantine Helladikos was flogged, and they dressed him in rags and put him on a donkey and paraded him through the City and then brought him to the Dalmatos monastery and locked him up in the so-called *katadike*.[1] Leo Katakalitzes and Abessalom, the son of Arotras, were blinded and sent into exile. Constantine the son of Eulampios and others with him had their heads cut off by the sword in the Sphendone of the hippodrome; this was done by the *hyparchos* Philotheos, the son of Lampoudes. **9** An extensive investigation was carried out concerning the whereabouts of Niketas, the *asekretis*, and of Constantine Lips; however, they were not found, and it was supposed that they had fled. But that man Aigides,[2] and many of his associates, who were valiant men, they put all to the stake[3] in a row, all the way from the Stone Heifer at Chrysopolis as far as Leukaton.[4] And these so-called guardians would mercilessly and without reason have killed many more people in high office at that time had some of the judges not held them back from their unjust impulse by saying to them: 'How do you presume to do such things when the emperor is still a child and you cannot get his order for it?'[5] The wife of Doukas they made a nun, sending her to her house in Paphlagonia, and they made her son Stephen a eunuch. **10** In the month of August Symeon, the ruler of Bulgaria, marched out against the Romans with a great crowd of people.[6] He arrived at Constantinople and surrounded it and built a palisade from the Blachernai as far as what is known as the Golden Gate, having the unrealistic hope that he would be able to seize the City without great effort. However, when he realised the strength of the City walls and the degree of safety provided by the mass of people and the weapons and the catapults that were employed, he lost hope and retreated to the area called Hebdomon and asked for a truce. **11** The regency council accepts the prospect of peace with great joy, and Symeon sends his *magistros* Theodore to discuss conditions. The patriarch Nicholas and the *magistroi* Stephen and John took the emperor with them and went to Blachernai and brought Symeon's two sons there, and they dined with the

---

1 I.e. in prison.

2 This man does not seem to occur otherwise in this text.

3 'stake': Greek διδύμοις ξύλοις, i.e. a kind of crucifixion.

4 I.e. close to Constantinople, on the Asian side of the Bosphorus/Sea of Marmara. The Stone Heifer was a famous statue.

5 If not evidence of the independence of the judiciary, this is at least indicative of the authority enjoyed by judges.

6 This was in 913.

emperor in the palace. But Nicholas the patriarch went out to Symeon, and Symeon bent his head to him. Having uttered a prayer, the patriarch, it is said, then put his own monastic cowl[1] on Symeon's head instead of a crown. Having been given countless precious gifts, Symeon and his sons then returned to their country without having reached an agreement on the afore-mentioned peace. **12** Since the emperor Constantine was a child and wanted his mother (earlier, the emperor Alexander had removed her from the palace), they once again bring her to the palace. When she gains power, she brings to the palace Constantine the *parakoimomenos*, and the brothers Constantine and Anastasios, with the by-name Gongylios, and at the suggestion of John Helladas the friends of the emperor Alexander are removed: John the *rector* and the man called Gabrilopoulos and Basilitzes and the others. **13** The *augusta* Zoe appoints Theophylaktos Domenikos to the office of *hetaireiarches*. John Helladas, the *magistros*, fell ill and, having been considered a hopeless case by the doctors, he went down from the palace and came to Blachernai where he died, burdened by the illness. On the advice of Domenikos the *hetaireiarches*, Zoe removes[2] the patriarch Nicholas together with his men after having told him in a fit of anger to mind the business of the Church [only]. Shortly after this, Constantine the *parakoimomenos* accuses Domenikos the *hetaireiarches* before the *augusta* of trying to usurp imperial power on behalf of his brother. They used his appointment as *patrikios* as a pretext[3] and, when he went down to the church to receive the customary blessing, they ordered him to stay in his house. Zoe promoted John Garidas to the office of *hetaireiarches* and Damianos, the eunuch, to the office of *droungarios* of the *vigla*. But Domenikos retreated to his house, lamenting to no avail. **14** The Bulgarian Symon was ravaging Thrace once more, and the *augusta* and those holding high office were concerned about how to prevent his presumptuous activities. At this point, John Bogas asked to be made *patrikios*, and promised that he would lead the Pechenegs[4] against Symeon. When his wish was granted and he had received many gifts, he went to the country of the Pechenegs and received hostages from them and brought these to the City. The agreement was that the Pechenegs should cross over[5] and defeat Symeon. **15** Also,

---

1 Cf. Wortley 2010, p. 194, n. 22.
2 I.e. from the regency council.
3 I.e. in order to get at him.
4 Semi-nomadic Turks coming into contact with the Byzantines from the ninth c.
5 I.e. cross the Danube and enter Byzantine territory.

Asotios arrived in the City.[1] He was a man of the greatest fame for his physical strength, and he was the son of the King of Kings. They say that he was able to hold an iron bar by its ends and, using his hands' extreme strength, bend it into a circle, so that the iron's rigid nature had to yield to his hands' violent pressure. On his arrival, he was received with great honour; he was then sent back to his own country. **16** In the month of September, in the third indiction, Pankratoukas the Armenian betrayed Adrianople to Symeon.[2] Shortly after this, Basil, the *patrikios* and *kanikleios*, together with Niketas the *protospatharios*, called Helladikos,[3] was sent [to Symeon] by Zoe with many gifts, and he received the city of Adrianople back. **17** Further, the emir Damian came to the island of Strobilos with warships and a great force and, had he not fallen ill and died, he would have captured the island.[4] The Hagarenes had to return home empty-handed. The inhabitants of Hellas and Athens were constantly vexed by Chase, the son of Ioube, and, unable to stand his recklessness and greed any longer, they subjected him to a violent death, stoning him within the sanctuary in the church in Athens.[5] **18** Seeing Symeon's uprising and his attack on the Christians, the empress Zoe, together with her leading men, makes a plan to achieve a treaty and a lasting peace with the Hagarenes, to make it possible to transfer all the armed forces of the East[6] in order to defeat and annihilate Symeon. The *patrikios* John Radinos and Michael Toxaras were therefore sent to Syria to conclude a treaty. When this had been done, they made the customary distribution of payment among the *tagmata*, and they brought these along together with the *themata* and crossed over to Thracian territory; this was while Leo Phokas the *magistros* was *domestikos*. **19** Constantine, the *protopapas*[7] in the palace, called Kephalas, and Constantine of Malelia brought the life-giving and venerable wood[8] out to Thrace, and everyone venerated it and swore on it that they would die for each other; and so they

---

1 This is Ashot II, king of Armenia 914–928 (and probably recognised as king already at the time of his visit to Constantinople in 914; he was the son of Smbat I). The purpose of the visit was to elicit Byzantine aid against his enemies, such as the Arabs.

2 This was in September 914.

3 Or: 'from the province of Hellas.'

4 Damian was the emir of Tarsos (or Tyros). He died, probably in 924, while attacking the island fortress of Strobilos in the Kibyrrhaiot *thema*.

5 This is presumably the cathedral church, i.e. the Parthenon.

6 I.e. transfer them to the West.

7 Head priest of church or other ecclesiastical unit.

8 I.e. a relic of the Holy Cross.

went in full force against the Bulgarians. John Grapson led the *tagma* of the *exkoubitoi*, and the *tagma* of the *hikanatoi* was led by the son of Maroules.[1] Romanos Argyros acted as *strategos* together with his brother Leo and Bardas Phokas. With them were also Melias[2] and the Armenians as well as all the other *strategoi* of the *themata*. With Leo the *domestikos* was also, amongst others, Constantine the *patrikios*, called Lips, who was his counsellor in all matters of importance. **20** On the twentieth of the month of August, in the fifth indiction,[3] the war between the Bulgarians and the Romans broke out at the Acheloos river and, since God's judgements are inscrutable and unsearchable, the Romans are routed with all their army. Full flight ensued, and a terrible, wailing cry was heard, and some were trampled down by their comrades, and some were killed by the enemy, and there was the worst bloodshed for a century. Leo the *domestikos* saved himself by fleeing to Mesembria. Amongst many others, Constantine Lips and John Grapson and a good number of other leaders were also killed in this battle. **21** At this time also, the *patrikios* Romanos,[4] who was *droungarios* of the fleet,[5] was sent to the river Danube with the whole fleet, in order to help Leo Phokas. John Bogas was also sent to bring down the Pechenegs for, as has been said,[6] the *droungarios* Romanos had been ordered to bring them over the river, to support Leo Phokas against the Bulgarians. However, Romanos and John Bogas started a dispute and a quarrel, and the Pechenegs, seeing them fighting each other and disagreeing, returned to their own country. **22** When the war had ended and Romanos and Bogas had returned to the City, matters were stirred up against them. This brought the *droungarios* Romanos into extreme danger. There was even a vote passed by his enemies to have him deprived of his eyesight. The alleged reason was that he had not shipped the Pechenegs over the river but had retreated quite hastily without even taking the fleeing Romans on board his ships, and that he had done so by negligence or even with malicious intent. And he would indeed have been blinded had not the verdict been annulled through the agency of the *patrikios* Constantine Gongyles and the *magistros* Stephen, who wielded great influence with the *augusta*. **23** Elated by the victory, the

---

1 Named Olbian Marsoules in Skylitzes (see Wortley 2010, p. 197).

2 For this Melias (Armenian Mleh), who fought against the enemies of Byzantium, see Wortley 2010, p. 217.

3 This was 20 August 917.

4 This is the future emperor Romanos I Lekapenos.

5 I.e. commander of the fleet based in Constantinople.

6 See above, § 14.

Bulgarians made a military expedition, which brought them as far as the City, and the *domestikos* of the *scholai* Leo went out against them together with the *hetaireiarches* John and Nicholas, the son of Doukas, and a lot of men, and they came to a Thracian village called Katasyrtai.[1] During the night, the Bulgarians unexpectedly fell upon them and, while the *domestikos* fled, Nicholas, the son of Doukas, was killed, and many others with him. **24** Seeing that Constantine the *parakoimomenos* was trying to appoint his son-in-law Leo to the throne, Theodore, who was the emperor Constantine's tutor, suggested to the emperor Constantine that he should take the *droungarios* Romanos into his private service. For Romanos had served the family since Constantine's father's time and was well disposed towards him. He suggested that Romanos should be with the emperor and protect him, and that the emperor should have him as his ally and assistant in every case of need. This had often been mentioned to Romanos, but he had always rejected the idea.[2] Now the emperor Constantine wrote a letter in his own hand and signed it with his signature and sent it to Romanos who, on receiving it into his hands, promised to attack the *parakoimomenos* Constantine and his family if necessary. **25** While this rumour was current, the *parakoimomenos* Constantine tried to force Romanos to set sail with the fleet. Romanos, however, refused to do so, saying that it was impossible to make the fleet sail off before they had received the payment they were entitled to. While Romanos was occupied with the preparation of the ships, Constantine the *parakoimomenos* went out as if to hasten his fleet's departure. Romanos greeted him with servile demeanour and eagerly promised to do as he was told. But when the *parakoimomenos* was ready to depart, he asked Romanos whether he had good-looking men of noble birth who would be suitable to row the imperial trireme. Romanos immediately signalled to his men, who were standing by, to come close; those[3] who knew about the plan were already standing very close to Romanos' trireme. Romanos walked behind the *parakoimomenos* Constantine, grabbed him and shouted: 'Seize him.' And at once they took him and put him on the trireme of the *droungarios* Romanos and kept him under surveillance. There was no one who tried to protect the man or was sorry for him, for all his supporters had fled. **26** On learning this, the *augusta* Zoe summons the patriarch Nicholas and her leading men to the palace, and she sends

---

1 This is most probably still in 917.

2 Presumably, the modesty of the future emperor is demonstrated by this.

3 The structure of the following sentences is loose and the translation somewhat free.

messengers to Romanos, eager to learn what had happened.[1] When these arrived, the people drove them away by throwing stones at them. The following morning, Zoe went out to the *heliakon* at the Boukoleon and shouted to her son and everyone: 'How did this plot happen?' The emperor Constantine's tutor, Theodore, said to her: 'This happened because Leo Phokas corrupted the Romans and Constantine the *parakoimomenos* the palace.' As a consequence of this, the emperor took Nicholas the patriarch and Stephen the *magistros* to be with him in the palace, transferring the power from his mother to himself. **27** The following day, the emperor sent John Toubakes to remove Zoe, the *augusta*, from the palace. But she held on to her son, crying and shedding tears, and moved him to sympathy and mercy towards his mother, and thus the emperor said: 'Let my mother be with me!' As soon as he had uttered this, they left her in peace. **28** The emperor and the patriarch summoned John Garidas to the palace and promoted him to be *domestikos* of the *scholai*; this they did out of fear that Leo Phokas should proceed to an act of rebellion. He [John Garidas] only agreed to this on condition that his wife's brother, Theodore Zoufinezer, and his son, Symeon, were promoted to the rank of *hetaireiarches*. Having received sworn assurances, he [Leo Phokas] went down to his house. However, immediately upon this, his relatives were removed from the palace.[2] When he saw them arrive at his house, fear overtook him and he lost his mind, and so he went straight away to Romanos and told him what had happened. Romanos made friends with him and gave and received pledges from him to the effect that they should be of one soul, and he acted in agreement and accordance with him. They even made an agreement of marriage between their families, so as to tighten the bond of love even more.[3] **29** Thus, on the twenty-fourth of March,[4] Romanos sends the *presbyteros* John, who was one of his men and most loyal to him, and Theodore, called Matzoukes, to the palace to speak on his behalf and to say, that 'what I did was not an act of rebellion, but I foresaw the attack by Phokas, and I feared that he would attempt a coup against the emperor; therefore I decided to come up to the palace and assume the protection of the emperor.' **30** At this juncture (this went against the wish of the patriarch

---

1 This train of events took place in 918 (see § 29).

2 The text is not fully clear at this point. Cf. Skylitzes (Wortley 2010, p. 201).

3 Despite this, Leo Phokas embarked on rebellion even after this (see below, Chapter 136, § 4).

4 24 March 918.

Nicholas[1]), Romanos was formally asked by Theodore, the afore-mentioned tutor to the emperor Constantine, to come with the whole fleet to the Boukoleon.[2] Having discussed the matter with his men (for the situation forced this upon him[3]), Romanos came in arms, with the whole fleet, to the Boukoleon; this was on the day of the Annunciation of the most Holy Mother of God, on a Thursday.[4] At once, Stephen, the *magistros*, left the palace, and Niketas the *patrikios*, Romanos' brother-in-law, came up to the palace and removed the patriarch Nicholas from there. When the people of the palace had received sworn assurances from Romanos, they sent the venerable and life-giving Cross of the Lord out to him, and he prostrated himself before it and gave them pledges by oath and went up with them, and a few other men, to the palace.

136 The Ascent[5] of Romanos

Romanos prostrated himself before the emperor, and he went with him into the church at the Pharos and swore loyalty to him, and he is at once made a *magistros* and *megas hetaireiarches*[6] by the emperor.[7] 2 Immediately there was issued a divine decree,[8] addressed to Leo Phokas, urging him not to have any sedition in mind, but to remain quietly at home for the time being. The *parakoimomenos* Constantine was also ordered to write a letter to Leo with a similar recommendation, to the effect that he should not plan any action against the emperor Constantine but remain loyal as his subject. Andreas, *primikerios* of the imperial *vestiarion*,[9] took

---

1 The patriarch is here once more playing at politics.

2 This palace had its own harbour.

3 Greek τὸ γὰρ ἄγον ἦγεν αὐτόν, a kind of proverbial expression.

4 25 March 919.

5 Perhaps: '[last steps on the] road to the throne.' His ascent had, of course, started long before. The Greek term is ἀνάβασις. In any case, this is a slightly anomalous heading for a chapter of this text, but perhaps this was only a marginal note referring to the act of going up to the palace, as described in the preceding paragraph.

6 Senior commander of the *hetaireia* (cf., however, Chapter 132, § 24, with note on *mikros hetaireiarches*).

7 Cf. to this chapter Skylitzes (Wortley 2010, pp. 206–224), and Ps.-Symeon 727.4–752.20.

8 'divine decree' (θεία κέλευσις): this is the technical term for a document issued in the name of the emperor.

9 *Primikerios* was used as a title for the highest-ranking official in many sections of the bureaucracy. In this case it is the chief of the imperial treasury.

these messages and brought them to Leo, who was in Cappadocia. Leo received them and, having read them, went to his house and remained there quietly. **3** In the fifth week of Holy Lent, in the month of April,[1] a gift symbolising the pledge of marriage was given by the emperor Constantine to Helen, daughter of Romanos, and on the third day of Easter, what is known as the Day of Galilee,[2] Constantine is blessed and crowned[3] together with Helen, by Nicholas the patriarch, and Constantine promotes Romanos to *basileopator*[4] and makes Christopher, son of Romanos, *hetaireiarches* in Romanos' place. **4** Shortly after this, Leo Phokas is fooled by some commanders and by the *tagmata* at his disposal into starting a rebellion, and he sent for the *parakoimomenos* Constantine as well as for the brothers Constantine and Anastasios, and for Constantine of Malelia, the *protasekretis*, to be with him. He assured everyone that he was doing all this in order to help the emperor Constantine. **5** Romanos, the *basileopator*, issued chrysobulls with the emperor's signature, as if they came from the emperor Constantine personally. These documents contained orders for the overthrow of Leo Phokas' plot and words to the effect that those who abandoned him and took refuge with the emperor would be considered to be in favour of the emperor. Romanos gave the documents to a certain shameless and daring woman called Anna and to a cleric called Michael, and he sent them to the camp of Leo Phokas, where they distributed them secretly to the whole army. However, Michael was discovered by Phokas, and he was mercilessly beaten and had his nose and ears cut off. After this, he was given appropriate compensation by Romanos, as was also the woman sent with him. Now, the first to desert Phokas and to join Romanos was the son of Barymichael. This signified the beginning of the collapse of this uprising and rebellion, and together with the son of Barymichael came Ballantios; both of them were *tourmarchai*. Then Leo Phokas arrived in Chrysopolis with a great many heavily armed people, and he posted squadrons all the way from the Stone Heifer[5] as far as Chalcedon, thereby intimidating those in the City. **6** So Symeon the *epi tou kanikleiou*[6] is sent by Romanos on a *dromon* carrying a written guarantee signed by the emperor Constantine, saying the following: 'Having found no

1 Probably 11 April 919.
2 9 May 919.
3 I.e. with the crown of marriage.
4 Cf. the use of this title for Stylianos Zaoutzes (see above, Chapter 133, § 13).
5 Cf. above, Chapter 135, § 9.
6 I.e. *kanikleios* (cf. Chapter 131, § 2, with explanatory note).

other of my subjects to be such an extremely vigilant and benign and faithful protector of my throne as Romanos, I have entrusted my protection to him (putting him second only to God), and I have decided to have him in a father's stead, for he has demonstrated a father's feelings and a parent's disposition towards me. This Leo Phokas I have always suspected of plotting against my rule, and now, by his very acts, I have found out that he indeed is a rebel and that he has attempted a rebellion against my power in the manner of an usurper. Therefore I no longer want him to be *domestikos*, and I declare that this rebellion was not provoked by me: he made this attack by his own decision and in an effort to appropriate the throne for himself.'
7 When this had been read out to the people, everyone began to retreat and go over to the side of the *basileopator* Romanos. Not knowing what to do, and in despair since he had failed in everything he had hoped for, Phokas fled to the Ateous fortress. There he was not received. During his continued flight, Phokas was apprehended in a village called Goeleon,[1] and Romanos sent John Toubakes and Leo, who was his relative, to bring Phokas back to the City. Seizing Phokas, these men blinded him, although they had not been authorised to do so. This they did by their own decision and to the vexation even of the *basileopator* Romanos. **8** In the month of August, the plans for a rebellion by Constantine Ktematinos and David Kamoulianos and Michael, the *kourator* of the Mangana, were disclosed, and these men were flogged and had their belongings confiscated and were paraded through the City; they were then sent into exile.[2] Leo, *magistros* and *domestikos* of the *scholai*,[3] was brought to the City, and he was paraded through the market place sitting on a mule. **9** It was discovered that the *augusta* Zoe had also been plotting against Romanos by means of poisoned food, which had been prepared by Theokletos, the *notarios* of the *hypourgia*.[4] And they remove her from the palace and bring her to the Petrion[5] and make her into a nun in the monastery of St Euphemia. **10** Theodore, the emperor Constantine's tutor, and Symeon, his brother, were invited to dinner by Theophylaktos, the *patrikios* and *komes* of the stables. While they were eating, John, the *droungarios* of the *vigla*, called Kourkouas, entered with a lot of men and, on the pretext that they were

---

1 These places are in Bithynia.

2 This was in August 919.

3 I.e. Leo Phokas.

4 A secretary (*notarios*) to the staff (*hypourgia*) of the person responsible for the emperor's table (*epi tes trapezes*, for which cf. above, Chapter 132, § 13).

5 Part of the city at the Golden Horn.

plotting against Romanos, had them [Theodore and Symeon] arrested and sent into exile at their own country estates, in the Opsikion. **11** On the twenty-fourth of the month of September, Romanos is honoured with the rank of caesar, and in the month of December, on the seventeenth of the month, on the Sunday of the Forefathers,[1] the emperor Constantine and the patriarch Nicholas crown him with the imperial crown. And on January the sixth, on the day of Holy Epiphany, Romanos himself crowns his wife, Theodora.[2] **12** In the month of May, on the seventeenth, in the fifth indiction, Christopher, the son of Romanos, is proclaimed emperor.[3] He is crowned on the twentieth of the same month, on the day of the Holy Pentecost, by the emperor Constantine, and only these two took part in the procession on that day. **13** In the month of July, in the eighth indiction, on a Sunday, the unification of the Church is achieved by Romanos, and all the metropolitans and clerics, who had refused to be in communion with the patriarch Nicholas and with Euthymios, were reconciled.[4] **14** On the eighth of the month of February, in the ninth indiction,[5] Romanos sends a messenger and has the *magistros* Stephen, the son of Kalomaria, exiled to the Antigonos island on the charge of striving for the throne, and he had him tonsured, together with Theophanes, the *teichiotes*,[6] and Paul, the *orphanotrophos*,[7] who were his men. **15** The emperor Romanos made a procession to the tribounalion,[8] and everyone under arms was gathered there. Suddenly, after the mustering of the troops, Romanos and Constantine return to the palace in great haste; for a plot had been reported by Leo, one of Arsenios' men, hatched by this very Arsenios and Paulos, the *manglabitai*. These were flogged and had their belongings confiscated and were sent into exile. The *paradynasteuon* at that time was the *presbyteros* John, the *rector*. It was he who made Leo, Arsenios' man, a *hebdomarios*[9] and introduced him to the emperor. **16** There was a certain Rentakios in Hellas at this time. A relative

---

1 I.e. the second Sunday before Christmas, when the forefathers of Christ are remembered.

2 December–January 920–921.

3 17 May 921 (the year of the indiction is not correct here in the text).

4 I.e. the reconciliation after the ecclesiastical schism and controversy brought about by Leo VI's fourth marriage. This took place in July 920.

5 8 February 921.

6 A guardian of a wall.

7 A person running an officially recognised orphanage.

8 I.e. the Kampos tou tribounaliou.

9 A palace official working under the *papias* (*hebdomadarios* according to some MSS).

of the *patrikios* Niketas, he was an uneducated man and had taken to violence against his father, whom he persecuted in order to kill him. His father fled from the assault and embarked on a ship and sailed out and was held in detention by the Cretans. This gave this Rentakios an opportunity, and he purloined all his father's possessions and, having travelled to the City, took refuge in the Great Church of God.[1] On hearing of Rentakios' disorderly behaviour and plundering, the emperor Romanos contrived to have him driven out of the church and chastised. At this, Rentakios sent false letters to the Bulgarians and claimed that he was willing to desert to them. But he was apprehended and questioned and then deprived of his eyes. **17** When, after the death of the *domestikos* Adralestos, the Bulgarians again went out on an expedition and came as far as Katasyrtai, Pothos, of the family of the Argyroi, was made *domestikos* of the *scholai*, and he went out as far as Thermopolis[2] with the *tagmata*, and sent Michael, who was the son of Moroleon and a *topoteretes*,[3] to spy on the Bulgarians. Without having been spotted, Michael hit upon their unit and killed many of the Bulgarians, but being wounded himself, he returned to the City and died there. **18** A plot was then reported by Theokletos, the *notarios* of the *hypourgia*. This was hatched by Anastasios, the *sakellarios* and head of the goldsmiths, together with Theodoretos, the *koitonites*, and Demetrios, the imperial *notarios*[4] of the *idikon*,[5] and Nicholas Koubatzes, and Theodotos, the *protokaravos*.[6] These, it was said, were plotting on behalf of the emperor Constantine; and, being discovered, they were flogged and paraded through the Mese and then sent into exile. As far as Theodoretos is concerned, he was flogged in private, in what is known as the Trikonchos of the palace, and then sent into exile. The *sakellarios* Anastasios they tonsured in the Monastery of Elegmoi,[7] and there he also died. Using this as a pretext, Romanos demotes the emperor Constantine and makes him second in rank,

1 I.e. in St Sophia.

2 These movements took place in Thrace, Thermopolis (Aquae Calidae) being present-day Burgas in Bulgaria.

3 A deputy commander of a military unit; cf. below, § 66, where it denotes a legate, i.e. a representative of the pope.

4 The epithet 'imperial' is sometimes used to distinguish the bearer of the title from someone's private secretary.

5 The *idikon* (or *eidikon*, either derived from *idios*, 'private,' or *eidos*, 'specimen/ware') seems to have been a storehouse of precious goods either belonging to the state treasury or to the emperor personally.

6 A steersman directly under the captain on a warship.

7 In Bithynia.

and promotes himself to the foremost position.[1] **19** Once more, Symeon goes to war against the Romans, and he sends a host of Bulgarians together with Kauchanos and Menikos and others, and he orders them to march against the City as quickly as possible.[2] Having passed through the mountains, these men came as far as Maglaba. On learning of their approach, the emperor Romanos considers how to prevent them from coming down to Pegai[3] and the Stenon and burning the palaces there. He therefore sends out John the *rector*, together with Leo and Pothos, both called Argyros. These were equipped with a sufficient number of men from the imperial forces and the *hetaireia* and the *tagmata*. They were also accompanied by Alexios Mousele, the *patrikios* and *droungarios* of the fleet, and his people. This was in the fifth week of Lent. **20** When these commanders had marshalled the men at their disposal in battle formation in the plains and the lower terrain at Pegai, the Bulgarians appeared from above fully armed and uttered a hideous and terrifying battle-cry and charged against them with utmost savagery. At this, John the *rector* flees at once, and Photeinos, the son of Platypodes, as well as many others, are slaughtered fighting for him. John barely managed to escape and embarked on a *dromon*. The *droungarios* Alexios Mousele also fled; being in full armour, when he missed his footing as he mounted the gangway of the *dromon*, he fell into the water and was drowned, together with his *protomandator*.[4] But the Argyroi saved themselves by fleeing to the fortress. The rest took to the sea, and some were drowned while trying to escape the hands of the enemy, and some fell victim to iron,[5] and some were seized by Bulgarian hands and made prisoners. Since there was no one to prevent them, the Bulgarians set fire to the palaces at Pegai, and burnt the whole of the Stenon. All this proves what a fearful thing it is when lack of reason and inexperience have rashness as their ally. **21** On the twentieth of the month of February, in the tenth indiction, Theodora, Romanos' consort, dies.[6] Her body was put to rest in the house of this same emperor Romanos, the house that had been made into a monastery

---

1 Perhaps in December 921.
2 In 923.
3 This should probably be Pege, at the Theodosian City walls.
4 The head of a group of special messengers serving a civil or military official of high rank.
5 I.e. were killed by the sword.
6 This was 20 February 924, supposing that the indiction should be the twelfth (*pace* Wortley 2010, p. 209, n. 26).

by him.[1] In the same month, Sophia, the wife of the emperor Christopher, is crowned.[2] **22** At the same time, the *kouropalates* Iber arrived in the City, and, making his way through the middle of the market place, which had been embellished gloriously, he was received with great pomp and honour.[3] They also brought him into the Church of the Holy Wisdom of God, and he saw its beauty and size and costly adornments. For, in preparation of his visit, they had embellished it and dressed it with curtains of golden brocade and with all kinds of adornment. He was amazed by the wondrous size of the church, and he expressed his very great admiration at the costly adornments and said that this holy place in truth was God's dwelling. He then returned to his own country. **23** In the month of June,[4] the Bulgarians made another expedition and came as far as the palace of St Theodora, which they consigned to the flames.[5] At this, the emperor Romanos called the leaders of the *tagmata* together for a lunch meeting (the man called Saktikes was also there), and he exhorted them and urged them to go out against the enemy and fight for the sake of their country. They willingly agreed to die for his rule and for the Christians. Thus, on the following day, the afore-mentioned Saktikes, in arms given to him by the emperor, demonstrated that his faith and courage were true. For, making his way behind the Bulgarians and bursting into their camp, he killed all the men that he found there. **24** On learning what had happened, the Bulgarians return to their camp and, when battle is joined, they rout Saktikes and the small group of men who accompanied him. He had fought valiantly and had killed many, but could no longer resist the mass of enemies, so he releases his horse's bridle and gallops off at full speed. As he crosses a river flowing nearby, his horse is stuck in the mud, and he is wounded in his seat and thigh. With the help of the men at his disposal, he barely manages to pull his horse out of the mud, and he gets safely to

---

1 I.e. in the church of the Myrelaion monastery, nowadays Bodrum camii, where Romanos himself was later buried (see Chapter 137, § 8, and cover of this volume).

2 I.e. she was given the title of *augusta* (senior empress), in order to be able to serve in certain ceremonies that required a woman with this title (cf. above, Chapter 133, § 31, where the need for an *augusta* is spelled out).

3 Or: 'the Iberian,' the ruler of Iberia in Georgia, given the title of *kouropalates* by the Byzantines. In this case, it may actually have been (the Armenian) Asotios, mentioned in Chapter 135, § 15, who arrived in the City and was given this title (cf. Wortley 2010, p. 209, n. 28).

4 June 924.

5 At the innermost part of the Golden Horn.

Blachernai. There he was put in the Church of the Holy Soros and, since his wound was fatal, died during the night. **25** At that time, on the orders of the emperor Romanos, the most honourable Petronas brought one sarcophagus with figures and two without sculptural ornament from the male monastery of St Mamas, the monastery close to what is known as the Xylokerkos Gate. These are the sarcophagi in which it is said that Maurice and his children were buried, and they were deposited in the emperor's monastery.[1] **26** A certain Chaldean, called Hadrian, as well as Tatzates, the Armenian, who was a very rich man, prepare a rebellion and plot against the emperor Romanos, and they occupy the fortress called Paipert.[2] This they did on the instigation and advice of Bardas Boilas, who was a *strategos* in Chaldea. The *domestikos* of the *scholai*, John Kourkouas, fought them, and he apprehended some of them, of whom the more prominent were blinded and had their belongings confiscated. Tatzates, however, had managed to escape to another, very powerful, fortress and, having received a guarantee that he would suffer no harm, returned to the City and was honoured with the office of *manglabites* and lived under surveillance in the complex of the Mangana. But, having planned an escape, he is captured and deprived of his eyesight. The emperor took pity on Bardas Boilas, since he was his friend, and he was tonsured. **27** Since the *patrikios* called Moroleon,[3] who was the *strategos* of Adrianople and very powerful and skilful at war, performed many valiant deeds against the Bulgarians, the Bulgarian Symeon, together with all his army, surrounded the afore-mentioned city and built a palisade around it and subjected it to a harsh siege. When there was no more grain in the city and a great famine weighed down on them (for they had no means of resupplying the city, and were pressed by great need), the citizens surrendered themselves, together with their *strategos*, to the Bulgarians. On apprehending Moroleon, Symeon put chains all over his body and had him punished with countless kinds of torture and, finally, put to death in a terrible way, worthy of his [Symeon's] most inhuman and cruel mind. He then handed over the guarding of the city to Bulgarians and retreated. However, these had heard that the Roman army was advancing on them, so they left the city and departed; and the city came once again under

---

1 On Maurice and his fate, cf. above, Chapter 108, § 2. For the monastery see above, § 21.

2 Or: 'Paiper,' in north-eastern Anatolia (present-day Bayburt).

3 'Mad Leo.'

Roman control. **28** Leo of Tripolis[1] went out against the Romans with battle ships and a great force. On reaching the island of Lemnos, he was suddenly attacked by John, the *patrikios* and *droungarios* of the fleet, called Radinos. When battle is joined, by God's help, the Hagarenes under Leo's command are routed, and the Tripolitan alone flees and is saved, although with difficulty. **29** In the month of September, in the second indiction, Symeon, the ruler of Bulgaria, goes on an expedition against Constantinople with all his forces, and he ravages Thrace and Macedonia, setting fire to everything and pillaging and cutting down forests.[2] Coming as far as Blachernai, he demanded that the patriarch Nicholas should be sent to him together with some of the leading men, for he wanted to discuss a peace treaty with them. There was a mutual exchange of hostages. The patriarch, Nicholas, was the first to go out; then followed Michael the *patrikios*, who was called Styppiotes, and John the *mystikos* and *paradynasteuon*. John the *rector* had been slandered before the emperor and had excused himself with an illness at this time, and had left the palace and been tonsured in his own monastery close to Galakrenai. **30** Thus, these men began to discuss peace with Symeon. But he sent them away and demanded to see the emperor Romanos himself. For he had been informed by many about the emperor's intelligence and valour and good sense. The emperor was much elated by this, for he longed for peace and an end to the daily bloodshed. **31** Therefore, he sent people to the beach at Kosmidion and he had a very solid landing stage[3] constructed in the sea there, to which the imperial trireme could sail directly and at which it could moor. Having secured this landing stage on all sides, he ordered a fence[4] to be erected in the middle of it, at which the leaders could talk to each other. Symeon, in his turn, sent an expedition to burn down the Church of the Most Holy Mother of God, the one at Pege,[5] and all land surrounding it. By this, it was obvious that he did not really want peace but that he had high hopes of deceiving the emperor. **32** The emperor came to Blachernai with the patriarch Nicholas, and he entered the Church of the Holy Soros. There he held out his hands in prayer, and fell upon his face and

---

1 This is the well-known renegade (first mentioned above in Chapter 133, § 40) who, after conversion, served different Muslim masters as a commander at sea. The present episode, datable to 924, is the last time he is mentioned by the sources.

2 This was in 923.

3 Or: (so Wortley 2010, p. 212) 'jetty' (ἀπόβασιν).

4 διατείχισμα.

5 This is the Church of St Mary of the Life-Giving Spring (Zoodochos Pege) outside the City walls of Constantinople.

sprinkled the holy ground with tears, beseeching the all-undefiled Mother of God to soften the unyielding and pitiless heart of the proud Symeon and persuade him to agree upon a peace treaty. So, having opened the holy casket, in which the revered *omophorion*[1] of the holy Mother of God was being treasured, the emperor took it out, and, wearing it as an impenetrable breast-plate, and surrounding himself with faith in the blameless Mother of God as with a kind of helmet, he went out from the church, armed with unfailing weapons. **33** Having adorned his force with shields and weapons, he arrived at the agreed meeting place, for the discussion with Symeon. It was on a Thursday that this happened, November the ninth.[2] At the fourth hour of the day Symeon arrived,[3] bringing an immeasurable crowd, divided into many formations: some with golden shields and golden spears, others with silver shields and silver spears, and others adorned with every kind of weaponry, all of them wearing heavy iron armour. These took up a position in the middle,[4] and they hailed Symeon as emperor in the language of the Romans.[5] All the members of the Senate stood on the walls and watched the proceedings. One could now see a truly imperial and high-minded disposition, and one had to admire the emperor's[6] fearlessness and great valour and how, although seeing such a throng of enemies, he was not frightened nor reduced to fear and did not retreat. Instead, he went as if he were going into a group of friends—so fearlessly did he go, almost offering his life to the enemy in order to save his subjects. **34** The emperor arrived first at the said landing stage, and he waited there for Symeon. When hostages had been taken on both sides, and the Bulgarians had checked the landing stage carefully, lest there should be some cheating or ambush, Symeon dismounted and went forward to the emperor. They greeted each other and started to talk about peace. **35** The emperor is reported as having said the following to Symeon: 'I have heard that you are a God-fearing man and a true Christian.[7] But I see that your deeds do not in any way agree with

---

1 Cf. Chapter 131, § 30, where Michael III employs the same robe, or veil, of the Virgin to chase the Russians away.

2 9 November 924.

3 However, he did not yet go onto the landing stage where the meeting was to be held (see below).

4 'in the middle' (μέσον αὐτῶν): this is somewhat unclear.

5 I.e. in Greek.

6 I.e. of Romanos.

7 There are certain similarities between this speech and that of Nikephoros I in front of the Abbasid caliph (see above, Chapter 125, § 6).

these reports. For a God-fearing man, and a Christian, is bound to cherish peace and love (for indeed God is, and is called, love). Instead, it is the way of an impious and unbelieving man to take pleasure in murders and in the unrighteous shedding of blood. So, if you are a true Christian, as we have been informed, make an end to the unjust killings and the unrighteous shedding of blood, and make peace with us, who are Christians, being, and being called, a Christian yourself, and do not allow your hands to be stained with the blood of fellow Christians. 36 You, too, are human, and you await death and resurrection and judgement and retribution. Today you exist, and tomorrow you will be dissolved into dust. One fever can quench all your wanton behaviour. What excuse for the unrighteous murders can you give to God when you appear before Him? How will you be able to face the formidable and just judge? If you do this out of love of riches, I will fill you to excess with what you long for. Just raise your right hand, agree to the peace, and declare yourself satisfied with the accord. Then you, too, can live a peaceful life, without bloodshed and worries, and there will be an end to the misfortunes of the Christians, and they will stop killing each other. For it is not right that they should take arms against their brethren in the faith.' 37 Having said this, the emperor fell silent. Symeon felt awe because of the emperor's humility and because of the speech he had given, and he agreed to make peace. They thereupon embraced each other and separated, the emperor giving magnificent gifts to Symeon. Now I will tell what happened next—something portentous, which baffled even those experienced in interpreting such phenomena. They say that, while the emperors were talking to each other, two eagles flew over them, screaming and clashing into each other and immediately separating from each other, and that one of the eagles went on towards the City, while the other flew towards Thrace. The experts in this kind of phenomena were of the opinion that it was not a good omen. For they said that it meant that the rulers would part without having reached a true peace agreement. On returning to his camp, Symeon told his commanders about the emperor's good sense and humility, and he praised his good looks and his strength and his fearless mind. 38 In the month of December, on the twenty-fifth, Romanos crowned his sons Stephen and Constantine in the Great Church.[1] So too his son Theophylaktos, a eunuch, was tonsured and made a cleric by the patriarch Nicholas, and ordained *hypodiakonos*[2] and appointed *synkellos* by the

---

1 This was in 923 or, possibly, 924.
2 I.e. sub-deacon.

patriarch; earlier, he had walked among the *hypodiakonoi*[1] at holy ceremonies. **39** In the month of April, on the nineteenth of the month, Romanos honoured John, the *mystikos* and *paradynasteuon*, with the titles of *patrikios* and *anthypatos*,[2] and for that reason envy was engendered against this man and some people brought accusations against him.[3] **40** On the fifteenth of the month of May, in the thirteenth indiction, the patriarch Nicholas dies after having been patriarch for a second period which lasted thirteen years, and his body was put to rest in the monastery built by him at Galakrenai.[4] **41** In the month of August, Stephen, the metropolitan of Amaseia, a eunuch, is made patriarch. **42** In the month of October the *mystikos* and *paradynasteuon* John was accused of coveting the throne,[5] at the instigation of Kosmas, the *patrikios* and *logothetes tou dromou*, who had given him his daughter for a wife. Because of this, John is removed from the palace, but he is then allowed to come into the emperor's presence again and serve him and conduct some necessary business with him. For the emperor Romanos had the greatest affection for this man, who served him in everything, and he did not want to reject him completely. However, as the accusers pressed the emperor and gave convincing proof of the truth of the accusations, the emperor conducted an investigation and, having understood that the accusations were true, decided to have the man apprehended and questioned. On learning what is coming, John takes flight and comes to the so-called Monokastanos monastery,[6] where he is tonsured. **43** Constantine, the son of Boilas, the emperor's table-mate and friend, also fled and, having come to Mount Olympos,[7] he dresses in monastic habit. For he too was afraid, since he was a confidant of the *mystikos* and was informed about matters of a secret nature. The emperor had the *patrikios* Kosmas flogged at the Horologion in the palace, and appointed a successor. In the place of the *mystikos* John, the emperor promotes the *protovestiarios* Theophanes to the office of *paradynasteuon*. **44** At this time, there was also a terrible earthquake in the *thema* of Thrakesion, and the earth opened in a great and terrible chasm, so that many villages and churches were swallowed

1 Greek ἐν τῷ τῶν ὑποδιακόνων τάγματι (*tagma* not being used in a technical sense).
2 The title of *anthypatos* (proconsul) is only used here in this text. It is probably only an honorary title at this time and does not entail any function.
3 19 April 925.
4 15 May 925; Nicholas' second period as patriarch lasted 912–925.
5 This was still in 925.
6 In Bithynia.
7 This is the Bithynian Olympus, present-day Uludağ.

up in it with men and all.[1] **45** In the month of May, on the twenty-seventh, in the fifteenth indiction, Symeon, the ruler of the Bulgarians, died after having made his son, Peter, ruler.[2] Peter was his son by his second wife, the sister of George Soursouboulis, whom Symeon had also left as guardian of his children. Symeon had made Michael, who was born from his first wife, a monk. John and Benjamin, Peter's brothers, were still wearing Bulgarian dress.[3] **46** On learning of Symeon's death, the surrounding peoples, such as the Croatians and others, decided to go to war against the Bulgarians. Now, since a very great famine, combined with an invasion of locusts, oppressed the Bulgarian people severely, they feared the onslaught of the other peoples, but most of all they feared the coming of the Romans. Therefore, they decide to go to war against the Romans, and they go to Macedonia in order, as is reasonable to suppose, to instil fear into the Romans. **47** Then, on learning that the emperor Romanos was about to go to war against them, Peter and George send a monk called Kalokyris, whose family came from the Armeniakon theme, on a secret mission, carrying a chrysobull. He spoke of what was written in it, namely that the Bulgarians would welcome a peace with the Romans and that they were eager to sign a treaty. And not only this: if the Romans should want this, they would even be willing to agree on a marriage contract. The emperor received this monk with the greatest pleasure, and at once sent the monk Theodosios Aboukes, together with the cleric Basil the Rhodian, on a *dromon* to Mesembria to conduct peace talks with the Bulgarians. After arrival, these men had the appropriate conversations and then set out over land with Stephen the Bulgarian. After them came also George Soursouboulis, and they arrived in Constantinople and concluded the peace and demanded that a [marriage] contract should be worked out with the emperor. **48** Having seen Mary, the daughter of the emperor Christopher, and been delighted by her, the Bulgarian envoys wrote to Peter to come as quickly as possible, having, even before this, worked out the agreement on the peace. Niketas, the *magistros*, a relative[4] of Romanos the emperor, was sent to meet Peter and bring him to the City. When Peter the Bulgarian approached, the emperor Romanos embarked on a trireme and travelled to Blachernai. There he watched Peter's arrival, and he greeted him with an embrace. When they had finished the appropriate negotiations,

---

1 This earthquake cannot be independently dated.
2 This was in 927.
3 An interesting piece of ethnographic information.
4 συμπε(ν)θερός.

the peace treaty and the marriage contract are signed. During these negoti-ations, the *protovestiarios* Theophanes acted as a go-between and monitored the discussions between the Romans and the Bulgarians in a sensible way. **49** On the eighth of the month of October, the patriarch Stephen went out together with Theophanes the *protovestiarios* and Mary, the daughter of the emperor Christopher, as well as with all the Senate.[1] They went to the Church of the Most Holy Mother of God, the one at Pege,[2] and the patriarch blessed Peter and Mary and placed the marriage crowns on their heads, while Theophanes the *protovestiarios* and George Soursouboulis acted as witnesses. Then a glorious and costly banquet was held, and all the customary marriage rites were performed in a spectacular manner, whereupon Theophanes the *protovestiarios* entered the City together with Mary, the daughter of the emperor Christopher. On the third day of the wedding, the emperor Romanos gave a splendid feast at the landing stage at Pegai,[3] which was decorated with silk fabric. The imperial *dromon* was moored at the landing stage, and on this Romanos dined together with Peter the Bulgarian and Constantine, his son-in-law, and Christopher, his son. **50** The Bulgarians insisted firmly that Christopher should be hailed first and then Constantine, and the emperor Romanos gave in to their insistence, and so it happened as they had requested. **51** Everything pertaining to the marriage had now been fulfilled, and Mary was about to take the road to Bulgaria with her husband, Peter. Her parents, together with the *protovestiarios*, Theophanes, accompanied her as far as Hebdomon and dined there together with Peter. When the hour of departure came, they embraced their daughter while shedding many tears—as is reasonable when one is deprived of one's beloved offspring. They said farewell to their son-in-law and committed Mary into his hands and returned to the palace. On being handed into Bulgarian hands, Mary travelled the road towards Bulgaria. She was at the same time both glad and sad: sad for being deprived of her dearest parents and the imperial dwelling and contact with her kin; glad because she had been joined to a man of royal birth and been named queen of the Bulgarians.[4] She now departed, bringing all kinds of wealth with her and an endless

---

1 This was 8 October 927.

2 Here, too, the Church of the Zoodochos Pege in Constantinople (cf. above, § 31).

3 The landing stage at Kosmidion (near Pege) at which Peter's father Symeon had met Romanos (cf. above, § 31)? If so, here, too, Pegai (at the southern shore of Marmara Sea) and Pege (more conveniently placed for anyone about to travel to Bulgaria) are confused.

4 The phrases describing the girl's feelings, with their antithetical expressions, smack of rhetorical exercise.

baggage train. **52** It was also at this time that ambassadors from Melitene came to the emperor Romanos, and they offered to agree upon peace and to offer tribute. Shortly after this, Abu-Hafs, the descendant of Amer and emir of Melitene, came together with Apolasath, who was a most noble *strategos* and a man of wealth in Melitene. Romanos received these with an appropriate show of honour and, when a peace treaty had been concluded, they returned to their country. From this time on, the people from Melitene went on military expeditions with the Romans against their Hagarene kinsmen, and in the victory processions they went with the Romans into the City, and led Hagarene prisoners in the processions—a sign of the godless Hagarenes' misfortune and a fact which caused some wonder and seemed strange. **53** On the death of Abu-Hafs, who had been a prudent and intelligent man, the inhabitants of Melitene rescinded the peace.[1] Therefore, the *domestikos* of the *scholai*, John Kourkouas, with the *themata* and the *tagmata*, and Melias with the Armenians, go to war against them and gather much booty on several occasions, and take prisoners from them in constant raids, and pillage them, and by this they reduced Melitene to such weakness that it could soon be destroyed and razed to the ground. But not only this: they also destroyed the neighbouring cities and land, which bore abundant crops and was very fertile and provided much income. Melitene itself the emperor made into a *kouratoria*,[2] and he arranged that many thousands [of *litrai*][3] in gold and silver should be paid yearly from there as a tribute. **54** Niketas, who was a *magistros* and the father-in-law of the emperor Christopher, was accused of having suggested to Christopher that he should turn against his own father and remove him from the throne. Because of this, Niketas was removed from the City and tonsured and confined to his country estate. **55** On the eighteenth of the month of July, in the sixth indiction, Stephen, the patriarch, dies, having served as patriarch for two years and eleven months.[4] **56** On the fourteenth of the month of December, they bring in the monk Tryphon, who lived the life of a hermit in the Opsikion and who bore witness to his faith in piety and holiness, and they ordain him patriarch for a fixed period of time, until Theophylaktos, the son of the emperor Romanos, should come of age; for they intended to ordain him patriarch of

1 These occurrences date from 931 and onwards. The final capture of Melitene took place 19 May 934.

2 A kind of imperial estate.

3 The unity is not specified in the text, and '*litrai*' is added by me.

4 He actually served 29 June 925–18 July 927. The indiction is wrong: the sixth year would correspond with 933.

Constantinople. **57** On the twenty-fifth of the same month,[1] unbearable winter weather came, and the earth froze for 120 days. This also resulted in a great famine, which exceeded all earlier ones, and many people died because of this—so many that the living could not carry away the dead. On[2] being made aware of this catastrophe, the emperor Romanos performed deeds worthy of his sympathetic and merciful nature. He comforted the need arising from the famine by many charitable donations, and he covered the porticoes[3] with boards and planks, so that the snow and the cold should not enter that way to the poor. At this time, he also had built what are known as *arklai*[4] in all the porticoes, and he arranged that money should be paid on a monthly basis to the poor who lay there and that the monthly *trimisia*[5] should be distributed to the poor in the churches. Thus, the sum given to the poor, in the *arklai* and in the churches, amounted to 12,000 [*litrai*][6] in minted silver. **58** This was not all that his sympathetic soul arranged in his care for the poor. He also decided that three poor people should dine with him every day and that they should receive one *solidus* each. On Tuesdays and Fridays, three poor monks dined with him, and each of them received the prescribed sum of money. He also adopted the custom of monasteries, namely that someone should read aloud during meals, thus offering a double table to himself and his guests, since the body was nourished by ordinary food, but the soul could delight at the suitable enjoyment of the words. And he paid close attention to these words and felt compunction in his soul and shed fountains of tears. **59** Who could describe the faith that he had in all monks, but especially those famous for their holiness and their piety? For he never saw a monk who cared for virtue without telling him with many tears about his own actions. Being a most ardent and orthodox believer, he embellished and brightened all the churches of the City in a glorious way with spectacular vestments and

1 This was on Christmas Day 927.

2 From this point, until the end of § 59, the text shows signs of being a kind of hagiographic *enkomion* on Romanos.

3 No doubt of official buildings in C/ple and, possibly, other cities.

4 Perhaps a kind of container; see O. Kresten, 'Arklai und trimisia. Lexikalisches zu den sozialen Maßnahmen des Kaisers Rhomanos I. Lakapenos im ›Katastrophenwinter‹ 927/928,' *Anzeiger der Philosophisch-historischen Klasse der Österreichischen Akademie der Wissenschaften* 137 (2002), pp. 35–52.

5 The *trimis(s)is* (or *tremissis*) was a third of a gold *solidus*. The definite article would seem to suggest that the custom in question is known to the reader, presumably because it is still in force at the time of writing.

6 The unity is not specified in the text, and '*litrai*' is added by me.

illuminations.¹ Further, he never stopped sending yearly contributions to the monks living in mountains, such as Mount Olympos and Kymina and what is known as the Golden Cliff and the Barachaios mountain, and he was concerned for them and took care of them, and those of them who were renowned for their deeds and contemplation he summoned to his presence, and reaped the benefit of their prayers. And this was not all: he did not stop providing the yearly payment, which he had decreed, to individuals who were living enclosed lives for the sake of God and who had shut themselves up in very small dwellings, as well as to all monasteries. These we have mentioned as some few examples of his countless moral achievements and acts of mercy. **60** Peter the Bulgarian was attacked by his brother John, who was acting together with other of Symeon's leading men. On being discovered, John is beaten and put into prison, whereas the others are subjected to no mean punishment. When Peter informed the emperor Romanos about this, the emperor sent the monk John, who had been a *rector*, to him, on the pretext that they should make an exchange of prisoners, but in truth to get hold of John and bring him to Constantinople. This indeed happened. For he [the monk John] arrived from Mesembria with [the Bulgarian prince] John on a ship and entered the City, and shortly afterwards [the Bulgarian prince?]² John threw away his monastic habit and asked for a wife, and the emperor gave him a house and great wealth and a wife who stemmed from Romanos' very own home region of Armeniakon, and he arranged a splendid wedding in the house of the caesar, and the emperor Christopher and John the monk (he who had been a *rector*) acted as witnesses. **61** In the month of March, on the second day, an architrave, set on the row of pillars standing in the Forum, fell down and killed six men.³ There was also a great and terrible fire in the portico outside the Forum, close to the Church of the most Holy Mother of God, and the candle factories and fur shops of the Forum were burnt down as far as Psichai. **62** In the month of August, in the fourth indiction, the emperor Christopher died.⁴ His father mourned him deeply and said that he had already reached old age, yet his [still living] sons were still babes. And Christopher's body was laid to rest in the afore-mentioned monastery belonging to his father. **63** In

1 'illuminations': Greek φωταγωγίαις.
2 The confusion in this passage is due to the fact that the monk and the Bulgarian prince carried the same name. Apparently both the prince and the monk travelled in monastic garb. The clarifying additions in square brackets are mine.
3 2 March 928.
4 August 931.

the month of August, in the third indiction,[1] they also removed Tryphon, the patriarch, from the throne, since he had accomplished the period agreed upon, and he withdraws to his own monastery and dies there. The Church remained without a leader for one year and five months, since Theophylaktos, the son of the emperor Romanos, had not yet come of age. For, as has been said, it was Theophalyktos whom Romanos intended to make patriarch. **64** A certain Basil from Macedonia, an impostor, spread a rumour that he was Constantine Doukas, and attracted many followers.[2] He was apprehended by Elephantinos the *tourmarches*, who was from Opsikion, and brought to Constantinople where Peter the *hyparchos* had his hand cut off. However, after this, when an opportunity presented itself once more, Basil goes to[3] Opsikion again, and he fitted a copper hand onto his arm in the place of the one which had been cut off, and he had an unusually big sword made for him, and he went around and fooled many of the people he met into believing that he was Constantine, the son of Doukas. **65** He also makes these people follow him, and starts a great rebellion against Romanos and, having occupied a fortress called Plateia Petra, he deposited every kind of foodstuff in it. Using this as his base, he ravaged the countryside and took hostage passers-by. In response to this, the emperor sent an army against him and had him and his men captured. And they brought him into the City and examined his case and had him severely beaten to compel him to tell the names of his fellow-conspirators. But he denounced many of those in high office falsely, saying that they had been with him. When it was found out that he had nothing true to say against these, he was committed to the fires in the Amastrianos. **66** The afore-mentioned Theophylaktos, son of the emperor, is ordained patriarch on the second of February, in the sixth indiction, and representatives[4] came from Rome and brought a synodical tome[5] confirming his ordination.[6] These representatives also placed him on the patriarchal throne. **67** The afore-mentioned granddaughter of the emperor Romanos, Mary, the wife of Peter the Bulgarian, often came to the City to visit her

1 Also August 931 (although the indiction is wrong, cf. preceding paragraph).
2 The uprising of Basil the Macedonian, the 'Copper-Hand,' took place in 932 or thereabouts.
3 'goes to' (καταλαμβάνει): or 'conquers.'
4 τοποτηρηταί (cf. above, § 17, where it is used in a technical sense denoting a military commander).
5 I.e. a kind of papal bull.
6 2 February 933.

father and her grandfather. On the last such occasion, when her father Christopher was already dead, she came with three children. And she received great riches from her grandfather and returned in honour. **68** Romanos, the emperor, brought a wife to his son Stephen. She was the daughter of Gabalas, and the granddaughter of Katakylas, and her name was Anna. Together with the marriage crown, the imperial crown was also set on Stephen's head.[1] **69** In the seventh indiction, in the month of April, the first expedition of the Turks against the Romans took place.[2] These overran the country as far as the City and carried off all the inhabitants of Thrace. The *patrikios* Theophanes, the *protovestiarios* and *paradynasteuon*, was sent to negotiate an exchange of prisoners with them. He approached them in an admirable and sensible way and achieved what he wanted, and he was much commended and admired by them for his intelligence and good will. On this occasion, the emperor Romanos also showed his magnanimity and philanthropy by not sparing any expense to set the prisoners free. **70** The emperor Romanos brought a wife to his youngest son, Constantine.[3] She was from a family of the Armeniakon *thema*, and her name was Helen, and she was the daughter of the *patrikios* Hadrian. When she died in the month of February, in the second indiction,[4] Romanos united Constantine with another woman, by the name of Theophano,[5] who belonged to the family of that Mamas.[6] **71** In the month of June, on the eleventh day of the month, in the fourteenth indiction, the Russians sailed down upon Constantinople with 10,000 ships.[7] The *patrikios* Theophanes, the one who was a *paradynasteuon* and a *protovestiarios*, was sent against them with all the triremes and *dromones* available in the City and, having prepared and made ready his naval expedition and fortified himself as much as possible through fasting and tears, he confronted the Russians, intending to defeat them in a naval battle. **72** When the Russians arrived and came close to the Pharos,[8] Theophanes, who lay in waiting at the mouth of the Black Sea, attacked

---

1 August 931.
2 April 934. The Turks mentioned are Magyars.
3 They married perhaps 14 January 938.
4 February 944.
5 Or: 'Theophanu.'
6 'that Mamas' (τοῦ Μάμα ἐκείνου): the expression implies that this was a family of significance or, at least, that it should be familiar to the reader.
7 11 June 941. For fuller commentary on this episode see Wortley 2010, p. 221f.
8 Or: 'Lighthouse' (at the entrance into the Bosporos from the Black Sea).

them in full force at the place called Hieron. He, in his own *dromon*, was the first to sail through the Russian lines, and he disturbed their lines and burnt a great many of their ships with Greek fire,[1] and the rest he put to flight. The remaining *dromones* as well as the triremes followed him and went forward and completed the rout, and many of the Russian ships sank with all hands, while many Russians were [mortally] wounded, but most of them were taken alive. The rest of them sail to the eastern shore, to the place called Sgora. **73** At this time, Bardas Phokas was also sent over land with an elite cavalry unit to intercept[2] the Russians. For the Russians had sent a rather considerable detachment to Bithynia in order to satisfy their need for food and other commodities, and the afore-mentioned Bardas Phokas met this force and attacked the men violently, routing and slaughtering them. **74** At this moment, John Kourkouas, the *magistros* and *domestikos* of the *scholai*, also came down together with the whole army of the East, and he annihilated many of the Russians, even catching stray soldiers here and there. This reduced the Russians to such fear of his attack that they remained gathered together in one place alongside their ships and did not dare to make raids in any direction. However, before the arrival of the Roman forces, they had performed many most evil actions: they had burnt the whole of what is called the Stenon, and of the prisoners they took some they impaled and some they pinned to the ground and yet others they used as targets and shot at them with bows. Every member of the clergy they apprehended had his hands tied behind his back and iron nails driven through his head. The Russians also burnt many holy churches. **75** When winter was imminent, the Russians, who lacked food and who feared the Roman forces that were coming against them, and even more the battle triremes, decided to return home and, trying to escape the notice of the Roman fleet, they set sail at night for the Thracian regions of the empire; this was in September, in the fifteenth indiction.[3] During this manoeuvre, they encountered the afore-mentioned *patrikios* Theophanes, for they did not escape the notice of this most vigilant and noble soul. At once, another sea battle is joined, and the afore-mentioned man sank very many ships and killed many men. A few, however, survived with their ships and were stranded upon the shore at Koile and managed to escape since night fell. Theophanes the *patrikios* returned to the capital

---

1 Here 'prepared fire' (ἐσκευασμένῳ πυρί).
2 Or: 'run parallel with' (παρατρέχειν).
3 September 943.

with a great victory and with very great spoils, and was received with honour and great glory and given the title of *parakoimomenos*. **76** The afore-mentioned John Kourkouas, the *magistros*, had proved most able in war and had won many battles and had extended the Roman frontier and destroyed very many cities of the Hagarenes. Because of the man's obvious qualities, the emperor Romanos wanted to offer John's daughter as wife to his grandson Romanos, the son of his son Constantine. This, however, led to envy against him [Constantine] from the other emperors, and he [John] is ousted from office. In his place, the *patrikios* Pantherios, a relative of the emperor Romanos, is made *domestikos*. **77** In the month of April, in the first indiction, the Turks attacked once again with very great force.[1] The *patrikios* Theophanes, the *parakoimomenos*, went out and made a truce with them, bringing some noblemen with him as hostages. This led to peace, which lasted for five years. **78** In the second indiction, the emperor Romanos sent Paschalios, the *protospatharios* and *strategos* in Lombardy,[2] to the king of France, Hugo, asking for Hugo's daughter as bride for Romanos,[3] the son of his son-in-law Constantine. The said Paschalios received her together with great wealth, and brought her to the City. The wedding was celebrated in the month of September, in the third indiction.[4] She died in the days of the sole rule of Constantine, her father-in-law, having lived with her husband for five years. **79** A violent and impetuous storm blew in the month of December, and what are known as the *Demes*[5] in the hippodrome fell down (these were opposite the imperial throne), and crushed the steps on which they were based and what are called the balustrades.[6] In the next year, in the same month, the emperor Romanos was brought down from the palace.[7] **80** When the city of Edessa, in which the revered image of Christ was preserved, was besieged by the Roman army and the city had been reduced to the greatest need, its inhabitants sent messengers to the emperor Romanos to negotiate the lifting of the siege, promising to hand over Christ's holy image. In return for doing so, they demanded hostages taken from the nobility and to receive a chrysobull

---

1 This, too, was in 943.

2 'Lombardy': i.e. from the Byzantine possessions in southern Italy.

3 This is the future Romanos II (main ruler 959–963), who married Bertha (Eudokia), daughter of Hugo of Provence, king of Italy.

4 September 945.

5 Probably the sections of the hippodrome reserved for the factions.

6 στηθέα.

7 This was in December 944.

guaranteeing that their land should not be ravaged any more by the army of the Romans. This indeed happened.[1] **81** When the holy image had been sent and was already approaching Constantinople, Theophanes, the *patrikios* and *parakoimomenos*, went out to the Sagaros river and met it with a splendid procession with torches and the appropriate signs of honour and the singing of hymns. On the fifteenth of August he entered the City with it, while the emperor was at Blachernai and worshipped it there. On the following day, the emperor's two sons, Stephen and Constantine, and his son-in-law, Constantine, together with the patriarch, Theophylaktos, went to the Golden Gate, and with an appropriate display of honour they received the image, and the Senate marched in front of them, and a very great procession with torches preceded them and they brought it on foot to the Church of the Holy Wisdom of God and, after it had been venerated there, it was brought to the palace. **82** In these days, an Armenian portent visited the City. It was a case of male children grown together, having come from one womb. They were fully grown with regard to all limbs of the body, but from the navel to the parts below the stomach they were fused together, facing each other. Living for a very long time in the City and being looked upon by everyone as portentous in some way, they were ultimately driven out as a bad omen. However, during the sole rule of Constantine they came to the City again and, when one of them died, some experienced doctors skilfully cut away the attached part hoping that the other one would live. He survived for three days and then died. **83** And, as has been said above, in all matters the emperor had boundless faith in monks. He especially honoured and revered Sergios, who shone among the monks. He was the brother of the *magistros* Kosmas, and the [grand-]nephew of the patriarch Photios. It was the nobility of soul that brought honour to this man rather than his physical valour. For he had brought virtue and knowledge to such an extreme that it was difficult to decide in which he excelled most: to such a high level he had trained himself in both. On him bloomed, apart from other advantages, the flush of modesty[2] and the charm of his character and his balanced mind. For he did not raise the eyebrows in the way of the wise men of our days. Nor did he seem pretentious or proud, but his speech

---

1 I.e. that the Byzantines left the city in peace thereupon (at least for the time being: it was captured in 1031 by the general George Maniakes, after the present text had been finished). For this episode cf. Wortley 2010, p. 224.

2 'flush of modesty' (τὸ τῆς διακρίσεως ἔρευθος): I take this as close to Modern Greek διακριτικός.

flowed sweeter than honey,[1] and his character was firm and stable, whereas he was humble of mind. This glorious man[2] the emperor always had with him, and he was a rule and a measuring-line, always regulating Romanos' life. This man entreated Romanos to take care of his children and not to leave them without an education, lest they should turn to evil and he, too, should suffer the same as Eli and have to pay for his children's lawlessness[3]— which is what happened. However, when his children removed him from the palace and exiled him to the island of Prote, Romanos again had Sergios to console him for his misfortunes and as his pain-allaying remedy against his sorrows. Together with him was at that time also Polyeuktos, who was a most pious monk and who also offered appropriate solace. It is he who is appointed patriarch by the emperor Constantine when the patriarch Theophylaktos dies.[4] **84** Since God wants to save man by many different methods, He allowed that also the emperor Romanos should meet with an unexpected disaster, so that he should be chastened by this and become aware of his own transgressions and be worthy of salvation. Thus, God allowed Romanos' son, Stephen, to rise against him as once Absalom rose against his father David.[5] As counsellors for this, Stephen used Marianos and Basil, called Peteinos, from among the monks, as well as Manuel Kourtikes. With the other emperors complicit in the plot, Stephen removed Romanos from the palace against his will and exiled him to the island of Prote and had him tonsured.[6]

137 The Sovereign Rule of Constantine

Thus his son-in-law, Constantine, was left as main ruler.[7] **2** At once, Constantine honours Bardas, son of Phokas, with the office of *magistros*, as a person who, over a long period of time and on many occasions, had

---

1 'his speech ... honey': this is an allusion to *Iliad* 1.249.

2 Greek ἀοίδιμος: this, too, is arguably reminiscent of Homer to a Byzantine, although it is actually not Homeric.

3 The story of Eli and his lawless sons is told in 1 Samuel 2.12f.

4 Theophylaktos died in 956. Accordingly, this is a reference forward in time, to a date after the end of the text.

5 On Absalom (or Abes(s)alom), who rebelled against his father, King David, but ultimately failed and was killed, see 2 Samuel.

6 Romanos was dethroned in December 944.

7 Cf. to this chapter Skylitzes (Wortley 2010, pp. 225–228), and Ps.-Symeon 753.1–754.18.

displayed courage in war; and he makes him *domestikos* of the *scholai*. He then made Basil, with the by-name Peteinos, *patrikios* and *megas hetaireiarches*. Marianos, of the family of the Argyroi, he stripped of his monastic robes and made him a *patrikios* and a *komes* of the stables. He also made Manuel, called Kourtikes, *patrikios* and *droungarios* of the *vigla*. 3 Not long after, God's righteous judgement came to these, since they had committed an outrage against the anointed of the Lord and unrighteously laid hands upon him and coveted the throne. For each of them was convicted of high treason and died a most pitiable death. I will tell their story in more detail in the following.[1] 4 Forty days later, on the twenty-seventh of the month of January, Constantine came to suspect the emperor Stephen and his brother Constantine, lest they should do the same to him [as they had done to their father], and, as was reasonable, he thought that if they did not spare their own father, why should they spare him?[2] He therefore invited them to dinner and, when they were already sitting at the table and the food was in their mouths, the so-called Tornikoi[3] and Marianos, the *patrikios*, as well as other men prepared to do so, apprehended them and brought them down from the palace and confined them to the neighbouring islands and tonsured them as clerics. 5 After a short time, Stephen and Constantine Lekapenos asked to see their father, and they came to the island of Prote and, when they saw him in the garb of a monk, they were seized by unbearable sorrow. And their father added his tears to theirs, and said: 'I fathered sons and I raised them, but they rejected me.'[4] Thereupon, the sons were exiled, Stephen to Proikonnesos, and from Proikonnesos to Rhodes, and from Rhodes to Mytilene; Constantine to Tenedos, and from there to Samothrace, where he was killed by his warders when he was planning a rebellion. Michael, the son of the emperor Christopher, was stripped of his imperial sandals and made into a cleric. 6 While the emperor Romanos was in the island, the patriarch Theophylaktos and Theophanes, the *patrikios* and *parakoimomenos*, made a plan to reinstall him in the palace.[5] They even informed him of this and lured him so as to agree, and they watched out for an appropriate moment to put their plan into action. But, as the plan was disclosed and the emperor Constantine was told about

1 To this compare the excursuses above (e.g. Chapter 132, § 2), telling about the awful death of persecutors. However, the promise to tell this story is not fulfilled in this text.
2 The sons of Romanos were ousted by Constantine VII 27 January 945.
3 Or: 'Tornikioi,' a well-known family clan.
4 Isaiah 1.2.
5 This attempt at reinstating Romanos may have taken place in 946.

it, he took revenge on those who had part in it. He exiled the *patrikios* Theophanes. The *protospatharios* George, who was also a *pinkernes*,[1] and Thomas the *primmikerios*[2] he had flogged and tonsured, and he paraded them through the City and then sent them into exile. **7** In the month of December, in the sixth indiction, some people attempted a coup against the emperor Constantine, for they wanted to bring the emperor Stephen back from the island to the palace.[3] When this plan was disclosed to Constantine by Michael, called Diabolinos, the emperor apprehended the rebels and had the noses and ears of some of them cut off, while he subjected others to unbearable beating. He then put them on donkeys and paraded them through the City and sent them into exile. **8** On the fifteenth of July, in the sixth indiction, the emperor Romanos dies on the island of Prote, and his body is brought to the City and laid to rest in his monastery.[4]

---

1 'cupbearer': eunuch waiting at the imperial table.

2 The functions of this Thomas are uncertain; for the title, cf. Chapter 136, § 2.

3 This attempt at yet another coup took place in December 947.

4 Romanos died 15 July (or June) 948. His body was laid to rest in the comparatively modest environment of the family's own Myrelaion monastery, where, among others, his wife had already been buried (see above, Chapter 136, § 21, and cover of this volume).

INDEX OF NAMES

INDEX OF TERMS AND CONCEPTS